THE
Cherokee Strip

A Tale of an Oklahoma Boyhood

MARQUIS JAMES

With a Foreword by William W. Savage, Jr.

University of Oklahoma Press: Norman and London

Also by Marquis James

THE RAVEN, a Biography of Sam Houston

ANDREW JACKSON:
(I) The Border Captain
(II) Portrait of a President

TO CYNTHIA

Library of Congress Cataloging-in-Publication Data

James, Marquis, 1891–1955.
The Cherokee strip : a tale of an Oklahoma boyhood / Marquis James; with a foreword by William W. Savage, Jr.
p. cm.
ISBN 0–8061–2537–3
1. James, Marquis, 1891–1955—Childhood and youth. 2. Historians—United States—Biography. 3. Enid Region (Okla.)—Biography. 4. Enid Region (Okla.)—Social life and customs. 5. City and town life—Oklahoma—Enid Region—History. I. Title.
E175.5.J3A3 1993
976.6'28—dc20
[B] 92-41739
CP

The paper in this book meets the guidelines for permanence and durability of the Committee on Production Guidelines for Book Longevity of the Council on Library Resources, Inc. ♾

Published by the University of Oklahoma Press, Norman, Publishing Division of the University. Manufactured in the U.S.A. First printing of the University of Oklahoma Press edition, 1993.

1 2 3 4 5 6 7 8 9 10

CONTENTS

Foreword
By William W. Savage, Jr.

Marquis James (1891–1955), born in Missouri and removed to Oklahoma Territory at the tender age of three, proved the poet's assertion that the child is the father of the man. Growing up in and around Enid, in what had been six months before his arrival the old Cherokee Outlet, James absorbed the lore of his elders and made it his own.[1] In Enid he first acquired and sharpened what would become the tools of his trade, launching there a career in journalism that would take him during the 1930s near the pinnacle of American letters. But, withal, he could not quite leave his past for his present, and in his conversations with family and friends he kept returning to the glory days of his youth, his boyhood in Oklahoma. Indeed, it was his daughter (the Cynthia to whom this book is dedicated) who prevailed upon him to write down what he kept talking about, inasmuch as it seemed to her considerably more interesting than his usual subject matter. James tells us that he had a detailed draft of *The Cherokee Strip* in hand by 1934. He worked and reworked it in fits and starts (or "takes," as he preferred to call them) for a decade before offering it for publication. He died a decade later. The chronology indicates rather emphatically that, no matter what else he might have experienced or accomplished, those years spent learning and growing in Oklahoma were never very far from his mind.

James acquired the greatest portion of his education informally. His mother taught him to read at age four and thereafter he pursued the printed word with something approaching mania. His father was a lawyer, and the family possessed a large library. In all likelihood, he gained more from perusing those volumes and the ones in the Enid Public Library than he did from the local schools, where he fared badly owing to his inattention to math and grammar. His father's death interrupted his formal schooling, at least to the extent that he had to find work in a printshop to help the family. He completed high school and spent a couple of years in classes at Oklahoma Christian University (now Phillips University), but in 1911 he left Enid to become a reporter.

During the next five years, James worked for twenty-odd newspapers in places like Kansas City, St. Louis, New Orleans, and Chicago, coming to rest eventually at the rewrite desk of the *New York Tribune*. He served a year and a half in the army during World War I, made the rank of captain, and devoted a good deal of time in the 1920s to helping organize and promote the American Legion. He wrote articles for the *American Legion Monthly* and, according to his widow, Jacqueline James Goodwin, was also on the staff of the nascent *New Yorker* magazine before he embarked upon a career as a freelance writer about 1925.

James spent four years working on *The Raven: A Biography of Sam Houston*, the intellectual origins of which are surely to be discerned from *The Cherokee Strip*. *The Raven* was published in 1929 and received the Pulitzer Prize for biography in 1930. James produced five more books in the next six years, including a two-volume biography (1933 and 1937) of Andrew Jackson, an opus that brought him another Pulitzer Prize in 1938.

James's studies of Houston and Jackson were enormously popular with the reading public, selling thousands of copies even in the midst of the Depression. Over the years, some critics have complained that James worshipped his heroes and was, therefore, incapable of much in the way of useful insight. James himself admitted that he was drawn to what he called "men of action" in selecting subjects for his biographies, and that may explain his preoccupation with personality and with matters involving individual honor. Nevertheless, historians have, on the whole, praised the vigor of his writing, the color and passion of his narrative. He remains, as they say, "readable." And as professional historians in our own time grow increasingly tedious, "readable" becomes more than the faint praise it was initially intended to be.[2]

If men of action were those who went somewhere and did something, perhaps James felt a certain kinship with them, owing to his own predilections for going and doing. Certainly he was footloose as a journalist, averaging four jobs a year in his heyday. Neither marriage nor family had much effect on his itinerary, perhaps because free-lance writing reinforced his need to move about. The Jackson biography, for example, required seven years of research, and that meant visits to archives and repositories throughout the United States. If we recall that he continued to make a living (and thus to support both family and his research) by producing magazine articles very nearly by the short ton, we see further evidence of steady activity.[3] James had slowed down a bit by World War II, turning his hand to corporate histories mainly for the money. *The Cherokee Strip* was an atypical James product for its time, sandwiched between books about the Insurance Company of North America and the Metropolitan Life Insurance Company. Still, whenever anyone asked, he would list travel among his hobbies, which included horseback riding and tennis. His death at sixty-four from cerebral hemorrhage underscored, perhaps, the pace of his life.

The Cherokee Strip is a personal book that tells us a great deal about Marquis James and his inability to sit still for very long. He was, after all, a boy; and boys are active. The epistemological problem of memoir may lead to skepticism about the accuracy of his recollection—is he telling us what he saw and did, or what he merely *thinks* he saw and did?—but intellectual historian Henry Steele Commager, in an introduction to a later edition of the book,[4] excused the whole exercise by calling it a fragment of autobiography that was part history, part poetry, and part imagination. In that way, Commager could include it among evocations of American boyhood ranging from *Huckleberry Finn* to *Two Years Before the Mast*. But those, too, were books about going and doing. Perhaps we only sense motion in James's memoir—though, even in narrow compass, he was a boy seemingly into everything. As well, his disposal toward activity is seen in those he admires: His father, a participant in the Run of '93; Mr. Howell, who had been places; the peripatetic Temple Houston; and those tramp printers, enviable souls all, even though they moved west to escape (for a brief moment) the technological obsolescence promised them by the linotype machine.

Perhaps more useful nowadays is the portrait James paints of a city aborning. Our tendency, especially in Oklahoma, is to regard the barely organized chaos of our various land openings as a momentary thing, passing quickly and leading directly to pastoral bliss in bucolic environs. What James presents is continuous hustle and bustle, a panorama of vigorous activity, be it social, political, or economic. He who rests in this environment, James warns, risks being passed by. His imaginative, if devious, attempts to stimulate newspaper circulation; his conversations with people who had traveled; his dreams of becoming a big-city reporter—all chronicled in the last chapter—provided not only the prelude to the career that followed, but also the capstone to James's reconstruction of a place and a time. Scenes of the old Cherokee Outlet lingered long in Marquis James's memory. And now, with their power to endure, his images become ours.

NOTES TO FOREWORD

1. The Cherokee Outlet originated in a provision of the New Echota Treaty of 1835 granting Cherokees removed from the East a "perpetual outlet west" so that they might never again find themselves surrounded by white people. The Outlet became irrelevant to the original purpose after the Mexican Cession, but the Cherokees retained possession and, after the Civil War, leased it to cattlemen. The federal government reacquired the land in 1890 and opened it to white settlement in 1893. What James calls the Cherokee Strip, then, was actually the Cherokee Outlet, a sixty-mile-wide parcel of land extending from the Arkansas River west to the Oklahoma Panhandle. There was a Cherokee Strip, but it was a two-and-one-half-mile-wide ribbon of land lying along the thirty-seventh parallel, north of the state line. Strip and Outlet were terms used interchangeably in the late nineteenth century, but were intended to mean only the Outlet. For further clarification, see John W. Morris and Edwin C. McReynolds, *Historical Atlas of Oklahoma* (Norman: University of Oklahoma Press, 1965), Map 20, and William W. Savage, Jr., *The Cherokee Strip Live Stock Association: Federal Regulation and the Cattleman's Last Frontier* (new ed., Norman: University of Oklahoma Press, 1990).

2. Essays on Jackson historiography are as abundant as Jackson literature. Any post-1940 discussion of Jackson is likely to contain an assessment of James and his work. But see Robert V. Remini's article on James in *Dictionary of American Biography, Supplement Five, 1951–1955*, ed. John A. Garraty (New York: Charles Scribner's Sons, 1977), pp. 363–64, since Remini is among the foremost modern Jackson scholars. James may have aroused scholarly ire by announcing his intention to elevate historical writing to the level of literature, an indication of his opinion of professional historians.

3. James was no stranger to voluminous writing. Before going off to World War I, he published a million or so words in various of the nation's pulp magazines.

4. New York: Viking Press, 1965.

PREFACE TO

The Oklahoma Edition

WITH the honor of countenancing an Oklahoma edition of this book goes a feeling of uneasiness. Already I know one Oklahoman who will be disappointed in this piece of composition unless she follows my suggestion, which was not to read it. She had said she was so glad the book was coming out because she never tired of hearing about Will Rogers. Unfortunately, Mr. Rogers's name does not appear elsewhere in these pages. I never heard of him when I lived in Oklahoma and, to my loss, did not get to know him later.

I have tried to restrict myself to what I knew about in the Strip's early days, and mine. Though the opportunity seems unlikely, if I could pick a place to grow up in again, when I did, I think I'd still pick the Strip. The object of this book is to give an idea of what the place was like in those days.

I imagine most writers have an audience in mind when they're working. That was true in the case before you, though writing this book wasn't work exactly. It was more of a diversion from other writing. And, owing to circumstances, the audience was a mixed one, I'm afraid. Some rather full notes for this book were made in London in 1934. I'd spent an evening in a company which included a storytelling county squire who'd been everywhere. Back in my hotel room I wrote a little that I thought might interest him. Other parts were written in Enid. That made it easier to get before me the gang at Waumpie Washburn's, the old *Eagle* bunch, and my contemporaries of the Congenial Dancing Club.

The book was written, as a good deal of my stuff is, in unrelated "takes" and assembled when I was in an assembling, rather than a writing, humor. Some things that appear in Chapter One were written almost last, and the other way round. Mizzou Edmundson, whom I knew fairly well, might not have got in at all except for a word Lee

Cromwell dropped one night on my very last trip home. Until then I just hadn't thought of Mizzou when thinking of the book. Before turning in I sat down and wrote quite a bit about Mizzou as I recalled him at different times. Maybe half of it survives, and, if so, that would be a fair proportion of first-draft copy.

When a fellow starts babbling trade secrets, I guess it's time to stop. Well, so long folks.

M.J.

Rye, New York
1945

Note of Explanation

Whoever gets very far into this book will understand that in Oklahoma Territory it wasn't good form to pry into a person's past.

As early Oklahomans nevertheless did have backgrounds, even a casual sketch like this would be incomplete without giving a few. I have restricted myself to my own forebears, to Mr. Howell, and to Aunty, the old slave. Of Mr. Howell I have told only what he himself told me, under no seal of confidence. Aunty is treated as one of the family.

Certain other case histories might have enriched the story. But that would have been too much of a good thing—distorting, by over-revelation, one aspect of the scene I have tried to recreate. The omissions are the fruit of no deliberate plan. During the ten and more years in which this book was put together, as a pastime as much as anything else, I don't believe it ever occurred to me to do otherwise.

The book as a whole is the result of no deep scheming. It was started on its way by a conversation with a small girl who said:

"Pop, why don't you write some of the things you tell about instead of what you do write?"

M.J.

Rye, New York
1944

I: The Claim

1893-1901

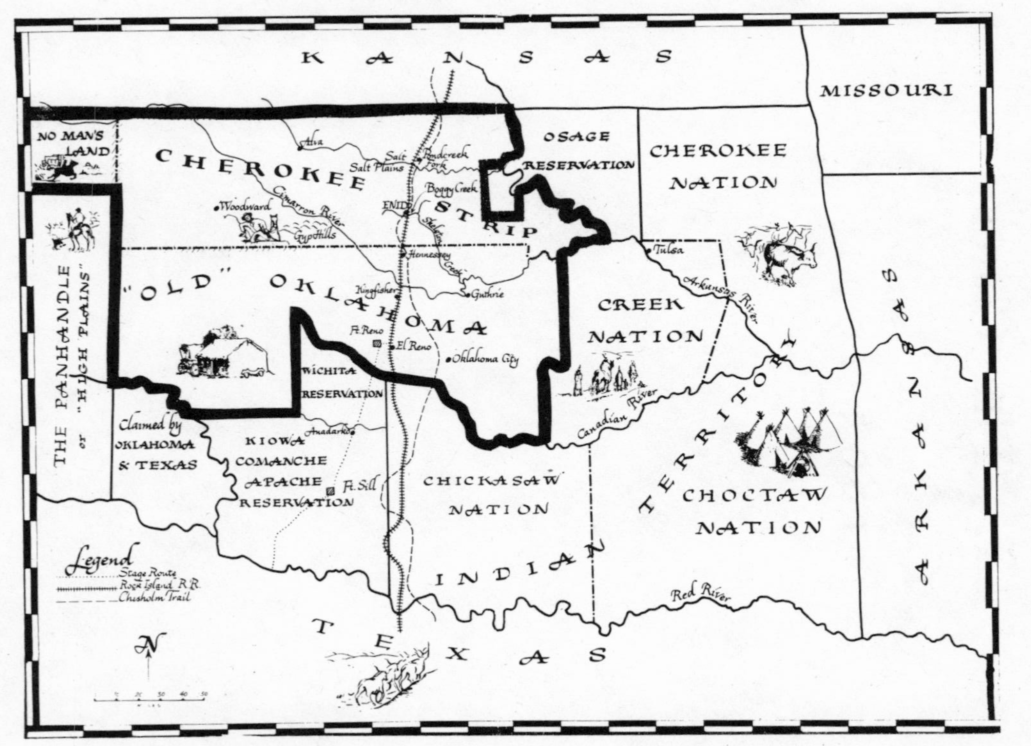
KANSAS
MISSOURI
NO MAN'S LAND
CHEROKEE STRIP
OSAGE RESERVATION
CHEROKEE NATION
Alva
Salt Plains
Salt
Pondcreek
Fork
Boggy Creek
ENID
Woodward
Cimarron River
Gyp Hills
Skeleton
Hennessey
Creek
Tulsa
Arkansas River
THE PANHANDLE or "HIGH PLAINS"
"OLD" OKLAHOMA
Kingfisher
Guthrie
Ft. Reno
El Reno
Oklahoma City
CREEK NATION
WICHITA RESERVATION
Claimed by OKLAHOMA & TEXAS
KIOWA COMANCHE APACHE RESERVATION
Anadarko
Ft. Sill
Canadian River
CHICKASAW NATION
CHOCTAW NATION
INDIAN TERRITORY
ARKANSAS
Red River
TEXAS
Legend
Stage Route
Rock Island R.R.
Chisholm Trail
N

CHAPTER ONE

Dick Yeager

I FLOPPED in a patch of new grass on the rim of the bluff in the horse lot and Prince trotted up and flopped by me. Prince was never very far from where I was. At nights he slept at the foot of my bed on an old lap robe which every morning I had to hang in the air. Prince had been after a cottontail. He was panting with his tongue out.

The rim was about my favorite place on the whole claim. You could look and look, for there was, indeed, much to see. Below lay the dark, plowed earth of West Bottom, which we sometimes called the Horseshoe from the way Boggy Creek curved around it. Lazying in from the Schrock claim on the other side of the Bottom, old Boggy's winding course was defined by a string of elms and cottonwoods whose branches the opening buds bathed in a pale green haze.

Mr. Schrock worked early and late. He had built himself a little house of lumber and turned the sod house into a stable. His whole hundred-and-sixty was under fence, and a good half of it broken and in crops. Later on you would see Mrs. Schrock helping her husband plant corn with a hand drill, a hill at a time.

"I declare," Mama would say, "there's a couple bound to get on in a new country."

Today Mr. Schrock was plowing, diminished by distance to a toy man with a toy plow and a toy team raising a plume of brown dust. I could have picked up all three and held them in my hand.

The claim north of Mr. Schrock's was Mr. Howell's. Mr. Howell had no fence, and he did not plow. From his dugout in the side of a little rise near the creek the prairie tilted gently until it met the northwestern sky. Bright islands of new grass were blotting out the winter-gray of this sloping plain. Out of sight beyond the crest was South Town—and all that went on there. Some days you could see the smoke of a Rock Island train and hear the whistle, too. Other times you could just see the smoke; other times just hear the whistle.

The new grass was soft to lie in. It tickled my legs and feet because this was the first time I'd had my shoes off. The sun felt good on my back. A glance down the face of the bluff at Boggy's green bosom made you think of swimming.

Prince pricked up his ears: cowbird on a hackberry limb beneath us. You know what a claim-jumper a cowbird is—laying its eggs in other birds' nests and all. That's what this cowbird was fixing to do. It was a robin's nest. I was fishing in my pocket for the nigger-shooter Mr. Howell had made me when I happened to look around, and there was Ad Poak coming over the rise in our pasture. He was riding Pat and he came from the direction of the East Draw.

The cowbird forgotten, I watched Ad let himself, without dismounting, through the far gate of the horse lot and then through the near gate. At the tie rail by the house he swung down and tied up. Pat was a stallion and would not stand without tying.

Mama was feeding the chickens. She beckoned Ad to come around in back. Ad walked toward her as if taking time to think. The wind was the wrong way to hear what they said but pretty soon it was plain, from the motions her sunbonnet made, that Mama was giving it to Ad for some reason. When she scolded, Mama talked so fast that her head would bob up and down.

The fact that it looked as if Ad had come from the East Draw was a matter of interest in itself, let alone maybe having done something there to be scolded by Mama. The East Draw was where the outlaws camped while waiting for Papa to come home. Sometimes one would be there for days. Arkansas Tom was supposed to be there now. That was what Ad Poak and the hired man had said. I wasn't allowed to go to the Draw and see for myself.

Just the same Prince and I *had* gone there, no more than two, three days before I heard about Arkansas Tom. I had looked down from the rim but I never saw any outlaw; only the ashes of an old fire by the plum thicket. I was good and winded by the time I topped the rise in the pasture which first brought in sight the top of the Big Tree, and then the hip roof of the barn, and then the roof of our house. As these friendly objects met my eyes I slowed to a walk, feeling more comfortable: not so much because I had been afraid of encountering an outlaw as of being caught doing something that wasn't allowed. Even Papa had told me not to go to the Draw alone.

"It would worry your mama, son," he said.

By and by I couldn't stand not hearing what Mama and Ad were saying; and so I started for home, running gingerly to favor my tender feet. As I ran I snatched off my hat and shook out my hair. Mama liked to see my hair down about my shoulders, though it was sure a bother to me, catching every briar and twig. Away from the house I kept it twisted up under my hat. Prince bounced ahead, his feathery tail riffled by the wind. Prince was a black dog, part spaniel. You should have seen him swim and dive.

It was just as I thought. Ad had been to the Draw, and he was wearing his gun. But the rest was something nobody would have thought: he had put Arkansas Tom off the claim!

Mama seldom stayed mad very long. Shucks, she was getting over it already, and just pretending. One brown hand brushed at the bonnet strings the wind whipped about her face. The other hand cradled a pan of kaffir corn against her hip.

"I still say that's no way to carry on around an outlaw. Dick Yeager seems to have gone to your head. You'll get it shot off your shoulders one of these days."

"Not by Tom Conway I won't; no, ma'am." Ad was a slow talker, different from Mama. He held on to his words as if sorry to see them go. "Too much of a cloud on his reputation."

"Ad Poak, will you be serious for once? 'Cloud on his reputation.' Now what am I to gather from that?"

"What I been driving at, Miz James, is that outlaw's just a courtesy title in Tom's case. Something picked up as a character reference here in the Strip. The judge can't be bothered with such trash."

Mama raised her eyes toward heaven, and tried hard not to

smile. "Strikes me," she said, "this Arkansas Tom has no monopoly on courtesy titles. Mr. Poak, just what have you done around here today? Now, Ad, I want you to put Pat up, fill Martha's water buckets, get some cobs for the cook-stove, and hear Marquis's reading lesson. Then it will be time to help the man with the chores."

"Yes, ma'am," said Ad. "What'll it be, Markey? *Robinson Crusoe* or *Tom Sawyer?*"

When we were out of Mama's hearing I said, kind of whispering to be on the safe side:

"Just tell me about the time you capterred Dick Yeager. I'll go get the shell."

It made it more real to hold in my hand the brass shell which had contained the bullet with which Ad Poak had ended Dick Yeager's career. It belonged to Mr. Howell's .40-.70 single-shot Winchester, his bear gun. Ad had given the shell to Mama as a keepsake. She kept it in a drawer of the sewing machine.

Two or three days later when Papa came home he said that Mama and Ad were both right, but Mama the righter of the two. A client was a client these days and entitled to considerate treatment. Papa talked slowly, too, and he never talked nearly enough. When Papa spoke I always stopped what I was doing to listen.

"But Ad meant well," he went on. "Aims to improve the tone of my practice. Like those city lawyers in St. Louis: clerk in the ante-room to shoo off callers who look like they might turn out to be nuisances. The Draw's my ante-room. And yet there's such a thing as an excess of zeal on the part of a law clerk. Ad brought in Dick Yeager, all right. But he brought him in in too poor condition to stand trial."

Martha entered with a pitcher of buttermilk. Martha knew how Papa loved fresh buttermilk. This time it was a part of her preparation to ask him to do something for Jerry.

Papa read Martha's mind. After thanking her for the buttermilk he went on talking to Mama and Ad. But the words were intended for Martha. "There's a client I mean to hold on to. Better put in my time keeping Jerry in jail than Tom Conway out. When that no-good nigger's locked up Martha can keep her mind on her work."

A shadow crossed Martha's round face—if you can imagine a shadow on a black face, as I can, having seen it so often. She set down the pitcher and silently returned to the kitchen.

Martha's name was not really Martha. It was Victoria, but Papa thought Martha more appropriate for the wife of Jerry Washington. Jerry was a dressy-up nigger who never worked, and the only colored person Mama permitted me to speak of as a nigger. When Jerry was in jail or carrying on with some high yellow on Two Street in South Town, Martha lived with us. When Jerry was loose and broke he would carry Martha off to Two Street where she would take in washing to provide him with a fresh supply of pocket money. By and by Jerry would get in trouble again or just go off and Martha would be back, looking melancholy and down.

2

I missed Martha the times she was away but I missed Mr. Howell more, and he had been gone a long while now—driving stage out of Fort Reno. No smoke came from the stovepipe which crooked from the dugout's window. Mr. Howell said the window was the place for the stovepipe in a dugout. Poke it through the roof and your roof would leak water when it rained. Mr. Howell's dugout didn't leak. In the winter it was snug and cozy; and in summertime as cool and nice as our cyclone cellar in the creek bank beneath the Big Tree. Prince and I went over there often, but the padlock was still on the door and everything hushed and lifeless. Before he went away Mr. Howell had no lock for his door. Prince and I could come and go, making ourselves at home on the neatly made bunk. Now I tried to peer through the window to see if the familiar room was the same, but it was too dark inside to make out anything.

Mr. Howell was the only person I knew who was always doing

something interesting and would let me do it with him: hunting and fishing; laying and tending traps for muskrat along Boggy Creek; cooking and eating in the dugout—or wherever we were when we got hungry. A trotline and a gun provided Mr. Howell with most of his victuals. He prepared them with the hunting knife he wore in a leather scabbard at his waist. Mr. Howell could cook as well on the embers of a fire outdoors as on the jack-stove in the dugout. He carried salt with him in a leather sack about half the size of Papa's tobacco pouch. Mr. Howell ate with the hunting knife. There was no fork in the dugout, and when Mr. Howell ate at our house Mama said he regarded a fork as an unfamiliar weapon. When Mr. Howell and I ate together I would use my pocket knife like he used his hunting knife. At home Mama not only made me use a fork but I had to hold it a certain way.

Mr. Howell taught me to have no fear of snakes, and how to kill them.

"They'll all run from you, never arter you; *sabe?*—don't keer what folks say. Allus carry a stick and just go at 'em. Rattlers an' moccasins the only pizen snakes in these parts."

We killed snakes nearly every day. The ones I killed I dragged back of the barn. Papa would count them and pay me a bounty of one cent each. One day I got a whole litter of nine little blacksnakes, no longer than your finger. Papa paid just the same. While not actually afraid of rattlers, I never went out of my way to look for one. Mr. Howell knew a cow-camp cook in Colorado who was bitten on the thumb by a rattler. He went to the chuck wagon and took a cleaver and whacked off the thumb. They seared the stump with a branding iron.

Mr. Howell and I would visit the old cowhand who worked for Mr. Jim Utsler. His face was creased and leathery. He walked as if it hurt him—I don't know whether from stiff joints or tight boots. But he could sure ride. He and Mr. Howell would squat on their heels in the shade of the big Utsler barn and talk about how the Strip was before the Run: all cattle range. The different brands they would trace on the ground with sticks. Right here along Boggy was the Circle J H outfit; down by the Cimarron the 2 S; over west toward the Salt Plains the Half Diamond R.

Mr. Howell and the old puncher talked about Nigger Green, a colored cowboy who followed the ranges from Old Mexico to Canada. Nigger Green had surmounted the barrier of race and adorned his name with bunkhouse legend. Without previous promise or later boast he performed superior feats. "Think *you* can ride him, Nigger?" partners would ask, indicating an outlaw bronc. "Mos' likely not, but might have a try." Nigger Green could ride about anything you could saddle.

Whatever their more obvious conceits, cowboys bragged of their horsemanship by understatement. Ask a cowhand if he rode and the answer would be: "Couldn't rightly say I do; take a stab at it sometimes, though." Any other reply was the mark of a tenderfoot. Good riders by eastern standards turned up in the West looking for jobs with cow outfits for the fun of it. They came from England, even—young fox-hunting gentlemen, good at five-bar gates. If, in all innocence, a tenderfoot would admit to experience in the saddle, the foreman would observe: "Now that's fine. Boys, here's a man who can ride. Suppose you bring out something and let him limber up." You can imagine what the boys would bring.

Most of all I missed Mr. Howell for the stories he told. It might be a wet day when he was tinkering with his traps, loading shotgun shells, greasing his boots or mending his clothes. Mr. Howell had two guns, the Winchester and the muzzle-loader. Papa's 10-gauge shotgun was at the dugout much of the time, an arrangement which kept our table supplied with small game. But usually it seems that Mr. Howell and I were out of doors when he talked—following the course of the creek, or resting on the slope of a buffalo wallow on the prairie.

He told how buffalo wallows were made and how he had seen buffalo on the plains as thick as blackbirds in the sky, and how he had made his living as a buffalo hunter, taking only the pelts and leaving the carcasses by the hundred for the buzzards. He told me about hunting grizzly bear in the Bitter Root Range, and about mountain lions. He told me about a fish he called a salmon that could jump as high as the dugout—up a waterfall, to get where it was going. I didn't know what a waterfall was until he took a stick and made a little one for me at our spring. Bears, he said, could catch fish—flip them out of the water with their paws, which was more than a man could do.

Mr. Howell had many Indian stories to tell. The bluish scar on his leg had been made by a Blackfoot arrow. Mr. Howell hadn't always fought the Indians, though. He'd hunted and trapped with them. He'd wintered in a Sioux village. That was a good tale, though nothing much happened.

Of course, you saw a good many Indians there in the Strip. They were usually on hand at our place at butchering time, looking for offal and scraps. They would pitch their tepees beside the creek along the section-line road which bordered our claim on the east. Mr. Howell and I often visited their camps.

"*How!*" Mr. Howell'd say and hold up one hand, with the palm toward the Indian he was speaking to.

"*How!*" I'd say after him.

Mr. Howell would squat on his heels and talk in the Indian sign language, mixed with grunts and ughs. This was the language Indians of different tribes used to talk to each other. He'd pick out a wrinkled old Indian who knew no English at all. I'd squat and watch.

"They's Injuns an' Injuns, Marquis," Mr. Howell told me. "Excusin' the old men, yore Cherokees, here, 'ud starve to death in the Comanche country. Fergittin' how to hunt. Leased their huntin' grounds to the cattlemen for cash money an' et store grub too long."

For Comanches, with their lean, sinewy bodies and straight, resentful glances, Mr. Howell showed more respect. "Finest hunters on the plains." Mr. Howell said that, despite its name, the Cherokee Strip was Comanche country, really; and so the unforgiving Comanches still regarded it. Away back, the Gov'mint had taken it from the Comanches and their friends the Kiowas and had given it to the Cherokees in trade for other lands taken from the Cherokees. As with all the history that he knew, Mr. Howell had this pretty close first-hand—from old Comanche and Kiowa and Cherokee bucks.

Comanches didn't come by our place so often, but when they

did Mr. Howell always went over and talked to them in Spanish. "Bad *hombres*, yore Comanches," he informed me, and summed the matter up: "Wouldn't trust one no further'n I could spit—excusin' Quanah Parker." Against Quanah Parker Mr. Howell had fought at 'Dobe Walls. But later on they had become friends. When Quanah left the warpath the Gov'mint was so glad that it fixed him up a big ranch near Anadarko on the Comanche reservation. Mr. Howell used to visit Quanah there.

Mr. Howell told how Quanah Parker had received his name—from his mother, Cynthia Ann Parker, a white woman, carried off by the Indians when she was a child in Texas.

Visiting a Comanche camp I'd stay close to the side of Mr. Howell long after the conversations, which I could not understand, had become tedious. There was no poking about on my own to explore the interiors of tepees, or to peer in the stew kettles the squaws stirred with sticks.

This circumspection amused Mr. Howell. "Marquis, they ain't stealin' young'uns no more." As far as that went, Mr. Howell allowed that Cynthia Ann hadn't had such a bad time at all, until the battle in which the Texas Rangers killed her husband and captured her. When the Rangers found out who their captive was, they took her to Austin and made a big to-do of restoring her to her people. For this Cynthia Ann did not thank them. The Comanches were her people then, and she wanted only to return to them and find out what had become of her boy Quanah. The whites wouldn't let her and Cynthia Ann pined away and died.

"I tell you, Marquis, it's the whites that's had a heap to do with making yore Comanche what he is, an' that's the way of it. Mind as how when I was on the high plains in the fifties, 'fore the Rebellion. Greatest runa game I ever see in open country, an' the Comanches troublin' nobody. The cowmen an' the nesters had ought to let them be."

The story of Cynthia Ann Parker was well known in our part of the country. The fact is I was more interested in the less familiar narrative which concerned her brother, John, on whose ranch in Old Mexico Mr. Howell had stayed for a spell. Captured the same time Cynthia was, John had grown up with a different Comanche band. He received a young Comanche's training as a hunter and a warrior. As described by Mr. Howell, this seemed a desirable mode of life. The Comanches hunted and fought on horseback with lances and arrows; and there was nothing they could not do on a horse. By and by this band of Comanches captured a Mexican girl. John married her and finally she persuaded him to leave the tribe and go to Old Mexico and set up as a rancher. To my mind that was quite a comedown.

Mr. Howell told other good tales about prospecting for gold in Colorado and in Californy; and about the big trees in Californy. Surely Mr. Howell had seen more wonderful things than any other man on earth. Our Big Tree was a cottonwood with bark so old and gnarly that a barefooted boy could go up the trunk like he could go up a ladder. The first crotch was almost as high as our chimney. As long as I could keep the top of the Big Tree in sight, I always knew which way home was. Strangers measured the distance around the trunk. It was fourteen feet and something. I heard Papa tell Doctor Fairgrieve that the Big Tree was the oldest living thing in the Cherokee Strip. Even Mr. Howell was stumped to think of anything larger on the plains, but I judged that beside trees in Californy the Big Tree wasn't much more than a bush.

Nor were Oklahoma outlaws, not even Dick Yeager or Jack Dalton, to be mentioned in the same breath with Mr. Howell's acquaintances, Billy the Kid (who was left-handed) and Sam Bass. And then there were tales of the cattle drives up the Chisholm Trail, and about the pony express, and about the Run, and about the North Town War.

Before Mr. Howell told about the Run and the North Town War, I used to think that nothing interesting had ever happened to Papa. Now I knew better, for Mr. Howell let it out that Papa had made the Run and that he had been in the North Town War. Yet I could never get Papa to tell about them—a regular story, that is. Of course, there was no one like Mr. Howell, always with a tale on the tip of his tongue. I comforted myself with the thought that Papa just wasn't ready with his story yet. Therefore

I listened whenever he spoke, so as not to miss his story when he should get around to telling it.

The North Town War was also called the Railroad War. The Rock Island Railroad wanted the town of Enid to be three and a half miles north of the place where the South Town people wanted it. The railroad owned most of the northern townsite. The Rock Island called its town Enid and the South Town people called their town Enid. So people could tell one Enid from the other nobody around where we lived said Enid at all. We said South Town and North Town. Papa was for South Town because our town lots were there and because it was closer to our claim.

The railroad would not stop trains at South Town. People had to get off at North Town. They were told that they were in Enid, the place they were looking for. If they insisted on going on to South Town they would have to get a rig, and no rigs could be hired for that purpose in North Town. When South Town people went to get the travelers, North Towners would try to upset the rigs and cut the harness. It was hard for Mr. Peter Bowers to get things for his store. For a while it looked as if South Town was a goner. Then the people decided that passengers and freight left at North Town should reach South Town whether or no. Every mule-freight was furnished with an armed guard, and a regular stage was sent to meet the passenger trains. Mr. Howell drove the stage, and he carried the Winchester in a holster beside his high seat.

In that way the passengers and freight got to South Town, though not without a ruckus now and then, as when a committee of South Town citizens had to throw a hint in the direction of Mr. Nat Campbell. Mr. Campbell was a lawyer. The word got around that he was a secret agent of North Town. When the committee called on Mr. Campbell he shut himself in the shack which served as his office and residence. The citizens pulled down the shack. They had a rope and I have heard Mr. W. O. Cromwell, another lawyer, say that one end of the rope was around Mr. Campbell's neck. Others who were present don't remember that part so well. Pretty soon Mr. Cromwell came to the conclusion that the committee might get worked up and do something to hurt the name of South Town as a peace-loving community. He asked the citizens to let Mr. Campbell go. When they refused Mr. Cromwell got a dry-goods box from Meibergen & Godschalk's and climbed on it. Pulling a paper from his pocket, he began making out to read the names of the citizens who were interviewing Mr. Campbell. Mr. Cromwell said that already he had started a copy of the list on the way to Guthrie, and if Mr. Campbell wasn't turned loose somebody would go to the pen as sure as shooting. They turned Mr. Campbell loose.

Still, Rock Island trains whistled through South Town without stopping. Red lanterns and dynamite caps on the track failed to stop them. Bullets failed to stop them: conductors would draw the window blinds and tell passengers to scrooch down away from the glass. One night someone sawed the pilings of the trestle and a freight train went into the south branch of Boggy. That was the first train to stop in South Town. If you know the right parties in Enid you can see the saw that was responsible. Some day it may go to the Oklahoma Historical Society.

South Town held a jollification at which there was a lot of talk about having the Rock Island licked. Mr. W. O. Cromwell went to my father. "James," he said, "this is bad medicine. If railroad detectives aren't in that crowd already they'll be there in a jiffy and sooner or later one of these blowhards is going to talk too much with his mouth. See what you can do to break up the meeting." Papa requested to be heard. He asked if the crowd wasn't overlooking something. This train which for reasons unfathomable had proved too heavy for the bridge contained a car filled with fine seed wheat. The car was smashed and the wheat spilled. Now everyone knew how dear and scarce seed wheat was. Didn't this look like a chance for a settler to get some real reasonably? The meeting broke up and the people went to get the seed wheat. Mr. Cromwell told me this story. As I say, Papa himself never mentioned such things.

Pretty soon the Rock Island agreed to stop its trains at South Town and the Railroad War was over—unfortunately, I thought—before Mr. Howell got a chance to plug anyone with his Winchester. Our Enid became Enid in fact, and the railroad Enid,

North Enid. No love was lost between the two towns for a long time thereafter, though.

I remember driving to North Town with my father and sitting alone in the buggy and being terrified at the sight of some children who trooped by. I expected them to cut the harness and set upon me. Children usually frightened me because I so rarely saw a child on the claim.

3

With Mr. Howell gone, there seemed to be more coyotes yapping around at night and getting the chickens. That was what Mama said. Mr. Howell kept the coyotes down, though personally he didn't have a very high opinion of coyote-killing. He bothered to shoot them only as a favor to Mama. "Take yore gray wolf, now. Mind as how in the early eighties they was so bad the cattlemen got the bounty up to twenty dollars. . . ."

My efforts to keep the image of Mr. Howell and the sound of his words before me were earnest efforts. Sitting in the dusty hay in the stable loft, I would draw up one knee and clasp my hands about it, as Mr. Howell did when leaning back on his bunk in the dugout. I would tell Mr. Howell's stories to Prince, pretending I was Mr. Howell and Prince was me.

"Reminds me, Marquis, of mule-freightin' outa Dodge City 'cross No Man's Land into the Panhandle. . . ."

That story was easy. All we did was catch and hang the Mexican horse thief. "Pulled out an' left him standin' on nothin' lookin' up a rope. Yessiree."

"Back in the winter of '75, Marquis, when me and my podner was scoutin' for Crook on the Tongue. . . ."

I had trouble remembering all that one and had to make up stretches as I went along. Once I got the hang of it, though, this making up wasn't so hard as a body might think. Moreover, it was a wonderful convenience. Sometimes when I really remembered the way Mr. Howell had told it I would make up differently because I liked the story better that way. It was the only way I had of saving the life of Mr. Howell's podner, who, unlike the Mexican horse thief, had not deserved to die.

You see, General Crook had told Mr. Howell and his podner to go up the river, ahead of the army, and look for signs of Crazy Horse. Pretty soon they came to a branch with steep rocky banks. Mr. Howell said he would scout the head of the branch and double back and meet his podner on the main stream. He didn't see any Injuns, but when he got back to the Tongue he found his podner lying on a flat rock, dead and scalped and his rifle and his belt gone. I would change that part so that it was Mr. Howell's podner who had kilt the Injuns instead of the other way around.

Thinking about Mr. Howell so much caused me to recollect a remark Papa had made, and it bothered me. It bothered me so badly that I asked Mama:

"Is it so, what Papa says about Mr. Howell?"

"What's that, Marquis?"

"'If old man Howell'd done all he says he's done he'd be a hundred and ten years old.'"

Mama laughed. "Mr. Howell's a good, kindly old man who's lived a rough and a lonely life. Lonely people have large imaginations sometimes."

Her words made me very sad. So it was true, after all. Mr. Howell, too, made up parts of his stories. That's what Mama meant, even if she didn't come out and say so. Suddenly I felt very angry at my father and mother. I told myself I would not, *would* not believe what they said about Mr. Howell.

Mama must have seen that something was the matter.

"You mustn't mind what your father says. It's the stairs, you know. It may be as your father tells it: that Mr. Howell was stumped and didn't know how to build a staircase after talking pretty big about the carpentering he'd done. And it may be as Mr. Howell says: that your father forgot to put a staircase in the plans."

Ever since I could remember I'd heard the grown people talk about our house not having any stairs, only a ladder that went up from the south porch. But Papa mostly joked about it, it seemed.

"Here I plan to build the first two-story residence in Garfield County. Get the lumber, only slightly less dear than good bourbon. Get it hauled from North Town. Carpenters scarcer than hens' teeth, owing to everyone in town wanting to build at once. Along comes old man Howell. By that time, I knew he'd advised Sherman at Atlanta and won most of our Indian campaigns and dug most of the gold in the West. But I didn't know he claimed to be a carpenter until I mentioned the fix I was in. Then it appeared that he was fresh from the Cripple Creek boom where he'd laid off digging gold in order to erect palaces for those who'd struck it rich already. So I turn him loose on my lumber and go to Guthrie for a jury trial. Come back and what have I? A two-story dwelling without a stairway."

"That was three years ago, Houstin," Mama would say. "Other carpenters have since been available, and we've no stairway yet."

"Too busy getting in our tobacco—twenty acres of the best tobacco in the Cherokee Strip."

"The only tobacco in the Cherokee Strip, unless I'm misinformed," Mama would say.

"A new country, Rachel. Twenty acres in tobacco, and when that tobacco goes to market I'll put a little something to it and throw that new addition across the front of the house and put the stairway in *it*."

"You've a lot of confidence in that tobacco."

"Naturally. This is the latitude of North Carolina, the finest tobacco country in the world."

The promise of a staircase in the new front addition kindled my interest in staircases, with which I had not enough experience for the novelty to wear off. Most of the stairways in Enid—we didn't say South Town so much any more—were on the outsides of the buildings where you could get a good look at them. But some were on the insides, as in the Rex Hotel and the Cogdal-McKee building where Papa had his office. I rather hoped ours would be on the outside. People would see it and stop talking about the James house which had an upstairs and no way to get there.

4

A trip to Enid was surely a marvelous treat, the stairways one saw being the very least of it. First off, on the edge of the prairie was a house here and a house there—and not so many of them sod houses, either. Quite a few were even painted. There was Doctor Feild's and across the road no farther than I could shy a rock was the house of Mr. Marshall who owned the lumber yard. Those little girls swinging on the gate would be the Marshall twins no one could tell apart. A little farther was the house of Mr. B. T. Thompson who had the Racket Store on the Square. Then there was Banker Fleming's and Doctor McKenzie's and Colonel John C. Moore's. Papa said Colonel John C. Moore had the best building site in Enid: on a bluff overlooking Boggy Creek and the whole town. The house was painted yellow, like ours. It had an upstairs. As I could see no ladder (and I looked sharply) there must have been a staircase *inside*.

Once we saw a lady milking a Jersey cow in Banker Fleming's yard.

"It's Mrs. Fleming," said Mama. "For all their money she gives herself no airs."

About some of the houses were planted little locust and maple trees. Instead of a picket fence Doctor McKenzie's house was enclosed by the tidiest row of bushes.

"That is a hedge," said Mama, "a hard thing to grow in this country; and the doctor'll need his windmill to keep up that lawn."

What Mama called a lawn was a front yard of grass no higher than buffalo grass but a prettier green.

The road from our claim was one of several roads leading from the flat prairie into Enid from the east. They all came together like the ribs of Mama's black fan and made one big straight road which was E Street. On E Street the houses were so numerous and so near each other that it would be hard to speak particularly of any one of them, unless Mr. Rick Messall's. Mr. Rick Messall was a saloonkeeper and, of course, very rich.

"At least he has the *manners* of a gentleman," Mama said of him.

Then you crossed the railroad and if very, very lucky got to see a train of cars pass. "Stop, Look and Listen!" said the white sign which was in the shape of an X. No one ever stopped. Enid people were not going to let the Rock Island tell them what to do. Pretty soon the stores began, with the buildings *touching* each other and no front yards at all, only board sidewalks shaded by wooden awnings. Then you came to the Square.

By this time my head would be in such a whirl that I'm afraid it would have been beyond me to tell you, all at once, about the Square. You never saw so many rigs or so many people. Rigs of all kinds: buggies and carriages, tops up and tops down; farm wagons of all kinds, from light spring wagons to big red and green Studebakers; enormous hayracks; movers' covered wagons; closed town hacks; the weatherbeaten yellow stage which now ran only from the Square to the Rock Island depot at train times; buckboards, carts, broad-tired drays, the splendid brewery trucks, and, oh, yes, the Moore phaeton with its colored driver handling the bays, and the colonel's daughter, Miss Mabel, leaning back with a folded parasol on her lap, looking like a picture in a book. Once I got close enough to see that Miss Mabel was freckled.

Behind a settler's wagon a calf or a steer or a colt might walk in the dust at the end of a lead rope. In the bed might be a few oinking shoats on their way to market; or chickens or turkeys or guineas with wings clipped and feet tied. Or a bed might be piled with watermelons, turnips or roasting ears; with fence posts or with jack rabbits dressed with the fur on. The fence posts and the jack rabbits usually told you a settler came from "the jacks," where jack oaks and jack rabbits were about all that grew. On the other hand a load of cedar posts would have been hauled, at some risk to the hauler, all the way from the Gyp Hills. The Hills were Government land, where you weren't supposed to cut timber. A cedar hauler had to keep an eye peeled for deputy marshals on the make for a little mileage money. I always looked twice at a cedar hauler out of respect for the chances he took. The fence posts on our claim were cedar.

Sometimes we sent a wagonload of watermelons to town. In the back of the buggy Mama would stow baskets of eggs packed in hay and crocks of butter to trade at Mr. Peter Bowers's. I made it a point to be present when she did her trading. After figuring with a pencil Mr. Bowers would shove his glasses up on his forehead.

"Mrs. James, I make it so and so much—not mentioning the usual little something extra. A bit of that nice China tea you like and——"

The storekeeper's glance would fall on me and his arm would reach into the showcase filled with candy. My eyes would follow the hand of the reaching arm. The trigger finger was missing at the middle joint: Dick Yeager had shot it off. Ah, the hand moved toward a big striped stick, a *big* one. Sometimes it stopped at a smaller stick.

Tie rails where people tied their teams and their buggy and their saddle horses ran nearly around the bare dust-blown five-acre Square. Considerate people moved their animals from one side to another to catch the shade of the buildings. When Mama or Papa sent me to move Tom it was an important thing. For a moment I could pretend that I'd driven to Enid all by myself. Inside the Square campers, with teams unhitched and stamping flies in the dust, made themselves at home about their covered wagons, cooking and toting water from the land-office pump or the courthouse pump, whichever was nearer.

On one street corner a crowd gathered about Colonel Joshua Mathis, the horse auctioneer. "Forty-five dollars I'm bid for this lively little mare. Do I hear a fifty?" A smaller crowd listened to a blind Negro in front of Jim Utsler's saloon and gambling house. The blind Negro was playing a guitar and singing a doleful song about Sam Bass.

Once Papa took me inside Jim Utsler's. Behind the bar was the biggest looking glass in the world. You could have seen a house in it. The floor was covered with sawdust and there were brass spittoons two feet high. On the walls were the horns of steers and snakeskins and old reward posters: "WANTED DEAD OR ALIVE." And there was a big picture of an Indian fight. I spelled out the words: "Custer's Last Stand." That must have been the very fight Mr. Howell told me about. But none of these was what Papa wanted to show me. He wanted to show me the fans that were attached to the ceiling. They were turned by little leather belts running from a wheel on a steam engine in a shed in the back, and they kept the place nice and cool.

Mama didn't fancy Papa's taking me into a saloon.

"But Jim Utsler's; you know you like Jim," Papa said.

Mama did like Jim Utsler, of whom she couldn't say, as she did of Mr. Rick Messall, that he had the manners of a gentleman. Jim Utsler was a rough and tough customer. With a scraggly mustache, tobacco-stained teeth, and rumpled clothes, he looked more like a cattleman than a high-toned saloonkeeper. He'd bought the claim north of us from the old cowpuncher who'd staked it, built a fine house and the largest red barn I'd ever seen. He'd loan anything: farm machinery, horses to draw it, a side of meat from his smokehouse, his white-faced Hereford bull.

"A lot of settlers are better off for Jim Utsler, and that's a fact. I reckon it makes up a little for those worse off on his account."

Mama's remark would bring before me a likeness of God, with a great beard like that of Colonel Joshua Mathis, the horse auctioneer. God would be bending over a thick book, balancing the good marks against the bad opposite the name of Jim Utsler.

Bullfights were occasionally held in a ring in the Square. The bullfighters were Mexicans. Though Mama would not go to a bullfight, Papa took me to more than one. But Mama loved the horse races, as she did everything that had to do with horses. The sin she said was betting. For a long while that was all I knew about betting. One time some man who was with us said such-and-such horse should win when I was sure that Mr. Ed Weatherly's filly would. The man offered to bet a nickel. He explained how it was to bet. The Weatherly filly won going away. Thus it was that I had two nickels to rub against each other in my pocket. Such a pity it was a sin.

It seems odd that I cannot recall ever having seen Ad Poak ride his own horse, Pat, in a race. Had I done so perhaps my career as a gambler would have made swifter if less fortunate progress. Surely I could not have refrained from betting on the big sorrel stallion no matter what other horses were running. I remember Mama returning from the Fair Grounds saddened because Pat had lost, or, if he had won, because Ad was unwilling to leave well enough alone. For Ad would keep on racing until in the end he had lost all his money and more besides. With Pat, he would return to the claim to clear away his debts. So Ad Poak, like Martha, was with us only on and off. For that matter so were Papa, Mr. Howell, and Will or Ira or whatever happened to be the name of the hired man. They came and went. Only Mama stayed all the time.

Besides reading to me and listening to me read and explaining the new words, Ad's duties about the claim were something Mama said she had never got clear in her mind. Mostly they seemed to consist of currying and clipping Pat and exercising him in the West Bottom. Ad was not a hired man. He did not sleep in the "boys' house." He was the only occupant of our upstairs.

All the same Mama and Ad got along fine. My mother had spent half her life in parts of the country where more men carried firearms than carried timepieces. Yet she had never fired a gun, which Ad declared to be a scandal. Ad spent a good deal of the time he could spare from Pat at pistol practice, fixing his marks to the chopping block in the back yard. He shot a bone-handled, double-action, nickel-plated Smith & Wesson .38. Mama said that was about the only use Ad made of the chopping block.

One time he came in with a little 16-gauge shotgun he had borrowed and began teasing Mama to shoot it. He told what shots his mother and his sister were—the sister who could "make a *git*-tar just talk." Finally he said that if Mama could hit her dishpan at twenty feet he'd buy her a new one. Mama sure surprised him.

"Happens I need a new dishpan, Ad. I'll just take you up on that."

Ad propped the pan against the chopping block.

As Mama aimed Ad kept giving her advice.

"Shut *one* eye, Miz James. Look the *same* way you point the gun—*toward* the dishpan."

With both eyes closed and her face turned from the target, Mama blazed away. She blew a hole in the dishpan you could have thrown a cat through.

Mama would say to Ad: "Why don't you go back to the good home you left and marry some nice Missouri girl and settle down instead of running wild in this forsaken part of the world?" Ad would read us his mother's letters. They seemed mostly about the colts they were raising on their farm in Missouri.

Getting back to my trips to Enid, I'd rather go with Papa than with Mama because he would let me twist my hair under my hat so that I did not look like a girl. Papa wouldn't get my hair cut off, though.

"It would displease your mama," he said. "Wait until you start school, son."

Best of all the ways to go to town was to sneak a trip in the wagon with Ad Poak. Barefooted, in the clothes I wore at home and with Prince at my side, I wasn't so fearful of the boys I saw in the streets. Once Ad and I ran smack into Papa, pitching horseshoes in the shade of the courthouse. With a happy shout he swung me to his shoulder.

"Gentlemen, I have the honor of presenting the Strip's own Huck Finn!"

Grateful for the welcome after my forbidden journey and enchanted to be the center of attention, I shook hands with Judge McAtee, Colonel John C. Moore, Mr. Sturgis, Doctor Fairgrieve and one or two gentlemen whose names were strange to me.

At one of them I must have looked closely, for his hair fell about his shoulders in glistening ringlets, as mine would have done were it not twisted up.

"Temple," Papa said, "this is my son. Marquis: Mr. Temple Houston."

Mr. Temple Houston made such an impression on my mind that I mentioned him to Mr. Howell.

"Temple Houston? Why, shore. Knowed his pappy, ol' Sam. Yessiree, knowed ol' Sam Houston, Bigfoot Wallace, an' all them early *Tejanos*. When I was a young squirt in the Rangers, 'fore the Rebellion."

5

Most memorable of my early excursions to Enid was the time I shook hands with Dick Yeager. Far from erasing a single detail of that meeting, or of the events which made it possible, I find by consulting the record that the intervening years have added details and performed other useful services.

This suggests that Mr. Howell's talent for elevating truth above the range of the familiar has not been lost on his most entranced listener. Indeed, I was all prepared to grace these pages with a story of Dick Yeager's pursuit and capture, and of my subsequent audience with him purporting to be based on my own recollections. I was almost as certain that I remembered those things as I am of anything. Then I looked up the date. Dick was taken on August 4, 1895. He died in the Garfield County jail on September 7. My fourth birthday was August 29, 1895.

So, the story I tell you now is of events I cannot remember, really. I pass it on from my memory (corrected by the record, where that is possible) of the accounts of others which were told to me, and told so often that they have come to seem a part of actual experience. My father's and Ad Poak's associations with Dick Yeager, and my meeting with him, embodied a claim to distinction which a child will keep bright.

Dick Yeager was any Cherokee Strip youngster's ideal of what an outlaw should be and do—an almost mythological figure, difficult to realize within the confines of acceptable evidence. The saga of how they hunted him down I must have heard a hundred times—from Ad Poak who fired the last shot; from other participants (who weren't hard to find since a thousand men took part in the chase first and last); and from Mama, who probably knew as many of the actors in the drama as any woman in Oklahoma Territory. Though too great a slave to facts to compete with Mr.

Howell, Mama lived in a day and in a part of the world where storytelling was still an important art.

Dick's end came as a result of one thing leading to another. First was only the holdup at the Cimarron River bridge of a Rock Island train which was carrying gold for the Army payroll in Texas. Bill Doolin's gang did that, and the best testimony does not place Dick on the scene. Later, in the Garfield County jail, Dick said he was there, but during his residence in our jail Dick said a lot of things. The Cimarron bridge holdup caused no great indignation in Enid. The Railroad War was too recent a memory for us to get worked up over the misfortunes of the Rock Island. That was distinctly something for Chris Madsen to worry about. Mr. Chris Madsen was the United States Marshal, the head of the Federal Government's law-enforcement establishment in the Territory.

Federal officers, appointed in Washington and sent down to tell us what and what not to do, were not popular with the rank and file of settlers. For instance, we didn't like the way they used the cedar haulers. Cedar haulers were products of the droughts and general hard times in the early years after the Opening. They were settlers who would drive into the Gyp Hills, cut a load of fire-killed cedar, light and easy to handle, drive thirty-five miles to Enid or to Alva, and sell the load for eight or ten dollars. The Gyp Hills, rising abruptly from the plain, were also called the Gloss Mountains from the way the shiny rocks in the steep red slopes caught the sun and glistened. Unfit for homesteading, the Hills were Government-owned and rarely visited except by cedar haulers or by outlaws on the dodge.

The law against cutting timber on Government land was a law settlers had no use for when in need of a little cash money. United States deputy marshals enforced the law spasmodically for the same reason. Deputies drew fees on a mileage basis—ten cents a mile as I recall—for the distance traveled with prisoners after an arrest. They were paid by the head. Escorting ten prisoners one mile was the same as escorting one prisoner ten miles. A couple of deputies would ride into the Hills, arrest a few outfits of cedar haulers, take them to Alva, the county seat of Woods County, thirty-five miles away, and put in for mileage on each man in custody. The vouchers approved, prisoners would be turned loose—inconvenienced only by the confiscation of their loads and the loss of their time. This leniency was not appreciated, however: settlers definitely didn't like the marshals' way of piecing out their incomes. So, after the Rock Island holdup, if Chris Madsen wanted to catch Bill Doolin that was Chris's affair.

Mr. Madsen accepted the challenge and got right busy. He was at the head of a small posse which killed a man the newspapers said was Rattlesnake Jim, a member of the Doolin gang. The publication of this item proved a boon to the real Rattlesnake Jim, whom they never got at all. Years later I saw him in my father's law office. When I left Oklahoma he was still above ground leading a different life.

One of Madsen's deputies, Bill Banks, killed Dan Clifton and Charlie Pierce, known, respectively, as Dynamite Dick and Tulsa Jack. They had been at the Cimarron bridge. Doolin and six companions reached the Gyp Hills but were not permitted the undisturbed enjoyment of that haven. Deputy Hec Thomas cornered the leader in a dugout and shot him to death. Of Bill Doolin I cannot pretend to speak from the best information. I still think of certain old-time Oklahoma outlaws in connection with attorneys who defended them, and from whom in later years I got some of the particulars that are related here. Bill Doolin's attorney was Mr. Scott Denton, with whom my father was on such distant terms that I never had a chance to hear him talk about Bill. But my impression is that Hec Thomas terminated the career of a southwestern highwayman to whom history has done less than justice.

Bill Radler was wounded and captured. Buck Wateman, Dick West, and Arkansas Tom got away. Retribution caught up with Buck and Dick shortly after. Buck was killed while robbing a Wells-Fargo express box in Woods County and Dick West after a Rock Island holdup at Siding Number One near Chickasha, in the Chickasaw Nation. Dick was killed by Mr. William D. Fossett, a friend of my father whom I came to know very well. Mr. Fossett was one of the great, though unpublicized, peace officers of the powder-stained Southwest: a man to mention with Wild Bill

Hickok and Bat Masterson. Dick West's reputation likewise has failed to survive, though in the nineties he was regarded as a highwayman who had reached the top of his calling.

Arkansas Tom, the third of the trio to escape from the Gyp Hills, was the only one the law never got its hands on. His reputation as a desperado didn't amount to much at the time and thereafter he was careful not to enhance it. Maybe this was because he was smart, and maybe because he'd had a scare thrown into him. Ad Poak's opinion of Arkansas Tom is recorded earlier in this chapter, and Ad wasn't a bad judge of such matters. In any event, the year I left the Strip Mr. Fossett told me Tom was still living in Oklahoma under a different name.

With Doolin dead, Radler caught, and Wateman, West, and Arkansas Tom on the loose, none of the party who had held up the train remained in the Hills. Yet the deputies and their small posses had quarry before them: Dick Yeager and Ike Black. It was thought then (and for that matter long after) that Dick and Ike had been at the Cimarron with Bill Doolin. Supporting this was the fact that they had been with the Doolin band at the time of the fight in which the leader was killed and Radler wounded and run down. Yet the most dependable evidence denies Yeager and Black any part in the Rock Island holdup. Their presence in the Gyp Hills with Doolin was a coincidence.

Ike Black was an outlaw of so little account as to be hardly worth the trouble of arresting except for mileage. Dick Yeager stood in a different light. Having killed a Kansas sheriff and twice broken jail in Guthrie, the Territorial capital, he had a price on his head. After the second jail-delivery, Dick had gone so thoroughly into seclusion that people about forgot to look for him. Well these two, Yeager and Black, were on their way from a hideout in Kansas to the Hills to lay low some more, when what should happen but they meet up with Bill Doolin and colleagues. After Bill had been killed and his band scattered, the officers kept right on going—in pursuit of Dick Yeager and Ike Black. At any rate that is how Mr. Fossett, who was in one of the original posses, explained the matter to me. He never did believe Dick Yeager as big a man as his reputation. Mr. Fossett entertained deep convictions on that subject, or he would not have mentioned it to me—knowing that Dick had been a client of my father and a childhood hero of mine. A strict constructionist in the rating of outlaws according to their merits, Mr. Fossett's point was that it had not been established that Dick ever held up a bank or a railroad train.

The pursuit of Dick Yeager might have continued as the pursuit of Bill Doolin had begun—a professional limited-participation affair with the Federal officers on one side and the outlaws on the other and the public taking little more than a spectator interest—had not Dick and Ike the poor judgment to kill a settler who got in their way. Kill one settler and you rouse up a swarm of settlers. That was what turned the chase of Dick Yeager into the greatest man-hunt Oklahoma ever had. The almost unbelievable endurance, the wilyness and the bravado of Yeager made it so. That's the rock on which his reputation rests.

6

The aim of Yeager and Black was to escape from the Gyp Hills to the Cherokee Nation. Time and again they ventured upon the intervening prairie and fought incredible pitched battles, the two of them against whole posses. They failed to break through; but the posses failed to take them. In these fights Dick seemed to bear a charmed life. Time and again men swore they had seen him knocked down by the impact of their bullets. On one of his captured horses was a saddle with nine holes in it. Dick stole other horses and kept on. But always he and Black were driven back to the Hills.

Ad Poak was with a posse, thus leaving Mama and me alone much of the time. Mama was not afraid. In her day she had met Jesse James and had known Cole Younger's whole family. She had never heard of an outlaw harming a woman. Certainly Dick Yeager would not have bothered us, though he knew the East Draw well.

Nearly every day brought fresh news of the hunt. Mr. Sam

Campbell's posse came by our place and, after scouting the Draw, unsaddled and watered their horses, fed and rested them. Some of the men sat around and cleaned their guns. Others stretched out under the Big Tree and slept with their hats over their eyes. A few moonlight nights later this posse came on Dick and Ike sleeping beside their picketed horses. One man fired too soon. He missed, awakening the outlaws who shot their way out of the trap. Yeager used only one pistol, carrying his boots in the other hand. A few days after that a man in a decrepit spring wagon, driving a seventeen-year-old horse and playing a mouth organ, rode through a line of vigilantes. Too late they learned that he was Dick Yeager. That happened on Skeleton Creek not far east of our claim. The occurrence made the posses more suspicious. When two men traveling south in a light covered wagon refused to explain themselves promptly enough, they were shot and one of them killed. It was printed in the papers that the victims were Dick Yeager and Ike Black. They turned out to be young farmers, brothers, from Old Oklahoma, who had been looking for gold along Boggy Creek. A little later a posse concealed in an angle of a corn field ambushed the right men as they dismounted at a settler's shack to ask for grub. Ike was killed, Dick wounded again and his horse captured.

At the point of a gun Dick got a fresh horse belonging to a settler named Blakely. Mr. Blakely described the fugitive as in no condition to ride far. Presently the horse was found. The bed of a dry creek revealed the track of a man who stopped frequently to rest and who appeared to be lame. It led into Alvin Ross's stand of corn. Sheriff Thralls of Enid spread his posse around the field and sent Ad Poak and Tom Smith to follow the track through the corn. The tassels were more than head high. Not a breath of air was stirring. This made it impossible for Ad and Tom Smith to move without rustling the corn. They kept their Winchesters ready. The track was very fresh and it twisted as if the person who made it did not know where he was going.

The track led to a small bare mound of bad soil where no corn would grow. Stretched out on this mound was the enormous form of Dick Yeager, apparently asleep. His clothes were tattered and stained with blood. He wore one boot and one shoe. At his right side lay a six-shooter and a rifle. Ad and Tom Smith raised their rifles. Ad said:

"Let's give the poor devil a chance."

With guns still leveled Ad called out:

"Put up your hands, Dick. We've got you."

The bandit opened his eyes and blinked. He did not say a word. His right hand moved toward his pistol.

Ad and Tom Smith fired. Dick rolled over one complete turn. But he had his pistol.

"Drop that gun," yelled the men.

Dick dropped it and stiffly raised his right hand.

"Both hands!"

"I can't, boys," said Dick Yeager. "That arm's broke."

The county jail was in the Square slantwise across the street from the Rex Hotel. A tight, slate-colored fence with four or five strands of barbed wire on top enclosed it. At each corner of the fence a deputy sheriff armed with a Winchester sat on a box.

There was always a crowd about the jail. People came on the cars from long ways off to see the celebrated desperado. Admirers brought hampers of fried chicken and cold bottles of beer. Dick enjoyed this attention, held court from a cot in his cell and entertained everybody. He admitted every crime that had been committed in the Strip since the Opening. He joshed the lawyers, saying they weren't worth the powder to blow them to hell. The lawyers were kind of disappointed because Doctor McKenzie said from the first that there would be no trial. Dick had been shot in almost every part of his huge body. He couldn't possibly get well.

Ad Poak had been given a job on the jail fence. He talked his way out of the hot sun and became the famous prisoner's personal cell-guard and chamberlain. He introduced visitors, helped Dick along with his tall stories, and consumed a share of the delicacies an appreciative public showered on the prisoner.

I had gone to town with Mama on one of her regular trips to Mr. Bowers's store when a little colored boy came to say that Papa would like to see us at the jail.

As Mama suspected, the message had come from Ad Poak.

Papa wasn't at the jail at all. We waited until a crowd of sightseers cleared out of the cell and Ad took us in.

Ad Poak was a small neat man with a silky yellow mustache Mama made fun of because it was so puny. About his neck was usually a figured silk handkerchief held by a ring made by cutting the center from a poker chip. I don't think Ad was much taller than Mama, whose head came little higher than Papa's shoulder. Any man taller than my father I knew to be real big. Well, you should have seen Dick Yeager. He was lying on his bunk, covered by a clean white sheet. But you could tell how tall he was. His feet stuck over the foot of the bunk. The cell smelled of medicine. Wet blankets were hung against the walls to keep down the heat. The brindle jail pup, with which Dick had made friends, was lying on the damp floor, panting. Dick's head was by the barred window. He was sucking a lemon.

"Dick Yeager, I hope you are comfortable," said Mama after Ad had said who we were.

Mama stood by the door of the cell.

"I am; tol'ably so; thank you, ma'am," said Dick Yeager.

Dick held out his hand. I marched to the bunk and took it. Mama stayed where she was.

"Young man," said Dick Yeager, "you can tell 'em you've shook hands with the bigges' outlaw Oklahoma ever had."

"Yes, sir," said I.

There was a chair in the cell, Ad's chair. He invited Mama to sit down.

"I'll stand; thank you, Ad," she said.

Mama was looking at Dick Yeager's face. It was covered with a reddish stubble of beard. His eyes were bright blue. In a moment Mama said:

"Dick Yeager, I hope you rest comfortably while you are here. Now, Ad, if you will excuse us."

Mama took my hand. While Ad was unlocking the door I looked at the gigantic figure on the cot. I wanted to say something, but it was Dick who spoke.

"Bub, jus' you recollec' what I tol' you: bigges' outlaw the Territory ever had."

When we got outside Ad said:

"Well, Madam, that was the coolest reception Dick's had so far."

The look of sadness in my mother's gray eyes stopped Ad's banter.

"What a tragic sight to see," she said, and added, "I reckon outlaws sometimes are just made by what happens to them."

Mama may have been talking to Doctor McKenzie. He, too, knew how outlaws sometimes were made: a cowboy who likes to brag gets in bad company and one thing leads to another. Could Doctor McKenzie have healed Dick Yeager's wounds it would have been only so they could have hanged him. Consequently the doctor, who wore an Old Testament beard and was a pillar of the Baptist church, tried to do something for Dick's soul. Dick wasn't interested.

Doctor McKenzie told Mama how Dick Yeager died. For a while Dick had seemed to fool the predictions of the doctors. He got stronger and spryer. Then one evening his fever began to rise fast.

"Dick," said the doctor, "this is your last night on earth. Is there anyone you wish to see or anything you wish to say?"

"Nobody to see, Doc; an' nothin' to say."

In the shallow top drawer of the rolltop desk in his office Papa kept Dick Yeager's revolver. It was the one he had carried through the one hundred and twenty-five days of the great pursuit. The pistol stayed there for years. One time after we had left the claim and moved to Enid, I opened the drawer to show the gun to a crony. It was gone.

"I gave it to a lady," Papa explained, "a rather nice-looking countrywoman I'd never seen before. She convinced me that she was a sister of Ellsworth Wyatt. That was Dick Yeager's true name. She wanted something to remember him by."

The gun was a cedar-handled, single-action, long-barreled Colt .45, with the "dog" filed for fanning the hammer. Dick's sister carried it away wrapped in a newspaper.

CHAPTER TWO

Mr. Howell

MUCH as I longed for his return, Mr. Howell would be of no help with my greatest problem. That was to get my hair cut. Mr. Howell sided with Mama. But then Mr. Howell wore his own hair pretty long. He told me that in the old days Indians respected a paleface with long hair because long-haired scalps were in demand. Two of the bravest men Mr. Howell had known wore real long hair: Wild Bill Hickok and Yellowstone Kelley. And there was Mr. Temple Houston. I had gathered from Mr. Howell that Mr. Temple Houston, though just a lawyer, possessed claims to renown not to be passed over lightly. He'd killed one man in the Panhandle and another in the Strip, at Woodward. Nor was there any denying the appeal of Wild Bill Hickok and Yellowstone Kelley, on the basis of their accomplishments as related by Mr. Howell. But in my case it didn't work. When I appeared in Enid with my hair down, the street boys didn't think of Wild Bill and his glorious deeds. All they did was yell:

"Aw, look at the little gur-rul! Nice little gur-rul!"

From this I came to understand that girls were undesirables whom it was a disgrace to resemble. I had only the street boys' word for this, for up to then I had known only one little girl. She was Virginia Ackerman and her hair was about the length of mine. The Ackerman claim was seven miles south of ours—a long journey over the prairie which we did not make very often. But as our place was on their way to Enid they usually stopped off. Virginia's father was an invalid and sometimes they would bring him along for the outing. He would sit in a chair and say nothing. Mrs. Ackerman, who had made the Run and staked the claim, was a big, jolly woman who talked a great deal in a throaty voice. She was Mama's best friend. So it was that Virginia Ackerman became the nearest I had to a playmate. We chased tumbleweeds, swung in the wild-grapevine swing by the spring, rolled in the hay loft and jumped from the loft door onto the soft manure pile.

Our infrequent visits to the Ackerman claim were even more noteworthy. It was a dry claim, without a tree or a drop of water except from a well. They lived in a sod house: the most wonderful sod house, the most wonderful house of any kind, I'd ever been in. Sod houses were mostly one room. I will not try to say how many rooms the Ackermans had, but it seems that I used to get lost in them. Mrs. Ackerman had helped in their building, lifting the sod with her own hands, to provide a home for the kinfolks and connections who composed the big, noisy, happy clan. It was at the Ackermans that I saw and heard my first piano—which I should be surprised to learn was not the first piano in a farmhouse in the county. After Sunday dinner dishes were out of the way, the family would collect about it and sing.

"I declare I envy Anna Ackerman," Mama would say. "Do the work of two men and then light in and have a good time."

On the edge of the bustle and laughter sat the silent invalid in his chair.

All at once my recollection of the Ackermans grows dim. I know that Mr. Ackerman was "sent away" and that he died and that somewhere along the line Mrs. Ackerman had to give up the struggle and abandon her claim. I have a memory of Virginia's coming to our place and seeming almost a stranger. Whether this was due to an elapse of time or whether to the prejudice against girls imbibed during the hair crisis I am at a loss to say.

My mother's reason for keeping my hair long was that "civilized" little boys wore their hair that way. I knew her to be right enough about that. It was all too plain from the pictures in *Scribner's Monthly* and even in the *Youth's Companion*. But then everything was different in those civilized places. There were street cars and the greatest houses you ever heard tell of and stores ten stories high. These houses were lighted by what you called gas, and everyone had a piano—in a room called the parlor.

The only parlor I knew of was Mills's Tonsorial Parlor in Enid where if it wasn't for Mama I could have had my hair cut. And then there were bathtubs to take baths in, though they didn't look like tubs. They looked like watering troughs. I would see the pictures of these things and Mama would tell me their names and all about them.

In these pictures the men wore different clothes from our men. Ever so many wore stovepipe hats. Mama said Papa had worn no other hat for years. That struck me as funny. I told Papa I bet he looked funny in one of those stovepipe hats and he said in his slow way, "Marquis, I expect I did." Colonel Havens was the only man in Enid who wore a stovepipe hat. They said he had been a congressman back in the States.

The ladies wore different clothes, too. Even Mama used to wear them. Upstairs was a leather-covered trunk with a broken hinge. In it were dresses which looked sort of like the dresses of the ladies in *Scribner's Monthly*. Mama cut them up to make quilts, finally. When these people rode they dressed more outlandish yet and had the queerest little saddles, like racing saddles. But mostly they went about in carriages finer than John C. Moore's or in funny little two-wheeled rigs Mama called hansoms. They rode on the cars and on steamboats. Mama used to take a steamboat from Cincinnati to St. Louis to see her folks in Missouri. I yearned to ride on a steamboat. I'd never even seen any kind of boat and couldn't remember having ridden on a railroad train. Mama was ever ready to answer questions about the pictures because she said she wanted me to know about civilized things.

In a book I saw a picture of a boy who was following a horse along a path beside a creek. The horse seemed to be pulling a funny-looking boat. I asked Mama what this could be. It was a canal, Mama said, and the horse was pulling a canal boat. The boy who kept the horse going was a poor boy whose father was dead, and his name was James A. Garfield. But he was a good boy, who worked hard and studied hard and obeyed his mother and got to be President of the United States. Our Garfield County, Mama said, had been named in his honor.

Now this boy, who was barefooted and wore clothes about like those I wore, did not seem so forbidding of aspect as civilized city boys. I regretted there were no canals in the Strip so I could start as a towpath boy and become President of the United States.

Though it had the breath of novelty, what Mama said on this subject of civilization could be a little disturbing. Until then the sod houses, the plains and Enid, plus what Mr. Howell spoke of, which all fitted in, were to me the order of the whole world. This world was populated by settlers, fringed with cowboys, stagecoach drivers, lawyers, outlaws, gamblers, saloonkeepers, storekeepers, horse traders, Indians and Mexicans. They comprised the social scheme of the universe. An example of how it hung together was the mutual dependence of outlaws and lawyers. The amplifications introduced by Mama and by *Scribner's Monthly* tended to create a situation too complex to cope with.

Getting back to the long-hair question, you see that while Mama's ideas on that subject differed from Mr. Howell's they came to the same thing as far as I was concerned.

"Marquis, I won't have you looking like a Comanche."

I tried to point out that a haircut would make me less like a Comanche. Comanches wore long hair. Mama was always telling me not to behave like a Comanche. If I yelled in the house, or picked my nose, or made a noise while eating, I was behaving like a Comanche. Mama's loose use of the term impaired my faith in her judgment.

I don't know just how it did happen, really. My own recollection fails me and I haven't Ad Poak's to fall back on as in the capture of Dick Yeager, for I suppose it wasn't a thing that Ad cared to talk about afterwards. And Ad was the only one present besides myself when I finally got my hair cut.

It was in the stable where Ad was clipping Pat. When he finished he took the clippers to me. Then Ad and I drove to town in the wagon. Ad didn't say much but he bought a bag of chocolate drops and after giving me one or two said the rest were for my mother. When we got home supper was waiting, but Mama didn't eat. She was sitting in her low rocker crying. By and by Ad went in and said he was truly sorry for what he had done. He said he thought he'd better pack his saddlebags and go away for a while.

"Yes, Ad," said Mama, "I think you better had."

Mama had seen my hair on the floor of the stable and had brought some of it in. She sat in the low rocker picking out Pat's sorrel hairs from mine, by the light of the lamp. Then she went to her bureau and got the box with the lid that latched on. I never fooled with that box, myself. Among the things in it were the pictures of my two baby sisters who had died.

Mama put my hair in the box.

2

The return of Mr. Howell must have been pretty soon after that. I know Mama and I were alone on the place: no Ad, no Martha, and no hired man. That sometimes happened. I would help Mama with the milking and other chores. The rest of the farm work didn't get done.

As the tobacco crop hadn't panned out, no front addition or stairway had been built. But our house had been enlarged, and in a way more nearly unique than building any front addition. North Town was dying out and many of the vacant houses were being moved to Enid. Papa went there and bought a house, and not just an ordinary house, but a store building. He had it joined on to our house. The building still had its big false front and its big store windows. It became our dining room and kitchen. I was proud of those big store windows and the false front. No one else had such a house to live in.

Papa planted sugar cane where the tobacco had been. With sorghum as high as it was one cane crop would about take care of the new front addition, he said.

One evening after she had finished the supper dishes Mama was reading in the low rocker and I was playing on the floor with Prince and Rublin and Idud. Rublin and Idud were the house cats.

They were black with white faces, and as nearly alike as the Marshall twins, Mama said. So we were all there together when I heard Mama exclaim:

"I declare, if it isn't Mr. Howell!"

Sure enough there he was in the doorway, holding his broad hat in his hand.

"Evenin', ma'am," said Mr. Howell, standing his rifle against the wall. Without comment he put down a wild turkey he had shot. Mr. Howell would have deemed it a breach of etiquette to come to our house empty-handed.

Mr. Howell was as tall as my father and slimmer. He would have been taller if he had stood straight, but he was stoop-shouldered. His gray hair came down over the collar of the red and white spotted calfskin vest he usually put on to visit at our house or to go to Enid. About the mouth his short gray beard was a little brown from tobacco juice. I suppose that was something water wouldn't wash out, for Mr. Howell was clean and tidy. When he came to see Mama he would put on a colored shirt he had washed in the creek and dried on the grass. It would be wrinkled, of course, because Mr. Howell had no flatiron. His pants were stuffed into boots that came half-way to his knees. The boots were low-heeled, and greased and soft. Mr. Howell did not clop-clop about like a cowboy. He walked with the long stride of an Indian, and you never did hear him until he was at the door. His voice was low and almost gentle. I never heard him say a swear word.

After admiring the turkey, Mama began to rally Mr. Howell about bringing his gun. Mr. Howell never left the dugout without a firearm—even to walk over to our house.

"You disrecollect the catamount I seed one night—in an elm by the spring," the old hunter said.

"Pshaw! That was in the fall of '94."

"Might come back," said Mr. Howell.

Before Mr. Howell accepted a chair he said:

"Soon as I see to the water buckets."

The first thing a man did coming on a place where women were alone was to see to the water buckets. A stranger would do it.

Usually this meant drawing the water from a well placed at some distance from the house, for the convenience of the stock. We used a spring by the creek, a good sixty yards away. The water buckets were my chore when Mama and I were alone. I could carry only one at a time and then I'd spill a good deal lugging it up the creek bank. Mama never sent me for water after dark. She was afraid I'd fall in the spring hole where the water was nine feet deep. I was not afraid of that. The last part of the way to the spring was under a natural arbor of elms overgrown with wild grapevines. At night that tunnel was as black as the inside of your hat. That's what I was afraid of. I wasn't so sure that the catamount had been gone since the fall of '94. The fact is I'd seen his shiny eyes fifty times.

But I loved to go to the spring in the nighttime with Mr. Howell. It gave me the wonderful feeling of passing safely through immense dangers.

Back from our trip to the spring, Mr. Howell told about driving stage out of Fort Reno through the Comanche country. He admitted it wasn't much of a tale.

"Country fillin' up. Railroads comin' in. Stages about played out. When we was buildin' *the* railroad, now—to Californy. The Union Pacific."

Mr. Howell had been employed as a hunter to shoot game for the track-layers' mess. He told us about that and I went to bed very happy.

3

Nowhere in his talk that evening did Mr. Howell mention what had really brought him from Fort Reno. Mama learned that from Papa. It was on account of Clark, the claim-jumper, who was trying to take away Mr. Howell's claim.

"Been writing him for a month," Papa said. "Never a scratch of a pen in return; and old Howell *can* write. He just turns up instead, taking his own sweet time."

"But the contest's good as won now—isn't it?" said Mama.

"Hardly that. But we can keep it going for a long while yet. Get a compromise of some sort."

Mama was alarmed. "Compromise! Why, I thought the shoe was on the other foot!"

"I know. We had Clark, and by that I mean his counsel, near the end of his rope after the last hearing. About ready to withdraw for three hundred dollars; but things have changed."

Papa went on to say that Clark had new money and new lawyers. "Rush & Steen, and you can imagine the difference they'll make."

"Houstin, you're not going to let that scamp Clark steal Mr. Howell's claim!"

"I can assure you no one will steal the old man's claim. But I've always said that with any kind of a lawyer on the other side it would be a hard case."

"And who's the old sly-boots who retained Rush & Steen for Clark?" Mama wished to know.

"I think none other than your good friend Jim Utsler."

Mama refused to believe it. Jim Utsler would have no part in stealing an honest old man's claim.

"No, Jim would not do that. Fact is, Clark's got a case. And I'm afraid George Rush is the man to find out what it is."

From earliest remembrance Clark, the claim-jumper, had played an interesting part in my scheme of things. Being a claim-jumper he was, of course, a menace. As everyone knew, a claim-jumper was not entitled to the respect reserved for an outlaw who held up banks or railroad trains or the Wells-Fargo. He was in a class with horse thieves. So Clark, because he was a claim-jumper, was a menace; but a menace in the way Mr. Schrock's bull was a menace. The Schrock bull was too old and lazy to chase you.

Clark had a sod house on the other end of the claim from Mr. Howell's dugout. He was a family man. One saw a woman and children about the sod house. Mr. Howell never spoke unkindly of Clark, though I knew he didn't like the way Clark plowed the end of the claim around the soddy and planted wheat.

"That's the way," said Mr. Howell, "to skeer off the game."

So we enjoyed all the excitement of having a claim-jumper in the neighborhood with none of the usual risks. When a claim-jumper contested your claim you either shot it out with him right away or hired a lawyer. That much I understood from the talk around me since the time I was old enough to listen to talk. As Papa was Mr. Howell's lawyer I could not regard Clark as a very serious hazard.

Actually, at this point in my story the Howell-Clark contest had dragged out four years—an unusually long time. And now things threatened to take an unfavorable turn for my father's client. A claim-jumper was a man who contested *your* right to *your* claim. Naturally it had not entered my head that Clark and his friends had grounds for regarding Mr. Howell in the same light as we regarded Clark.

Gradually I became aware of the drift of events. It was as if the Schrock bull had suddenly taken on new life. A danger yet to be met rather than a danger that had been met and overcome, as in all his tales of adventure, seemed to imperil Mr. Howell. I gathered this from what I heard Mama and Papa say from time to time about the contest. It was Jim Utsler, all right, who was putting up the money for Clark. Mama was awfully worried. Papa would say:

"Rachel, if you didn't have a worry on your mind you'd invent one."

But the cloud was easily dispelled when Mr. Howell and I were together at our old occupations. He never mentioned the contest and I'd forget about it.

4

In the West Bottom we raised watermelons and muskmelons for the market, but the house melon and garden patch was back of the barn on the edge of the cane field. One day I took a corn knife from the tool shed and went out to get me a watermelon for my own use. I was forbidden to carry a corn knife which had a blade longer than my arm. But it was the best thing there was for cutting a melon. One swipe and your melon was in two.

I was going along thumping melons for a ripe one when all at once my foot seemed to come down on something like a needle. I thought I had stepped into a mess of sandburs.

But when I looked there was a rattler. I knew all about rattlers never being supposed to strike without warning. And I knew the sound of a rattler as well as I knew the notes of a quail. It was figured later that maybe this one didn't have time to rattle. I must have stepped right into his mouth. I lit out for the house, yelling. I was sure I was going to die. That was all I could think of.

Mama whipped off her apron and tied the strings around my leg above the knee. She made me lie on the sofa in the front room and put Martha to watch me. There was not a man on the place or a horse in the lot. The nearest habitation was Mr. Howell's but he had no horse. The next nearest was Jim Utsler's, exactly half a mile away by the short cut through a field and a draw. Mama made for the Utslers. One of the Utsler boys jumped on a horse and started for town. A son of Clark, the claim-jumper, who worked for the Utslers, drove Mama home. When she got there she found that Martha had taken off the apron strings because I had cried that they were too tight. Mama put them back, yanking them so tight that I screamed.

Then Mama went to the porch to watch the road from town. Following the line between the Utsler and the Howell claims, the road ran along the crest of a rise so that for quite a piece you got the silhouette of anything that passed over it. I could always pick out our buggy and Tom, especially with Papa driving. Anxious to get his nose in the manger, Tom would break into a gallop if you would let him—and Papa always did.

Herb Utsler's instructions had been first to find Papa. If he couldn't do that right away to find Doctor McKenzie. If he couldn't find him to find Doctor Feild or some doctor.

Mama was watching to see whose rig would show up. Every now and then she would come inside and try to get me to stop yelling.

At length she said: "It's your father."

I made some half-hearted attempts to stop crying. Papa had told me about the Spartan boy with the fox under his coat. But I wasn't much interested in being a Spartan just then.

I can close my eyes now and see Papa's buggy, careening along that crest with Tom at a dead run. Of course I never saw this really (being inside the house), but I've heard Mama tell of it often enough. She said Doctor Fairgrieve was as badly scared as I was. "I say, Mrs. James, we touched earth just four times between the courthouse and your house." That would have been once every half mile.

Doctor Fairgrieve lanced my foot. About that time Mr. Howell showed up in a great lather. Why hadn't Mama sent for *him*? He knew all about snake bites.

When Doctor Fairgrieve told Mr. Howell to go down below the spring and get some of that sulphur mud, Mr. Howell said:

"Do you want to kill the young'un?"

It's a good thing I didn't hear this for I think that where snakes were concerned I had more faith in Mr. Howell than in anyone else in the world. Mama said:

"Mr. Howell, for goodness' sake do what the doctor says."

They put the mud on my foot, changing it every little while. Best of all, presently they took Mama's apron strings off my leg. Doctor Fairgrieve said:

"Judge, after that ride I could do with a drink."

"Get this boy out of danger and I'll buy you all the whiskey in Enid," said Papa.

Next day I must have been out of danger for Papa sent Doctor Fairgrieve off to Enid to collect his fee. At first Mama had been disappointed because Papa hadn't brought Doctor McKenzie, but Papa said Fairgrieve was the best doctor in town. Mama admitted she'd never heard of a person getting over a rattlesnake bite easier than I did. She gave Doctor Fairgrieve the credit for knowing about the poison-absorbing qualities of that smelly sulphur mud. Otherwise Doctor Fairgrieve didn't come up to Mama's ideas of a doctor. He was a gaunt, red-faced Englishman with a very big nose. He owned neither horse nor buggy, which were as much a doctor's belongings as his pill-box. Within walking distance of Enid's Square were enough patients to keep Doctor Fairgrieve in whiskey.

Then came the real good part about a snake bite. *I* had a story to tell and there were grown folks (not merely Prince and Rublin and Idud) to gather and listen. With a little practice I made it quite a tale. In the first place Papa had learned a surprising thing. He had visited the melon patch and come on to the corn knife. But that was not all. He found the rattlesnake, cut plumb in two. He carried the rattles to his office where he showed them to everyone, and told them they were from the snake that had bitten his boy, who hadn't left the melon patch until he'd killed the snake. So it was Papa, really, who put me on the track of telling this story properly.

Until his discovery I had not known that I'd killed the snake or tried to. Indeed, it must have been with some misgivings that I had mentioned the corn knife at all. Supposing myself in the shadow of death, perhaps I had thought it prudent to tell about the knife. For the rest, it seems that Mr. Howell had taught me so well to go after every snake I saw that it had become second nature. It must have been a part of my spasm of mortal terror to lash out at the rattler. Having a corn knife in my hand, one lick was enough. This I figured out later, of course. It was not a part of the early editions of my snake-bite story, the first narrative effort of mine to reach the audience I thought it deserved.

While I was getting back the use of my foot Papa was at the claim more than usual. He would bring Doctor Fairgrieve to look at the foot. Often he would bring others who would give me a chance to tell my story. Telling this story was the most natural thing in the world. You had an experience and you made a story of it. Listening to such stories had been about the sum total of my life up to then. Now I had my own to tell.

Ad Poak came and stayed a few days. Neighboring settlers I barely knew came. Jim Utsler's pretty young wife came with her stepdaughters who were nearly as old as she was. They brought a case of red soda pop, a present from Mr. Utsler. Bottles were tied on a fishline and hung in the spring to cool.

By and by the foot was well. One evening Mr. Howell said:

"Fotched the boy around slick as grease, didn't we?"

"Yes," said Mama, "that sulphur mud was surely a godsend."

"Knowed it would be," said Mr. Howell, in the mild, even tone which lent plausibility to the most extraordinary statements. "Mind as how the first time I tried out the mud cure for snake bite. Down in West Texas. When I was with the Rangers."

5

Besides Ad's going away and Mama's feeling so badly about it there was another reason my haircut hadn't brought all the serenity I'd counted on. Now I knew that I'd have to go to school. That's what Papa told Mama.

"They had to come off," he said, meaning my curls. "The boy's past school age now."

Sure enough, no sooner was I well of snake bite than the fatal morning came. I was told to put on my shoes and stockings because Papa was going to carry me to school in the buggy. Poor as was my opinion of school, I had not counted on the additional torture of shoes and stockings.

I knew where the schoolhouse was, and long ago had marked it as the place where on some evil day I should have to go. That thought would be in my mind as long as the school was in sight.

The East Hill School was a low building which had once had a coat of white paint. It stood on the very edge of town where there was only a house now and then and where the roads from the country began to come together to make E Street. That part of Enid was called East Hill because of the dip E Street took to cross Boggy Creek before it got to the Square. Though the road from our claim did not go directly past the schoolhouse it went close enough for me to see all those boys and girls in the school yard.

As Papa and I drove along I said that I hadn't known I'd have to wear shoes to school. He said he'd get me a pair of shoes I'd *like* to wear. Only they wouldn't be shoes. They'd be boots—red-topped, copper-toed boots. He'd had a pair when he was a boy and he'd worn them to school and they were the envy of every boy there. For the first time in my life I displayed a mild interest in footgear.

"I'll see Mr. Joe Meibergen and put in the order today," he said.

Papa introduced me to Miss Edna McKenzie, the teacher. Miss Edna said something friendly to me and I got the idea that Papa intended to stay there with us. But he looked at his watch and said he'd have to be getting along to see Mr. Joe Meibergen and that Miss Edna would take good care of me. It was all I could do not to cry. I would try very hard to keep from crying before Papa because he said he wanted me to be a Spartan.

I expected Miss Edna to ask me to read or that she would read to me or tell me a story. That was what lessons were like at home. Instead she led me to the door.

"Now, Markey, you run and play till the bell rings," she said and left me.

A girl chasing another girl nearly knocked me over. I moved out of the doorway. The yard was filled with children, most of them bigger than I. Nearly all the boys and some of the girls were barefooted. They were chasing balls, running and wrestling and tumbling. They were shouting and laughing. A boy was riding a pony and other boys were clinging to its tail.

They all seemed to know each other. I knew no one. To that moment, really, I had lived in a grownup world. How to take the first step toward an acquaintance with one of these children I had not the slightest idea. I stood mercifully unnoticed until I heard the bell. Miss Edna was standing on the doorstep ringing it. It was a little like the dinner bell at the Rex Hotel.

"Last bell! Last bell!" the youngsters shrieked, bolting for the door and buffeting me in their rush. I was about the last one in. The other children scrambled for seats. I stood until Miss Edna pleasantly indicated a seat for me.

I liked Miss Edna's smile. It made me feel less frightened and I sat down. But it also did something else. It discovered my presence to the other children. Their glances were upon me. There were giggles and whispers: "New boy! New boy!" My eyes appealed to Miss Edna. Her solacing smile was turned on someone else. I threw my head on my desk and burst into tears.

In this way it was that I made a sad beginning in a strange and hostile world. I do not know how I survived the taunts of the next few days.

Very quickly, though, I learned to discard the discomfort of shoes. After that first day I usually walked to school, taking the cut through the Utsler draw. I'd stow my shoes under the little bridge over the creek and on my way home wash my feet and put them on again.

By and by I began to get to know a few youngsters of my age. The country children brought their dinners in pails while the town kids went home at noon. This gave us country kids a chance to get acquainted and I got to know Harry Davis and Jeff George and Eva Britton, who was a girl. I got to know Jay Radcliffe and Sherman Rooney, though they were town boys. And the funny thing is that I got to know Enid's youthful celebrities, the Marshall twins, Ruth and Octavia, who were always dressed so nicely and exactly alike. I learned to tell them apart by a sort of twinkle Ruth had in her eye. Once as I passed their house after school she asked me into the yard to swing in their swing.

"I'm glad you're getting to know such genteel children," Mama said.

When Jeff George came home with me to stay all night I was afraid Mama might not think all my acquaintances so genteel. Jeff could swear terribly. The girls would put their fingers in their ears. Jeff was Buck George's brother and the only small boy in the school not afraid of Buck. Buck was the meanest of several large boys who would hold our heads under the pump, twist our arms until we squawled, or throw us on the ground and sit on our faces. Buck's face was freckled, his eyes as small as a pig's, and he had buck teeth. He rode a pony to school, carrying Jeff behind. He wore his spurs all day long and would stick the little kids with them. Buck must have been twelve years old and he was in the Third Reader. But he never bothered Jeff or bothered me when I was with Jeff. I asked Jeff why this was.

"I nearly kilt him once," Jeff said.

"How?" I asked in amazement.

"With an ax."

My fear that Jeff might rip out a string of cusswords before Mama proved unfounded.

"Give me a southern boy for manners," Mama said. "Marquis, you would do well to copy your little friend Jeff."

I wished I could fight like Jeff.

During the dinner hour when there were so few of us on the school ground I learned to take part in a few games: tag; hide-and-seek; prisoner's base; pom-pom-pull-away. I bought marbles which big boys stole, or confiscated under the pretext of finding them. "Losers weepers; finders keepers." I had never before played a game with other children, except keeping house with Virginia Ackerman. We both had dolls. At school I got it in my head that the object of a game was to win. This seemed more important than sticking to the rules when the other fellow wasn't looking. I was soon caught at this. My playmates raised a cry:

"Cheatin' dog! Cheatin' dog never wins!"

I was so humiliated that I wanted to crawl in a gopher hole. I did not recover until another boy had been caught fudging and I could join in the cry:

"Cheatin' dog never wins!"

My performances in the classroom attracted some little notice though this did not help to put me at ease on the playground. It never does. I could read anything we were required to read. I could read the Fourth Reader, along with the big boys and girls. That was as far as the East Hill School went. I enjoyed the stories in McGuffey's Readers and read them all straight off, without waiting to get to them in the course of daily lessons. Though I knew all the letters at sight, one day it was discovered that I could not "say the alphabet." That is, I could not name from memory all twenty-six letters—let alone name them in any particular order such as a, b, c, d. Miss Edna set me to learning them with the children in the "chart class." These children read from no book but from a large chart. They were below the First-Reader kids.

I must have had some knowledge of numbers, acquired from

my mother as a part of learning to read. Now Miss Edna taught us something else about numerals which was called "saying twos," and "saying threes": "two times one are two; two times two are four; two times three are six," and so on. I memorized those rapidly and liked to say them. It was like saying a jingle. But Miss Edna didn't let you stop with saying them. She made you "use" them.

"If Eva had three apples and Harry had three apples and Merwyn had three apples, and they all put their apples on one desk, how many apples would be on the desk?"

I would stand utterly perplexed while feet began to shuffle and hands to go up about me.

"Three times three are what?" Miss Edna would ask.

After counting to myself from three times one I would be able to answer: "Three times three are nine."

"That is right, there are nine apples. You know that now, Markey?"

"Yes, ma'am," I would say, glad to slide into my seat.

I didn't know it, of course. I was talking about numbers, and Miss Edna was talking about apples.

I could not write. Not even my name. I could not read "writing," only "print." So here again I had to begin with the chart class, and at the blackboard and over my slate painfully learn a slightly different character for each letter; not only learn to name them but learn to make them. This did not confound me as did "using" numbers, which went by the name of arithmetic. It merely bored me. My writing was the sloppiest in the class and I was always having to do it over. My feeling seems to have been that others should do the writing and I do the reading. It still seems sensible.

Even the instruction I received from my mother could be a means of diluting reality. When she insisted that I say "panther" for "painter," "creek" for "crick," "bear" for "b'ar," "buffalo wallow" for "buffalo waller," and "Indian" for "Injun," my feeling was that Mr. Howell knew better. Surely a man who "seed a painter" had an experience more vivid than one who merely "saw a panther"—in a circus cage, perhaps. What person who spoke of "buffalo wallows" had seen one made and had slept on its slope? "An' thar was the ol' she-b'ar with two yearlin' cubs acomin' thu the bresh by the crick." Put that in Mama's words and something went out of it.

One of Mr. Howell's expressions my mother respected. That was "peetrified," as in the peetrified-forest story. The word "petrified" was never used in our family. One was "peetrified" with amazement. A tough cut of meat was "peetrified."

The finest thing that happened during my early days at East Hill was a switching Miss Edna gave me. She had three punishments: standing in a corner, staying after school, and switching. Only boys were switched. Miss Edna would do a pretty good job of it and usually small boys would cry. By this time I had got over crying when Mama switched me at home. I'd think of the Spartans.

One day another boy and I fell into disfavor. Miss Edna called us to the front of the room and took a willow switch from her collection behind the stove. The other boy got it first and began to bawl after a couple of licks. Then came my turn. Though Miss Edna stung my bare legs worse than Mama'd ever stung them, I didn't let out a peep. I had cried once in the schoolroom and had resolved never to do it again whatever happened, though crying when licked was not considered altogether disgraceful for a small boy. There was a theory that you didn't get licked so hard that way. But big boys never cried. Once Miss Edna wore out two switches on Buck George.

When school let out that evening larger boys I didn't know very well took notice of me.

"Laid it on, didn't she?"

"Didn't hurt none," said I.

I heard some girls talking, and Eva Britton said:

"Goodness, he's *brave*."

I was sure she meant me.

CHAPTER THREE

The Icehouse

THE red-topped boots were fine in the wintertime when a norther howled through the Utsler draw and poured over our pasture, laying flat the tawny grass. With a norther blowing we used to say there was only a barbed-wire fence between the Strip and Canada. Every few winters the thermometer would hit zero. Any freezing weather seemed plenty cold. Neither our wardrobes nor our houses were prepared for it, though sod houses were warmest. Several times a winter there would be ice. Mostly it was "rubber ice"; that is, it would sway and crack under the weight of us boys. But the older boys from the northern states would get out their skates.

The Frantz brothers of Enid set up a brickyard in the Utsler draw and Pete Cheney ran it. It was good to stop at the brickyard and warm my hands and ears. Mr. Cheney would say to stand close to the kiln. Mr. Cheney was a tall, sallow-faced man with a lump on his jaw made by his quid of tobacco. He wore a sheepskin coat with the wool inside. I admired Mr. Cheney for the distance and accuracy with which he could spit tobacco juice, but his swearing awed me. He could not invite me to come by the kiln without half of what he said being cusswords. Consequently I was a little afraid Mama wouldn't like my stopping at the brickyard. She said it was all right, though; Pete Cheney's swearing didn't mean anything because he came from Kentucky.

"Those Kentucky poor whites learn to swear so young it's hardly a sin."

That was the winter I heard about the Civil War. This was the war Mr. Howell called the Rebellion and Pap Crosslin called the Confedrit War. Pap Crosslin had tended our sugar cane.

I came to learn about the Civil War in this way. One night Papa came home while Mama was reading to me by the cookstove. He took me on his lap and said that the Spaniards had sunk our battleship and that there was going to be a war. He told me just how this had been done—told me so plainly that next day Miss Edna asked me to tell the school. Mama was excited and said that she hoped that she had seen her last war. I was excited because I had never seen a war and wanted very much to see one.

One day a gentleman named Captain Huston came home with Papa. He wore a blue uniform and rode a nice horse, some sixteen hands high. Mama went out and admired the horse, but she seemed worried for fear that Papa was going to the war with Captain Huston. Papa said no, that he was too old, but that he hoped to furnish Captain Huston with a couple of substitutes. They were Papa's clients. I was sorry that Papa himself did not go. I could think only of the stories he would have to tell.

From what Papa said from time to time I was able to follow something of the fortunes of the Rough Riders, which his clients had joined. But this war was not fought in our pasture as I had got an idea it might be. It was fought in a place called Cuba. At school we played at killing Spaniards. If we didn't like a boy we'd all yell "Spaniard" and pile on him and stay until the boy said he was dead. Before the war this was called dog-piling.

Still, the Spanish War was far away and the only persons I knew of who were in it were the cattle rustlers Captain Huston had accepted as Papa's substitutes. But it served to bring up the subject of war and got Mama to talking about the Civil War, which had happened when she was a little girl. That was the war that seemed close at hand to me. I got to know the people who were in it. Mama's father went and her two brothers went. One was Birney ("your Uncle Birney"), Mama's special playmate. My Uncle Birney was on Sherman's march to the sea—so was Mr. Howell—and he was in what Mama called "the battle above the clouds." I tried to imagine a mountain (rising out of our pasture, say) so high that it went above the clouds. It seemed more like something Mr. Howell might tell about than Mama.

Papa was in the Civil War, too; and three of his brothers were in it. Two were killed and one was captured and put in Andersonville prison. He got home so thin his own folks didn't know him. After that Papa, who was the youngest of the brothers, went to the war.

One morning during the war Mama was on her way to school and she saw a man hanging in a tanyard. He was a bushwhacker the people had caught and hanged during the night, leaving him there as a warning. I had no idea Mama knew such wonderful war stories.

That was the interesting part of the Civil War. The dull part was about its being to free the slaves and all. I did not understand this very well. Mama said that folks used to own colored people, as if we owned Martha. Her father had owned Negroes, but had set them free and had gone to war to set the others free. Yet Mama did not hate the Rebels any more. She said that most of them were good people who had fought for what they believed in. Pap Crosslin and Colonel John C. Moore had been Rebels.

Until Mama told me, I had not known that Papa had been in the same war with Pap Crosslin and Mr. Howell, or, for that matter, in any war except the North Town War. When I asked him to tell about it, he laughed and said that I had heard it all from Mama. But he would tell about the Rough Riders.

2

In the barn lot I saw a saddletree stripped bare and asked Mama about it. She took the tree and disappeared through the barn door. An old dried-out unused saddle that had hung in the barn as long as I could remember was missing from its peg.

"Of all things. This belongs to your father's saddle. Who on earth stripped it?"

She learned that a neighbor had stripped it. He wanted some leather for shoe soles for the young'uns and Papa had told him to strip the saddle.

Mama certainly gave Papa the what-for.

"Houstin James, you get that saddle leather right back. I want that saddle for Marquis."

Papa said the saddle was no good. A stirrup was gone and the cinch was broken. He said he would get me a proper boy's saddle one day.

"But that's the saddle you made the Run in. It'll be an heirloom for Marquis when he grows up."

It was too late about the leather. The man had cut it up. But I was the gainer by the day's events. First was the promise of a saddle of my own. And, of course, there would have to be a pony. You wouldn't put a new saddle on Billy, the big, jug-headed, spavined, dirty-black plug used for light plowing and hauling wood, and the only horse I had to ride. He didn't even belong to us. A man had left him in our barn and never come for him. The second thing was that Papa told me about the Run.

Of course this was a story everyone knew—the commonest story in all the Strip. By now I didn't bother to listen to it, sometimes. But I listened to Papa because it was Papa telling a story and because he told it so differently. Never before had I known that there were so many, so very, very many people in the Run. Somehow, I'd only thought of there having been just a few—like Mr. Howell and Mr. Schrock and Clark the claim-jumper and Jim Utsler's cowboy and Mrs. Ackerman and so on. But no, there was a whole world of people in the Run. More than I had ever seen in Enid on circus day. Papa covered the prairie with them.

He said the Run was the biggest horse race that ever had been; and for the biggest purse—all the Cherokee Strip. He asked me to think of four or five horses lined up at the post at the Fair Grounds. They break and are away. Well, sir, in this race there were thousands of horses and thousands of riders and drivers, and they stretched in a line across the prairie as far as you could see. Papa asked me to look to the east and look to the west and imagine all those horses strung out ready to break. Most of the horses were under saddle. The others were hitched to every kind of rig. Light rigs—buckboards, spring wagons and sulkies—were the best.

But there were covered wagons, lots of them, and even people on foot.

They broke with a yell and at first you couldn't see a thing for the dust that was raised where the grass had been trampled away along the starting line. In this blinding cloud the wheels of rigs locked and there were spills at the very start. When the racers got out on the grass, the dust went down, except along the Chisholm Trail. The riders took the lead, mostly, with the fastest driving horses and lightest wagons next. And on they went. There were no roads, mind you, except the Trail, and no bridges. You got down and up draws and across creeks and ravines and gullies as best you could. Or you headed them. Wagons stuck in the streams and stalled in draws. Rigs broke down from the rough going. By and by the horses that had been ridden or driven too hard began to play out. Horses that had started slower began to edge ahead.

The thing to do was to get to Enid first, and get the choice of town lots, or of the claims close by. It was seventeen miles by beeline from the nearest point on the starting line north of Hennessey, in Old Oklahoma, to Enid's south line. With five miles to go, of the thousands who started about a hundred held the lead. Most of the others were far behind, some dropping out all the time to stake claims along the Trail or to veer east or west. The rest pressed on to get nearer Enid. The hundred leaders dwindled to fifty, nearly all on horseback, though a few buckboards were still keeping up.

A small man on a small and fleet cow pony was gliding past rider after rider. The man was Walter Cook, a twenty-two-year-old cowpuncher from the Chickasaw Nation. Pretty soon he was ahead of everyone. He kept his lead and was the first man to reach the townsite. He could have had any town lot there. But the little cowhand was out for bigger game. Sweeping past the land office he staked the claim—one hundred and sixty acres—adjoining the Square on the north: the prize quarter-section in the whole Cherokee Strip.

Two or three minutes later Albert Hammer dashed up, threw

himself from his heaving horse, and without batting an eye staked the same claim. Then came Ben Clampitt in a swaying buckboard behind a foam-flecked team that was beating its own dust in a high south wind. All the way Clampitt's race had been a sight to see. A lean old Texan, he had rigged his buckboard with leather stirrups like those on a racing sulky. Mounted behind the driver was a hired hand with a pitchfork who in the crowded early stages of the race had jabbed to the right and left, keeping competitors at a distance and making a clear track for Ben.

Next came Bill Coyle; and after him people just swarmed in. Before night there were three hundred claim-jumpers on the quarter-section Walter Cook had staked first.

"What happened, Papa?" I asked breathlessly, knowing that a dose of lead was the thing for claim-jumpers caught in the act.

"A lot of things happened. First off, the claim-jumpers got together and began to divide the claim into town lots. They called the place Jonesville. Now, if you're the better man, you can put one claim-jumper off your land. But you can't put three hundred of them off. Walter Cook could have had a share of the town lots, a big share, but he insisted on having his claim. He was just a boy, you see, and green. There were contests and contests and in the end the organized townsiters came out on top. Walter Cook, who had won fair and square the greatest horse race in the world, never got a thing."

I always think of Walter Cook, whose path was to cross mine before I left Oklahoma, as a victim of democracy in its most primitive form: the law of the pack.

In addition to an active indignation over the injustice to Walter Cook, my father's never long-winded or oft-repeated accounts of the Run gave me a feeling of the dash and scope of that contribution to the Southwest's boisterous history which I have had from no other source. When old enough to understand a map of the United States I chanced to note that the Cherokee Strip was larger than the State of Massachusetts, and, lopping off Cape Cod, about the same shape. That made me feel pretty good, for the histories made so much of what had gone on in Massachusetts.

There were a hundred thousand people in the Run, and they came in from all four directions. About fifteen thousand started from the Hennessey section of the south line. All who staked near Enid (either Enid) came from there. Yet Mr. Howell, in his story, mentioned only perhaps a half dozen riders besides himself—his immediate competitors. Other storytellers did the same. Each was pretty much the hero of his own story. Only my father brought before me a picture of all those hard-riding thousands. And he did it without mentioning himself.

My father had not seen Walter Cook, Albert Hammer, Ben Clampitt and the rest pile onto the Strip's most sought-after claim, for he was two miles away and with other things to attend to at the time. The scene he laid before me must have been reconstructed from testimony in Oklahoma's most famous series of claim contests. Then, too, Papa would have had the benefit of Mr. Pat Wilcox's story. Nobody had so good a view of the birth of Enid as Mr. Wilcox, an observer whom the research of half a century has not proved mistaken on an essential point. Before the Run there was one building in Enid, the L-shaped land office, one room of which was set aside for the post office. Young Mr. Wilcox was assistant postmaster. As soon as he had washed his dinner dishes, he climbed to the roof and began scanning the southern skyline.

When I was older I got Mr. Wilcox to tell more than once what he had seen: first a haze faintly discernible above the crest of the slope we called South Hill. The haze grew larger and denser. His eyes on this looming dust cloud, Mr. Wilcox did not see Walter Cook, who was ahead of it, until Walter had topped the rise and was tearing down the slope inside the townsite. Ben Clampitt and the others who followed next engrossed the attention of the observer. Then Mr. Wilcox happened to glance to the west. Riding easily on a fairly fresh horse was a man in light blue overalls—without doubt, thought Mr. Wilcox, a sooner who had hidden out in the blackjacks. The man mixed with the crowd which by nightfall had swelled to ten thousand, and Mr. Wilcox was unable to spot him again.

3

From my mother I learned of Papa's own part in the race. It was the kind of story that Mama, with her love of horses, would tell with relish.

Especially for the Run, Papa had bought a race horse in El Reno. It was wind-broken but otherwise a sound and strong animal, capable of carrying my father's more than two hundred pounds.

"In his young days your father was a real fancy rider," Mama would say. "And for a man of his size very easy on a horse."

This was no small tribute. My mother was about as accomplished a judge of riding as any woman in our part of the country.

The Run was a young man's undertaking. My father was crowding forty-nine, a good twenty years older than the average man who entered the race on horseback with serious intentions of reaching Enid in time to stake anything. A year and a half of law practice in Old Oklahoma and the Indian nations had made him fairly used to the saddle again. Nevertheless, he took three weeks to condition himself and to find out what he and his horse could do. He knew the ropes well enough to get himself the best possible place on the starting line—smack on the Chisholm Trail, just north of Hennessey, in Old Oklahoma.

You could begin your race anywhere you could get to on one of the four borders of the Strip, which was about a hundred and sixty-five miles east and west by fifty-eight miles north and south. Papa picked the Hennessey section because it lay closest Enid, which he figured would be *the* town of the Strip. There was also the Trail to follow. It made for easier riding and led straight to the desired townsite. On a prairie experience is necessary to preserve a sense of direction.

Mama's understanding was that Papa spent about three days and nights on the line, holding his place. The wonder is the wait wasn't longer, considering the premium on places in the neighborhood of the Trail. I have heard men tell of spending three weeks on the line. Probably they were with covered-wagon outfits, but, unless close to water, they must have got pretty tired of it. The sheets of some of the wagons were scrawled with notices of intention such as "Oklahoma or Bust." Substituting "Texas" or "Oregon," the phrase had been western usage for a good fifty years.

The line was patrolled by soldiers to prevent anyone from crossing over before the opening gun. The country had been evacuated by the cattle outfits which formerly leased it from the Indians. Excepting land-office and post-office staffs and soldiers on the site of each county seat, the Strip was depopulated. That was the theory, and it came tolerably close to being the fact. Nobody knows how many sooners did manage to hide out in the promised land before the opening gun was fired, but probably not more than you would find trying to obtain their ends by illegal means in any collection of a hundred thousand persons. (Walter Cook, you understand, lost his claim by strictly legal procedure.)

After a man had staked a claim he had to "file" at the nearest land office. In order to file he was required to exhibit an evidence of registration permitting him to make the Run in the first place. Registration slips were issued from booths along the line. It was in no way difficult for a prospective sooner who knew the country to register a week before the Run and sneak up a draw through the thinly patrolled line. He could camp in the blackjacks west of Enid, for instance, and ride out with the first honest comers—as Mr. Wilcox suspected the man in light blue overalls had done. A cavalry troop encamped on the Enid site had reconnoitered the surrounding country for three weeks. Though the lieutenant in command was sure a number of sooners had eluded him they must have formed a minute proportion of the whole body of settlers.

The Hennessey stretch of the line broke five minutes before the official gun. Somebody may have discharged a firearm by accident. My father was in the saddle and ready. Waiting only to see that there was no turning back the tide, he, too, set off, keeping to the Chisholm Trail and reining his horse to a pace it could maintain for fifteen or sixteen miles and have a spurt left for an emergency.

The Chisholm Trail was the name cowmen gave to the Oklahoma section of the Abilene Trail, greatest of the southwestern cattle thoroughfares. It ran from San Antonio, Texas, to the railway terminus at Abilene, Kansas, a distance of eight hundred miles. Though little used for cattle drives since the completion of the Rock Island Railroad through the Cherokee Strip in 1889, the famous prairie road was still distinct. Like a carelessly laid ribbon, which your eye would lose in the dips and pick up in the rises of the undulating plain, the Oklahoma part stretched almost due north. On level places it was like several ribbons side by side. These markings were the Trail's core, made by the wheels of chuck wagons, calf wagons, freighters and stages. When wheels and hoofs wore through the sod, creating a "high center," teamsters would start a new road alongside the old. For two or three hundred yards on either side of these ruts the grass had been beaten down by the feet of the cattle. This on level stretches. To ford a stream or cross a draw the Trail narrowed.

The race was going well for my father. At first many riders and some drivers passed him; but this he had counted on. In the fullness of time, without increasing the pace of his horse, he began to pass them. When Papa calculated that he had gone about fifteen miles he was feeling the strain, and his horse was feeling it. Ahead of him were perhaps fifty riders in sight whom he doubted his ability to pass. (Fifty out of fifteen thousand starters from Hennessey.)

Glancing to the east my father saw the top of a distant string of trees. That meant a stream, an asset of great value to a claim: also an asset of great value to my father, who liked trees. They were the thing he missed most on the plains. Turning his horse from the Trail, he crossed the Rock Island track and the bed of a dry creek. He urged his tiring mount up the rise. On the other side he saw only a shallow draw, its naked sides exposing coarse sandy soil tinted from red to orange. Was this a wild-goose chase? Holding a northeast course he made for the next rise. He was traveling over short-grass prairie, knobby-surfaced and with washes of bare red soil: a good place for a horse, especially a tired, wind-broken horse, its breath coming in rasps, to stumble; and no good to grow anything. The crest of this second rise brought a welcome sight into view: the trees he had seen from the Trail; and beyond them more trees.

Watering the roots of the first trees was a disappointing stream, hardly more than a yard wide. (This was the driest season of the year.) But better trees were beyond; indeed, what seemed a veritable forest, in terms of the plains, with a noble green mass—surely the granddaddy of all the trees in the Cherokee Strip—dominating the whole. The first of these trees were soon reached. The creek was wider there: ten or twelve feet across. The illusion of a grove had been caused by the way the creek curved in the shape of an S. Papa followed the course of the stream in the direction of the Big Tree. He crossed the creek once and found that, to reach the Big Tree, he must cross again or double a loop. He started to double the loop and came upon a steep ravine. The ravine wouldn't have been much to head, but Papa didn't take the time. Precious minutes had been lost feeling his way toward the trees. On the next fold of the prairie to the south other riders were in sight. Unseen riders might be coming up the draws. Papa wanted that creek, flowing in the shape of an S with good bottom land in the loops; and he wanted the Big Tree. His horse barely made the steep yonder side of the ravine. A few rods farther, at the high point on our pasture, luxuriant in red top, Papa dismounted and set his stake on what proved to be the Southeast Quarter of Section 17, Township 22, Range 6 West of the Indian Meridian.

It was 12:53 P.M., September 16, 1893. As the Hennessey line had broken at 11:55, my father had ridden seventeen miles in fifty-eight minutes without injuring his horse. A note of pride would touch Mama's tone as she spoke the last four words. Walter Cook covered eighteen miles in fifty to fifty-five minutes—he carried no watch and no one seems to have timed him exactly.

Something else my father had had to watch out for during the last part of his ride were the markers, designating section and certain quarter-section corners. Twenty years before, surveyors had checkerboarded the Strip with these little monuments. Where there were any, roughly cut sandstones sticking six or eight inches above the ground were used; elsewhere, "pits and mounds." A pit-and-mounds marker consisted of a hole about three feet deep, surrounded by four piles of earth and sod indicating the points of the compass. Virgin prairie sod is thick and durable. Except where beaten down by cattle, these mounds could still be picked up by a person who knew what to look for easier than the stones hidden by grass.

Before the Run much of the Strip had been burned over. I have heard this laid to sooners, in an effort to drive off rightful homesteaders. It appears, however, to have been the work of the troops—with the object of rendering markers more readily visible, of preventing prairie fires with possible serious consequences during the chaotic first days of settlement, and of smoking out sooners. The fires had been set too late. In areas they were burning on the day of the Run, and for some time after. I have heard men tell of riding through lines of flame, and of droves of rabbits, coyotes, and snakes fleeing the fires. Near North Town a woman was burned to death trying to save her team.

Streams, arid gulches, green bottom-land grass and so on stopped the fires in places. Where my father was had not been burned at all. Stone and pit-and-mounds markers were mixed in together, and all hard to see. Later examination disclosed the three designated corners of his quarter to be marked with stones—in all likelihood not visible more than a few yards away. As there was no time to search out these markers before he staked, my father had to estimate his boundaries by eye—while in motion on horseback, taking his bearings from the last marker he had seen. In the matter of acquiring title to the Big Tree luck was with him, too. Only three corners of any quarter-section were marked. Lines had to be run to determine the fourth. When they were run on our place the Big Tree was found to be less than a hundred yards from the Utsler boundary. Of course my father could have tried to make sure of the tree by setting his stake right under it. But he would have sacrificed the advantage of observation—for claim-jumpers and sooners—which his commanding position in the pasture afforded.

Having driven his stake, Papa set up a pup tent to which he

affixed an American flag. I would like to know who gave him that flag, which was the last thing my father would ever have thought of taking along. From the tent he could see almost the entire claim, barring the East Draw and where the bluff hid the creek. He removed his saddle and, leading his horse so it would cool off gradually, began a tour of his estimated boundaries—probably looking for the markers. In the East Bottom he found a man preparing to set his stake. Cases of lead poisoning developed from a number of such meetings that day. But this man was no sooner or intentional claim-jumper. He rode with Papa to higher ground and took a look at the tent and the flag.

"You beat me out, stranger," said the man. "I'll strike eastward a piece."

Papa wished him luck, and never saw the man again.

4

Overhearing what passed between Papa and Mama on the subject, I was aware that Mr. Howell's contest was not going so well as Papa could wish. He kept saying that it was a hard case.

To my mind a hard case was something difficult for a lawyer to manage, right or wrong having nothing to do with it. For practical purposes I did not rate justice highly. Too often cheatin' dogs *did* win. Justice on the side of Walter Cook hadn't helped him any. It didn't seem to be helping Mr. Howell. The good things of life belonged to the strong and to the clever. As I was not strong I tried to be clever. I cultivated tough little Jeff George, who became virtually my bodyguard.

My second year at school passed with fewer hard knocks than the first, though Miss Edna, who seems to have been clever, too, deprived me of one source of satisfaction. That was the prestige derived from taking a switching without whimpering. She stopped licking me and substituted a more effective punishment. As I disliked penmanship next to arithmetic, my hand was still miserable. For breaking rules she would require me to go to the blackboard and write "disobedient" twenty-five times, in five neat columns, of five words each:

Dis-o-be-di-ent
Dis-o-be-di-ent
Dis-o-be-di-ent
Dis-o-be-di-ent
Dis-o-be-di-ent

If a letter was not roundly and properly formed I had to do the word over.

Still, in the world at large, I made progress. I took to swimming at the Stump. The Stump was Enid's favorite swimming hole. It was on the west side of our place at the deepest pool in Boggy. An elm stump at the end of the water was dandy to dive from. In summer there was hardly a day but what people came from town to swim at the Stump. They wore the bank bare of grass. Previously the Stump had been forbidden to me because the water was so deep. But under the guidance of Mr. Howell, Ad Poak, and my father I had become a good swimmer. Water was a scarce article in the Strip and very few boys had my opportunities for learning. There were shallower places than the Stump where when younger I had gone in with Prince, who loved water; and so for five months of the year I suppose I was in Boggy Creek nearly every day.

Mr. Howell told time by the sun. When we were out shooting or fishing he would hold up a bony hand to shade his eyes and say, "Promised yore ma to git you back by noon. We better mosey 'long." Mama said that Mr. Howell's sun-time was more accurate than the noisy and energetic little clock on the shelf above the kitchen stove.

Mr. Howell began to teach me to shoot. I used the muzzle-loader with a light charge. The Winchester or Papa's 10-gauge would have kicked me over. The muzzle-loader was longer than I was and so heavy I had to rest the barrel on something. But I learned to sight and to squeeze the trigger, not pull it. Mr. Howell said what I needed was a .22 for frogs and squirrels. One time we met a boy with a .22. I could handle this little rifle without a rest. It did not kick at all.

"What yore pappy ought to buy you is a .22," said Mr. Howell. The statement thrilled me and for a moment I could feel a .22 of my own in my hands, simply because Mr. Howell had said Papa should buy me one. I got him to ask Papa to get it. I thought that would be better than asking for myself. It wasn't though. Papa just said, "Wait till you get a little older, son." But Mama was horrified. As nearly as I could tell she didn't want me to have a gun, ever. So I continued to snag frogs with a fishhook baited with a piece of red flannel. I brought home so many fish that Mama wouldn't eat any more. But she still liked a mess of frog legs.

Freshets would overflow part of the West Bottom, especially the grove. The grove was a stand of young cottonwoods where Papa had cleared the ground and set it to Bermuda grass. It was fun to wade about when there was a freshet. One time, as the water was going down, I discovered the Bermuda grass to be alive with buffalo fish which had been carried from the creek. Tangled in the grass, they couldn't get back. Buffalo fish had small mouths and would not take a hook. Consequently I had not seen many of them before. Mama said they weren't fit to eat, but Mr. Howell said they made good eating. Mr. Howell and I filled two washtubs with buffalo fish, cleaned them and took them to town behind Billy. I sold mine at Cap Bond's restaurant for two dollars. It was the most money I had ever earned and I think the first money excepting snake bounties.

One day Papa brought the news that Mr. Howell had lost his contest. Mama was terribly upset. Papa assured her that Clark had not "stolen" the claim. "I always said it was a hard case." What made it so hard was what Papa called Mr. Howell's "carefree attitude" toward the leave-of-absence and homestead-improvement regulations. "I knew George Rush would have a look into that." Mama said she hoped to goodness that Papa wasn't going to stand by and see a good old man turned out to starve.

"Old man Howell *starve?*" said Papa. "Rachel, old Howell's as well off as he ever was: and that's better than most of us. He's got a gun and a fishline, and plenty of places to use 'em."

Papa got the lumber and Mr. Howell built himself a shack on

our land in the West Bottom, not far from where the dugout had been. He moved in his plunder and fixed up the new place real nice. It was twice the size of the dugout. There was a board floor, and windows to let in plenty of light. But somehow it wasn't the dugout.

Mama took the loss of Mr. Howell's claim harder than Mr. Howell did. I have heard her say that he never mentioned it except to remark that he wasn't cut out for a settler, nohow.

The grove where we caught the buffalo fish got to be quite a place for Sunday-school picnics and baptizings from town. Taking the grove and the Stump together there was nearly always a crowd on the claim in the summer. School had made me less bashful and I often mixed in and got acquainted. Picnics were fine because there was always something to eat—for me and Prince both. I liked baptizings, too; colored baptizings best of all. They sang and shouted and had such a good time. Mama would come down and watch a colored baptizing. She loved to hear colored people sing.

Some gamblers from Enid and their lady friends had a picnic in the grove. How did I know they were gamblers? For one thing, Mizzou Edmundson, who hung out at the Red Front, was there. But anyone could tell a gambler by his stylish clothes. Prince and I sat at a distance watching them. Mama had nothing to do with gamblers and I knew that she would not want me to. They drank from bottles, and I had never heard ladies laugh and talk so loudly or seen them loll about so. Pretty soon one of the men began to toss a coin in the air and shoot at it with a pistol.

That gave me an excuse to move closer so they could see me and not shoot my way. They were very friendly, really, especially the ladies. The man who was shooting could not hit the dollar he threw into the air. He stuck it against a tree and there he hit it and sent it flying into the grass. It had been hit smack in the center. The bullet hadn't gone through, but had fairly doubled the dollar up. After looking at it for a moment the gambler flipped the coin to me.

"Here, bub; it's yours."

That is how I got my third dollar. I had better judgment than to show it to Mama. I didn't think she would let me keep a gambler's money. What to do with an almost perfectly good silver dollar, which Mr. Howell had straightened, seemed a problem. I don't remember what I did do with it. Perhaps I carried it around until I lost it, proving that no good comes of tainted wealth.

5

Although the sugar cane didn't build any front addition with a stairway, visitors to our house remarked what a fine place we had. Mama was quite proud of her red rambler roses. The young orchard, too, was a pretty and an unusual sight. It was next to the horse lot, on the slope that led to the pasture. Manured and watered, the pruned rows made quite a showing. The peach trees were nearly ready to bear.

Mama was growing fond of our claim. Certainly this quarter-section of land was as favored by nature as any I ever knew in that country. There were fifty acres of prime bottom land watered by Boggy's two loops. In a country where fresh fruit was a rarity we had wild grapes and wild plums in abundance, besides the strawberries, blackberries, gooseberries and currants we cultivated. Mama would put up enough preserves for all winter. Every fall at butchering time our smokehouse was filled. That was a lively event. I ate pig tails roasted on the coals of fires used for lard-rendering and soap-boiling. I foundered myself on cracklings and could not bear the sight of that delicacy for years. Pork, chicken, and fish were our staple fare; turkey and game a change; beef-steak from town a Sunday treat. Although we used the frontier expression "light bread" to distinguish bread made of wheat flour from simple "bread" made of corn meal, I think we usually had light bread on our table.

We had the boon of natural shade, the Big Tree being the claim's crowning glory. Reared under its branches, I could not appreciate the fuss people made over trees and especially that one. Native-born plainsmen, used to getting along without trees, regarded it merely as a curiosity. I have heard tell that other people sometimes went mad on dry claims, with nothing to hear but the ceaseless prairie wind and nothing to see but the bending grass on the featureless plains. Long afterwards my mother would recall the rapture of the Ackermans at the sight of our trees. They were Virginia people.

We seemed to have more company. Although Ad Poak didn't live with us any more, he came often. Papa's lawyer friends from town came; also Mr. and Mrs. Peter Bowers, Mr. and Mrs. W. E. Cogdal, and Oklahoma's Delegate to Congress, Mr. Dennis Flynn. For Papa's part in the congressman's campaign for re-election Mr. Flynn gave Mama a black rocking chair with arms on it.

My sisters from Chicago came: Sister Zoe and Sister Nan. It seems funny to speak of your own sisters as company, but that was what they were to me. They had been to the claim before this—a fact I have been meaning to mention but somehow Sister Zoe and Sister Nan didn't seem to blend in with what I was writing. They never blended into my life on the claim. Until I was grown I addressed them as "Sister Zoe" and "Sister Nan," never "Zoe" and "Nan." Their husbands were "Brother Elliott" and "Brother Perry." So my sisters were nothing like the sisters other boys had. Not only were they company but rather special company, for they dressed like the ladies in *Scribner's Monthly*. I remember picking flowers in the pasture with Sister Nan when the wind, making a sail of her stylish long skirt, nearly blew her over. How I watched my manners when they were about. If they stayed long, the pose became tedious to maintain. But their comings were enjoyable because they brought presents. The *Youth's Companion* had been my present from Sister Nan since I can remember. Its "Children's Page" was one of the primers Mama used to teach me to read. My file of the *Companion* for several years back was a treasured possession.

Nan tells of asking what I intended to be when I grew up.

"President of the United States," I said.

That would have been the influence of James A. Garfield. And there is a suspicion in my mind that I may have deemed it the kind of answer to please a fashionable lady from Chicago. I am pretty sure that at this time of my life presidential aspirations had made only fitful headway against the ambitions with which Mr. Howell had filled my mind: to be a stage driver, soldier, scout, bear hunter, gold miner or Texas Ranger.

A day came when Mr. Howell took down sick. He seemed dreadfully ashamed, and declared it the first time he'd been laid up ("excusin' mishaps") in forty years. Mama wanted him to move into the boys' house, but he wouldn't hear of it.

"You'll be aimin' to git a doctor, next."

Mr. Howell lay on the bunk in his shack. Mama went over every day. I got his water from the spring and carried him victuals. I heard some wonderful stories about the times he'd been laid up before: chaw'd by a b'ar; and once the stage had upset. Finally he was able to hobble over to our house to eat.

"I declar', Mrs. James, you've a healin' hand," he said.

"I'm a doctor's daughter," said Mama.

"I don't hold with no doctors, ma'am. But you've a healin' hand. An' that reminds me of a pack-train boss I knowed in Salt Lake. The year after the Sioux campaign."

Mr. Howell was past seventy years old. His strength returned slowly. He puttered about, low in mind. It was the lack of "altitood," he said, that held him back. What he needed was a whiff of mountain air. Thought maybe he ought to go back to prospectin'.

One day Mr. Howell returned from Enid driving two respectable plug horses attached to an old light covered wagon. So there had been more than anyone suspected in the leather money belt which was the last thing Mr. Howell would shed when we went swimming. He announced that he was pulling out for Colorado.

Nothing Mama or Papa could say was any use. He'd been in the Strip six years and that was too long for anybody to stay in one place. Yessiree. Besides, he was never meant for a nester, nohow. There were men who followed the frontiers as other men follow the sea.

Though weak and slow, Mr. Howell was no more than three

or four days repairing the wagon, mending the harness, and stowing his gear. Leaving the loaded wagon beside the shack, he walked over to tell Mama and me good-by. Not many words were said. Those old-timers made little of leave-taking. Mama and I watched the wagon disappear over the hill. One of the telling influences on my early life, if not my whole life, had ridden out of it.

Mr. Howell died in his light covered wagon on the road to Colorado. When we heard of it he had been buried for weeks. Up to then I had been sure of his return. Or that I would join him in Colorado. We had had a sort of pact.

This was the first death to touch me and the first non-violent death of my recollection. (Mr. Ackerman's was too vague to count.) Prince and I would go over to the dugout. The dugout and not the shack meant Mr. Howell to me. Weeds flourished on the roof and all around. Pretty soon the roof caved in. Winter rains beat the ruin into the sloping plain. In the spring Clark ran his plow over the site and by July all that remained was a place where the corn tassels dipped a little.

The second natural death that I recall was that of Doctor Fairgrieve. The chain of misadventure which had brought that surgeon and Shakespearean scholar from London to die of drink in a sun-drenched Oklahoma town is more than I know. Perhaps my father, the doctor's closest friend in the Territory, did not know it. In the Strip one did not make inquiries along that line. You pushed discretion pretty far by asking a man where he came from. You never asked why he'd left.

6

One day it turned out that we were rich. Papa had won a big case. He bought a new buggy and new harness for Tom and there were five hundred dollars left over. With outlaws getting scarcer, that was a lot of money for a lawyer to have all at once. Much of his pay would come in the shape of a town lot or a cow or a steer or a sow; groceries at Mr. Peter Bowers's, clothes at Meibergen & Godschalk's, or having a horse shod by Mr. Hackett the blacksmith. Nearly all our crops were put in and gathered by farmers working off fees. (Farmer, instead of settler, was getting to be the word.)

As with the gambler's dollar, the question was what to do with this money. Papa always had to do something with money; Mama said it burned holes in his pockets. Of course we could build the new front addition and have a stairway. But Mama was not for that. She wanted to "stock the farm"; buy brood mares and Guernsey cows and raise colts and calves. The front addition could wait. Here was a chance to start a stock farm, like her father's in Missouri. And, yes, I could have my pony and saddle.

The prospect of a pony won me to Mama's side. Otherwise I'd have been for the new front addition—in order to get the stairs. I had been very disappointed over what happened to the rock quarry, which had represented Papa's latest attempt to provide the addition. The rock quarry was opened in the ravine which he had crossed on horseback in the Run. Papa thought that the red stone beneath the gravel would be capital for building. It was fun to watch the blasters drill holes and fill them with dynamite, and the stonecutters with chisels and mauls work the rough masses into smooth, regular shapes. The first stones were taken in low, broad-tired small-wheeled wagons to Enid where they were putting up a new building on the Square. But Papa's stone never went into that building. There came a rain and a terrible freeze and some of those red rocks cracked, just sitting there in the street.

As it happened I did not get my pony because Papa decided to use the money to build the icehouse. Mama was simply thunderstruck. She said it didn't freeze hard enough in the Strip. Papa said it froze hard enough to crack rock. He went on to say how much money was spent in Enid in one summer to buy ice which was shipped all the way from Wichita. It was enough to get all the stock anybody should ever want.

What Papa did he did fast. Work on the icehouse started right away. The grandeur of the undertaking enthralled me. Half a dozen mule teams and two-wheel scrapers began widening and throwing a dam across Boggy Creek. The driver of a two-wheel scraper can be a lordly personage. Coat off and cuffs turned back, Papa was in their midst, directing. His quiet tones formed a contrast to the "Gees!" and "Haws!" and "Git-along-thars!" of the mule skinners. The result of this labor was the largest body of water I had ever seen. On the bank rose the icehouse, with double walls filled with cinders. It was as high as the Rex Hotel, and in an unfinished state a marvelous thing to climb.

As if this was not enough excitement for one summer, the East Bottom was planted in cotton. The Negro family that had charge of it lived in the boys' house and did their cooking in the back yard. This tribe took in all ages from a gray-wooled "uncle" to a pickaninny learning to crawl. Young and old worked in the field, the baby playing in the dust between the rows. I shall never forget the bright hues of the garments or the bright laughter of those colored people. Or their singing in the evenings. There was a boy and a girl about my age. During cotton-picking time I worked with them because I enjoyed their company. When the cotton was hauled away, with the last of the family perched on the last wagonload, our place seemed silent and empty.

And there stood the icehouse: empty, and also silent—after a summer of hammering and sawing and bustle of building. We waited for ice. It happened, though, that there was no ice that winter—only a twister that took a corner of the roof off the icehouse. So ended a year worthy of note. A man more given to boasts than my father might have made something of it: not only was he the sole person to try to raise cotton or to cut ice in Garfield County, but he tried both at practically the same time.

The icehouse roof was repaired, though I did not pay much attention to it, for that was the summer I herded cattle, or at any rate cows—milch cows from town. Of a summer, townfolks pastured their cows in the country and boys found employment driving the herds to and fro, morning and evening. There were several herds in our pasture. My schoolmate Jay Radcliffe drove one. Leonard Bacon drove another. Leonard's father was a preacher who ran a dairy. He had two thumbs on one of his hands.

As the pasture was fenced, all I had to do was keep an eye on the bull. Often a town boy or two would spend the day with me to save himself a trip. We would practice riding tricks and throwing lariats. In the evening when the other boys returned, some mounted and some afoot, all the town cows would be rounded up and the different herds cut out and started on the road with some distance between herds to keep them from mixing together again. For this work a pony would have been a handy thing. All I had was Billy. The experience should have made me quite a rider for a kid, but it didn't. Billy had the hardest gait of any horse I have ever been on. He trotted at nearly any pace, indicating an early training which his disreputable looks belied. A sustained trot is an unnatural gait for a horse, and one that must be taught. Your western cow pony trotted a few steps and broke into an easy lope (it differs from the eastern canter) that was like sitting in a rocking chair.

The next winter it froze and froze good. Papa took no chances. At the first cold snap he put men on the pond with pumps to keep water on the surface of the ice so that the freezing weather would thicken it faster. In that way we got ten-inch ice. The cutters worked night and day, fearing a thaw. It was a spectacle people drove from town to see. Every now and then a cutter would fall in and then dry out by the crackling fire on the bank. The icehouse was filled to the rafters.

This was not all that happened that winter. The Wichita people who had been selling ice in Enid at fancy prices began to build a branch plant in town. When Mama heard of that, she started to set hens on a scale she had never attempted before. Some lumber left over from repairing the icehouse roof was used to make a great shed for the brooders.

We bought an ice wagon and a team of horses as big and sleek as brewery-truck horses. The wagon was the most gaily painted apparition I had seen on wheels outside a circus. We also bought a second team and a smaller wagon, but this was merely a farm wagon made over. My first trips in the big wagon were made on Saturdays. By the time school let out for the summer I was able to drive the team anywhere except downhill: I was not strong enough to set the brake. As there were only two hills in Enid, East Hill and South Hill, I took to driving fairly regularly, leaving the man to ride the back step and carry ice into the houses.

This occupation gave me a feeling of importance I had not known before. On my high seat, handling the reins that lay on the flat backs of the team, I felt superior to the run of other boys for the first time in my life. There were usually boys following the wagon for a piece of ice to suck. I do not believe the note of respect in their tones was altogether a fancy of mine, for until now ice in summer was a thing few people saw in Enid. Not that my powers of fancy had been entirely overcome by the magnificence of reality. My imagination would change the ice wagon into a stagecoach.

Leaving Enid and turning into the quarter-line road between the Utsler and the old Howell claims, you made your way along a ledge—wall of a canyon on one side, foaming river on the other. Prime place for a holdup or ambush, specially this trip with all that gold dust aboard. On the straight stretch just before Horseshoe Bend the nigh leader r'ars. Arrow in his rump. Injuns! I cracks my whip an' we hits the Bend at a dead run, two wheels in the air. . . .

My self-esteem does not seem to have suffered from the fact that there was an ice wagon other than ours on Enid's hot and dusty streets: the wagon of the "artificial" ice company. That wagon was driven by a man. The artificial wagon driver spread lies about our ice. He said it came from dirty creek water with wigglers in it. The men on our wagons told people the artificial ice was slow poison. You just had to go to the plant and smell the stinking stuff they made it of.

There was a good deal of argument as to whose ice was colder, and therefore would last longer. It stood to reason that ours was colder, having been frozen in practically zero weather. Still, some people wouldn't believe it until Mr. John Reilly made his experiment. Mr. Reilly bought a hundred-pound cake of our ice and a hundred-pound cake of the artificial ice and put them side by side on the walk in front of his Kentucky Whiskey House. All afternoon long people stood around and watched the melting cakes. Bets were made as to which would go first. When night came it looked like a dead heat. But the test wasn't over yet. Next morning our cake was twice the size of the artificial cake, which proved that there was something about man-made ice that couldn't stand the night air. We were officially declared the winner and wagers were paid on that basis. Several years later I heard Mr. Sam Evans, the druggist, tell what it was about the night air that affected the artificial ice. Some of Papa's friends had poured a kettle of boiling water on it.

As this wasn't publicly known at the time, the artificial-ice people cut the price of their ice. We cut the price of ours. They cut again and we cut again.

We sold all our ice, but at such low prices there was no money to put ice in the icehouse during the coming winter should it freeze hard enough to make any. So Papa retired from the ice business.

But while Papa had been selling ice at a loss, Mama sold poultry and eggs at a profit. She had always done this to make her pin money. That summer she went into the business in earnest and sold a thousand chickens, turkeys, and ducks. They brought in a good deal; but it was not enough. The icehouse took our claim and the best of the town lots. When told that we were moving to Enid I am not so sure but that I was more glad than sorry. The summer on the ice wagon had sharpened my taste for metropolitan life.

II: Enid

1901-1909

CHAPTER FOUR

The Cogdal-McKee Building

THE Cogdal-McKee building was on Grand Avenue in the south block of the east side of the Square. Downstairs were the National saloon and Parker's bookstore. On the second floor to the left of the stairs was the office of Mr. W. E. Cogdal, the owner. His door bore the sign:

Real Estate &
LOANS

Mr. Cogdal now owned the claim, too.

To the right of the stairs was Papa's office. The sign said:

HOUSTIN JAMES
Atty-at-Law

I thought "atty" should have been spelled out.

In other rooms were the offices of Moore & Moore, attorneys-at-law (Colonel John C. Moore and his son, Mr. Charlie); Mr. Henry Sturgis, attorney-at-law; the Hunter Realty, Mortgage & Investment Company; the Western Union Telegraph Company, and the Police Court. That left two rooms in which Papa and Mama and I slept, amid furniture brought from the claim which rather crowded us. We owned a house in Enid, a small unpainted house which the icehouse had not gobbled up. There had been some mention of moving into it. Papa said the family living there would have no place to go if we did. I was glad. The house was away out on East Hill. I wanted to be in the middle of things. The Cogdal-McKee building satisfied this desire in every particular.

It was solid brick and the most imposing of the ten or twelve buildings that made up the block. So the block was called the Cogdal-McKee block. If my recollection serves, the Cogdal-McKee block contained five saloons, one grocery, two dry-goods stores, one Mexican tamale and chili joint, Cap Bond's restaurant, one barber shop (Mills's Tonsorial Parlor), the Citizens Bank and Parker's bookstore.

Upstairs a hall split our building down the middle. At the rear end was a small porch and stairs leading to the pump in the back yard which supplied the building with water. From the porch you got an interesting view.

Public drunkenness had lately been declared an offense against good morals in Enid. (Mama said it was about time.) As a convenience to patrons some saloons enclosed their back yards with high fences where the tipsy could lie on the ground until fit to venture abroad without risking a night in the calaboose. Boys roaming the alleys would peer through the knotholes. This was unnecessary for me. Our second-story porch overlooked the enclosures of the National, the Monarch, and Gillespie Brothers. Gillespie Brothers was the best for sights. At Sunday-school time on Sunday morning you might see the forms of men who had been there all night, still as stiff as cordwood.

On the other side of the alley back of our building stood the calaboose, or town jail, a filthy little tin-covered structure, scorched about the barred windows as a result of an attempt of a prisoner to burn his way out. I became acquainted with the connected functions of the calaboose and the Police Court. Attendance at the sessions of the court added considerably to my knowledge of the world in a fairly short time. Men were brought in for being drunk in public, fighting or stealing things of small value. Now and then I heard the story of a good cutting scrape involving colored residents of Two Street or Happy Hollow. A white man seldom had a lawyer to speak for him in Police Court. All the Negroes had. He was Enid's colored attorney-at-law, Devotion L. F. Banks. Devotion L. F. Banks wore a seedy Prince Albert coat and gold-rimmed spectacles. He always made a big speech, hard for me to follow on account of the long words. Apparently Judge

Roach, too, found them hard to follow. Anyhow he frequently interrupted. "That'll do, Banks. I find this nigger guilty."

One time some young ladies were brought into court. Before reading the complaint Judge Roach looked over the glasses perched on the end of his nose.

"Marquis, I think I will excuse you for the present," he said.

If the judge thought to spare me from the knowledge of what the young ladies were there for, he could have saved himself the trouble.

I made the acquaintance of inmates of the calaboose. One slipped fifty cents and a dime through the bars and asked me to run an errand. The dime was to keep. With the fifty cents I bought a small bottle of whiskey at the back door of a saloon and delivered it to the prisoner.

Stronger proof than the fact that he was in jail was needed to persuade me that a person should be shunned by his fellows. Dick Yeager had died in jail. Other of Papa's clients had been in jail—but the county jail or the Ohio State Penitentiary and not the dirty little calaboose in the alley. (Having no penitentiary of its own, Oklahoma sent its convicts to Ohio.) To my mind a man might be in jail merely because he had gone into court with "a hard case," or, like the Negroes before Judge Roach, because he lacked the services of a sufficiently persuasive lawyer. Judge Roach gave the father of two of my schoolmates a stiff sentence. He was a cocky, undersized Irish teamster, frequently in trouble for drinking and fighting.

I now went to Central School, in the great new brick building heated by contraptions called radiators. Only a few of my classmates had I known before, at East Hill. Among the strangers were the prisoner's children—pert, forward little girls with short pigtails. Word that their father was in the calaboose sent a buzz through the fourth grade. I fancied it up to me to show that I felt they had nothing to be ashamed of.

After school I sidled up to the girls who were laughing and carrying on as if, in truth, ashamed of nothing under the sun. Perhaps my gallant intentions were awkwardly expressed. At any rate the elder and prettier and bolder of the sisters began a chant half the playground could hear:

"Markey wants to be my fel-la! My fel-la!"

Taking to my heels I bade chivalry a farewell calculated to last forever.

2

One of the first things I noticed about town life was the need for money. As a country boy I had been accustomed to spend money whenever in town. As I did not go too often, my funds were usually equal to the demands on them. But being in town every day I soon ran out of cash.

The second floor of the Cogdal-McKee building solved this problem. Tenants saw to the sweeping of their rooms, but Mr. Cogdal kept the hall and the front stairs swept. For twenty-five cents a week I swept them every few days, and the only person who complained that they were not clean enough was Mama. Papa paid me a quarter a week for sweeping his office and cleaning his spittoons. Mr. Charlie swept the office of Moore & Moore, but I cleaned the spittoons at the pump in back for five cents each. Mr. Sturgis slept in his office and swept it. Judge Roach paid two-and-a-half cents apiece for cleaning the spittoons in the Police Court room. I could not complain over the reduced rate because there were so many of them and I cleaned them so often.

The Western Union office was almost as fascinating as Police Court, and our building was never shut of the clack of the instruments. The telephone had seemed marvelous enough when they put one on the wall of Papa's office and I could talk to Jay Radcliffe clear out on East Hill. But one who understood the code could talk on the telegraph to Fort Worth or Kansas City. Mr. Seward, the manager, said that the company gave him no money for cleaning spittoons. I offered to clean them for nothing if he would teach me the Morse code. He said he would see about it. I began cleaning the Western Union spittoons and sure enough one day Mr. Seward wrote out the alphabet with a Morse sign after each letter. Had it been a guide to buried treasure I don't think I could have taken better care of that piece of yellow paper.

Another place I made myself handy was Parker's bookstore. Mr. Parker would let me sit on the back stoop and read second-hand books from his shelves: Oliver Optic, G. A. Henty, *The Prince and the Pauper*, the endless *Elsie Dinsmore* series, *Black Beauty*, *Beautiful Joe* and *The Great Northfield Bank Robbery & Other Daring Deeds of Jesse James*; also old copies of the comic magazines *Life* and *Puck* and *Judge* and of the funny papers with the doings of Happy Hooligan, Foxy Grandpa, and Buster Brown.

There was more to Enid, of course, than the Cogdal-McKee block. I had driven the ice wagon all over Jonesville (as they called the part of town that rightly belonged to Walter Cook) and the Kenwood and Weatherly additions on the West Side. But it was funny the things you *didn't* see from the ice wagon. I suppose that was because the wagon stuck to the streets, mostly. Alleys were the place to see things. You looked in the back doors.

Take the front door of Mr. Fred Luft's harness shop on Broadway, as they called E Street now. Well, on the sidewalk was a rather lifelike dummy of a dappled-gray gelding. Sometimes Mr. Luft would have a nice set of single harness on it, sometimes a saddle and bridle. This was all very well to see once or twice, but the novelty wore off. The same with Mr. Luft's show windows: just harness and saddles and the gear that went with them. But look in Mr. Luft's back door from the alley and you could see him and Mr. Daniels working on a set of harness or a saddle. You saw them cut and punch and rivet and shape and stitch the leather. A thing took form under your eyes. You went back in a day or so and what had been just a saddletree was half a saddle. You went back later and there it was, done; and a beauty.

That was it. From the back doors you could see people make

things. You could see Uncle John Dollar making a pair of boots or Mr. Divers mixing his colors and painting a sign. At the Model Carriage Works you could see them fashion spokes and assemble a wheel. Jack McCutcheon, the tinker, soldered pots and pans and fixed umbrellas, guns, and bicycles. It was something to see him take a Colt apart, cut a new spring and put the parts together again, and snap the trigger to show that the Colt worked.

Looking in the back door of the Enid Bakery you could see Mrs. Oligschleger bake bread, taking loaves by the dozen from an oven you could have shoved a barn door in. Mrs. Oligschleger and her husband spoke German to each other. It was the first I knew that anyone except Indians and Mexicans spoke a language different from ours. I asked Mr. Oligschleger to teach me German.

"I got other things to do," he said, though his wife did most of the work.

Mrs. Oligschleger taught me to count to ten and to ask for bread or cake in German. When her husband was around she would make signs for me to go away. When he wasn't around she would tell me about life in Germany when she was a girl and sometimes give me a cooky.

On reading of a man who spoke sixteen languages I, too, resolved to become a great linguist. Having at my command a few words of Cherokee, Osage, Comanche, Spanish and German, I imagined the rest should be easy. I got to telling boys that, counting English, I spoke seven languages already. The seventh was what I called the "deef-and-dumb language." You talked it with your fingers. This accomplishment I had learned from Deefy, a smelly old deaf-mute hermit who lived in a hovel near the Old Government Springs and read all the time. He would read anything straight through—a seed catalogue or anything else.

In the back of Bumstead's ice-cream parlor they made ice cream in the biggest freezer you ever saw. It took two boys my size to turn the handle. Sometimes I would be one of those boys, and we'd each get a dish of ice cream for doing it.

Watching Mr. Divers I became interested in what he called lettering. I watched him paint about a dozen signs reading:

See
F. S. KIRK
for
COAL WOOD & FEED

The signs were to tack on fences and walls.

I got an old brush Mr. Divers had thrown away and some paint. I found a cast-off tin sign, painted out whatever was on it and substituted:

See
HOUSTIN JAMES
about
L A W

Papa gave me a nickel for the sign. But he put it back of his desk and showed it only to other lawyers.

Behind Gensman Brothers (Farm Implements & Gen'l Hardware) I watched a man uncrate and start to put together a McCormick reaper.

"Bub, like to do me a favor?" he said.

"Yes, sir."

"Run over to Jack McCutcheon's and tell him Billy Gensman would like to borrow his Number 5 left-handed monkey wrench."

Mr. Gensman had me repeat the name of the tool so I should make no mistake, and I went off feeling myself a cog in the wheel of Enid's busy life.

Jack McCutcheon looked up from his littered bench. He was a small stooped man with bright, dark, pleasant eyes that looked through silver-rimmed specs.

"Declare," he said, "I loaned that wrench to Grant Yeakey. Go ask him for it, lad."

Grant Yeakey was drilling a well several blocks away. He sent me to the Model Carriage Works. They sent me somewhere else. And *they* sent me to Hackett's blacksmith shop.

Mr. Hackett used to shoe our horses. He was an enormous, solemn man, partly bald and with a short graying beard. I'd never seen him smile and would as leave have approached a stranger. Pulling lightly at his bellows he began to ask questions which brought out all the places I'd visited.

"Son," he said, "I reckon you been far enough on a wild-goose chase."

I just looked at Mr. Hackett.

"They been foolin' you," the blacksmith said.

I did not understand.

"They ain't no left-hand monkey wrench," said Mr. Hackett. "It's just a thing they send greenhorns after."

I began to back out of the blacksmith shop, feeling as if I was sinking in quicksand. So I was just a greenhorn. Just a hayseed. Just a dumb country jake. And half the town knew it.

"Wait a minute, Markey," said Mr. Hackett, still as unsmiling as Brother Porter at the Methodist church. "If any butcher ever sends you for a *meat auger*, you tell him you'll be glad to lend him *yours* in exchange for a nice slice of *whale steak*."

"Yes, sir," said I, and bolted from the scene of the exposure of my humiliation.

I waited for years for a butcher to send me for a meat auger but one never did.

Other boys "peddled" newspapers and sometimes I would gather with them at the *Eagle* office where they waited for their papers. One time I wandered through the back door of the *Eagle*. There were people about, all doing things I did not understand. I was careful to keep out of their way. I had learned to keep out of people's way when they were working and to be careful about asking questions. Some would answer you, some would not, and some would chase you out.

A man was standing before a rack which supported a big shallow box divided into a lot of smaller boxes. He was taking little things from the boxes and putting them in rows in something he held in his other hand. The man looked as if he might be friendly. Finally I asked what was he doing, please, sir. He stopped and looked down as if trying to decide whether to answer. Then he said, "Settin' a handbill," and went on about it.

I knew a handbill, but I didn't know what settin' one was.

Pretty soon the man went over to a table with a marble top,

something like the top of Mama's bureau. There he put the things he had been arranging in rows. When he returned to his boxes I went to the table and looked at what he had put there. They were letters. After a little I caught on to the fact that they spelled words, but backwards. At the top in real big letters was

!NOITCUA

Presently the man had another batch of words he had made from the boxes. He added it to the batch on the table. I could read at the bottom:

SIHTAM .J
reenoitcuA

That was not too hard to translate:

J. MATHIS
Auctioneer

You saw it on handbills all the time.

This was real exciting. I watched the man do a number of things to the words he had arranged backwards. At length he fastened them in a machine which he ran with his foot. He would put a sheet of paper in the machine and it would come out a handbill. One fell to the floor and I asked if I could have it.

Outside I read the handbill through. I am sure I had never read a handbill through before. But this was something special. I had seen it made. I had discovered the art of printing.

3

That summer Mama and I went to Chicago to visit my sisters. The pictures in *Scribner's Monthly* had been no hoax, no glorified left-handed-monkey-wrench proposition to fool a country boy. There they were in breath-taking reality: the elevated railway; theaters; the Masonic Temple, which was the highest building in the world (we went on the roof and looked down); Marshall Field's; Lake Michigan and the ships (we took a trip to Milwaukee on one named *Christopher Columbus*); the menagerie in Lincoln Park; the Field Museum. Some of the most vivid impressions of a city that I possess at this day were acquired in Chicago in 1901.

You would have thought that I should have had a world of things to talk about when I got back to Enid, but it doesn't seem to have been that way. Too much was happening at home.

The day after our return a street show came to town and President McKinley was shot. Papa and I were coming out of the tent as a boy passed the handbills telling about the shooting. The handbill interested me from the point of printing. There was a line drawing of the President on it. I wondered how the printer had been able to assemble each of those little lines to form such a good likeness of Mr. McKinley. Visiting a printing office I learned of the existence of cuts.

Nor was this all. Things had been happening in Enid all summer. There was an automobile in town now; a boy had lost three fingers picking up a cannon cracker on the Fourth of July; Johnny Baxter's father had tried to poison Johnny's mother.

Herschel Goltry, whose father owned the automobile, was in my Sunday-school class. I did not like him. Every time I went to say something about the automobiles in Chicago, he'd chime in about *their* automobile.

I forget the name of the boy whose fingers were blown off. When the bandages were removed he carried his hand up his sleeve so you could not see it and would charge a piece of candy or a marble for a look.

Mrs. Baxter was a dressmaker and milliner. The family lived back of her shop. Johnny told me how his father had tried to do the poisoning. It seems that Mr. Baxter was carrying on with the seamstress who worked for Mrs. Baxter. So one morning he lifted the lid of the coffee pot and put something into it. Mrs. Baxter saw him. Thinking her husband up to no good, she emptied the pot and made fresh coffee. Then she called Johnny and his sisters and told them to ask for coffee for breakfast.

When the family sat down Mr. Baxter said he wasn't feeling very well and guessed he wouldn't have any coffee. When the kids asked for coffee Mrs. Baxter said that, as their father wasn't drinking any, she guessed there would be enough. Mr. Baxter got very excited. He said the kids couldn't have any coffee. But the eldest, Beulah, already had poured herself some and was drinking it. Mr. Baxter grabbed the cup from her and spilled out the coffee. Then he ran into the next room and got his hat and coat off the nail. That was the last Johnny had seen of his father.

Mrs. Baxter took the coffee she had poured out to the drugstore to be examined.

"Enough poison in it to kill a horse," John said proudly.

The greatest thing I had missed by going to Chicago was the fire. The whole south side of the Square and the block south of us on Grand Avenue had burned. Every boy had a thrilling story to tell of the fire and every boy had a store of loot from the ruins. When I got home the ruins had been picked pretty clean, but I had the good luck to dig out the frame of a baby buggy. I got the wheels off and put them under my bed. I talked of making me a wagon for coasting down East Hill but never got around to it. Still, the wheels were something to show when a boy asked what you'd got out of the fire.

Dewey Evans had made the best haul from the fire. I deemed it a privilege to be numbered among Dewey's acquaintances. He belonged to a gang of boys Mama called hoodlums. They did not go to school. It was hard to tell from their faces whether they were white or colored. One or two of them were bootblacks who toted their little boxes in and out of the noisy saloons. They fought terribly among themselves but stood together against the rest of the town. Roaming the alleys they were the terrors of boys with reasonably clean faces and clothes.

Dewey was the only one I wasn't scared to death of and I was a little scared of Dewey. He lived with his father in a shack made of dry-goods boxes and tin in the willow thicket between Two Street and the Rock Island track. The father was a handyman about saloons and sort of feeble-minded, people said. Dewey seemed to rustle most of his own grub, making out well enough by washing dishes in restaurants in exchange for what they would give him to eat.

It was in Cap Bond's kitchen, a few doors removed from the rear of the Cogdal-McKee building, that I had made Dewey's acquaintance and learned of his ambition in life. It was to be a short-order cook.

"They make good money," said Dewey.

This ambition exalted Dewey in my estimation. Not that I was without ambitions. Since moving to town two had been added to the list: railroad brakeman and telephone lineman. I loved to watch the brakemen, walking along the tops of moving trains. They came from far places, they went to far places, and their manner and their talk, their very signals to the engine crew, were so casual. It was a lineman's climbing irons that made his work attractive. I knew a lineman—Hal Roach, the Police Court judge's son—and would follow him from pole to pole. But these ambitions, like all my others, appeared as remote of attainment as stars. On the other hand Dewey, a dishwasher already, seemed on the highroad to the realization of his.

It was in the rear of Cap Bond's that Dewey mentioned that he had got something out of the fire.

"You'll keep mum if I show you," said Dewey, "or I'll skin you alive."

Reaching deep into a pocket of his pants, which were too big for him, Dewey hauled out—a gold watch. Alice could have been no more astonished when the Rabbit hauled out a watch. Dewey let me take it in my hands and hear it tick.

The questions that rose to my lips were unuttered. How on earth did one get a perfectly good gold watch out of a fire? I knew that if Dewey wanted me to know he would tell me. He never did and I cannot recall that either of us ever referred to the watch again.

Not long before Christmas I came across Dewey looking into a store window.

"See anything you want for Christmas, Dewey?" I said, mean

ing it as a joke. I knew Dewey didn't expect anything for Christmas.

"Naw," said Dewey, and after a pause: "Wantin' ain't gittin', nohow."

"You better write your letter to Santa Claus." I can't imagine how I could have been so bold, even in fun.

"Santy Claus be good God-damned," Dewey said and moved away, wiping his nose on his sleeve.

Although I had heard Dewey use worse language I was rather shocked. I didn't see how good-God-damning Santa Claus improved matters for anybody.

A greater shock came one time when I was on my way to evening services at the Methodist church. In the shadow of a house across the street from the church I heard Dewey and some of his fellow-hoodlums singing "Nero, my dog, has fleas" to the tune of "Nearer, My God, to Thee." Then I heard Dewey's voice above the others imitating the tone and cadence of Brother Porter, the preacher. "Thy kingdom come, on a big bass drum; high, low, jack and the game."

Truly I was appalled. I expected something dreadful to happen to Dewey on the spot: God to strike him deaf and dumb, or at least knock his hat off with a jab of lightning. But nothing at all happened, and the last I saw of Dewey and his friends was when they trooped across Maple Street and disappeared into the alley behind the Hubbard House, probably to bum a handout off the colored cook. I think I was a little disappointed not to bear witness to some sort of display of celestial wrath.

After a moment's reflection, however, I was grateful to God for overlooking Dewey's transgressions. If God could do so much in Dewey's case, maybe He could overlook the matter of the apples in my case. They were the apples I had swiped from a barrel in front of Buttrey's grocery. They weighed on my mind.

We were Methodists—that is, Mama was—and I attended the Methodist Sunday school. Mama and Papa usually went to the Congregational church, though, because Papa liked the Congregational minister's preaching better. Mama admitted that

Brother Porter's sermons could be pretty long and dry, and she seemed pleased to get Papa inside any church.

"But Brother Porter is a good, sincere man," she'd say, sticking up for the Methodists.

"Without question he is," Papa would agree, "and most useful in the service of the Lord. To hear him one should get credit for an act of penance as well as for going to church."

Feeling myself in need of penance I had decided to take in one of Brother Porter's sermons. But, meeting some other boys, I had stopped at Bumstead's and bought an ice-cream soda water with the nickel intended for the collection. Dewey's blasphemous performance further delayed me, and when I reached the church the service had begun. So I took my place among the bunch of boys you always found sitting on the church steps, whispering and nudging each other and half-way listening to the service through the open windows. These boys always knew the text of the sermon, which they would repeat at home as evidence that they had been to church. A boy arriving late could get the text from another boy, for repeating the Bible verse helped you to remember it.

After getting the text I repeated it a couple of times to myself and then sat down and tried in earnest to follow the thread of Brother Porter's discourse. From Dewey's experience it was pleasant to know that the Lord was in a good humor that evening. But, with a theft on my conscience, I didn't want to push Him too far.

4

From what I have written it would seem that the broadening influences of urban culture came from Enid's alleys and streets. This was not entirely true. With the Donly Hotel I had not only a back-door but a front-door acquaintance. This made my education in one respect more extensive than that of Dewey who, I do not believe, had ever passed through the front door of a hotel. Though Mama got our breakfasts on a gasoline stove in the rooms in the Cogdal-McKee building, we ate our dinners and suppers at the Donly. To eat a meal at a hotel was an event for a boy. I know of no other boy in Enid who ate at one regularly, as I did for more than a year.

The Donly Hotel was the new name for the Rex. A massive three-story building with a pressed tin front painted to look like brick, it was the most conspicuous landmark in Enid and the Strip's most important hotel—that is, until recently, when the Frantz Hotel, three stories and real brick, was built in the next block. When we lived on the claim I had occasionally eaten at the Rex with my parents. I cannot say that the meals were altogether enjoyable because I had to watch my table manners so.

By now I was at home at the Donly. When my parents' mealtimes were not to my liking I would eat alone. It made me feel grown up to stroll from the dining room into the hotel office with a toothpick between my teeth and casually tell Mr. Donly, behind the counter, to "punch one dinner." He would take our meal ticket from the rack on the wall and punch it. For a while I got to taking school friends with me to eat. It was a pleasure to interpret for them the bill-of-fare which a waitress would rattle off as if it was one long word. My hospitality exhausted a meal ticket so quickly that my parents made inquiries. I could have no more guests without permission, not often given.

"Mr. Donly's dinners cost fifty cents apiece," said Mama.

I observed the manners of traveling salesmen. They had jokes for the waitresses. At the end of a meal they would gather up all the little dishes the different victuals had come in and stack them on their plates so the waitress could carry them away more easily. Stacking the dishes showed that a man was no hayseed. Then they would saunter about the office with toothpicks between their teeth and their thumbs hooked in their suspenders. Or they would go on the sidewalk under the awning and sit in chairs and tilt back. I tried to copy these evidences of sophistication.

It was, therefore, a matter of disappointment to me when Mama succeeded in getting Papa to buy a house for us to live in and we left the rooms in the Cogdal-McKee building.

CHAPTER FIVE

The Secret Society

Our house was at Sixth and Maine, catty-cornered across from the Park; or what East Hill called the Park. Really it was just eight or ten acres of bottom land which the north branch of Boggy meandered through. On the banks of the creek were some fair-sized cottonwoods and elms. For the rest, the Park was a willow thicket, except for the clearings about the shacks of the squatters, who were nearly all Negroes. Old Aunty, who helped Mama get straightened around in our new place, lived in one of the shacks. Though her skin was not much darker than my mother's, whose French blood showed in her complexion, Aunty was a Negro—what you called a "white nigger."

On the side of the Park opposite our house a bluff thirty feet high formed the right bank of Boggy. It was on this bluff that John C. Moore's residence occupied the site Papa so admired. The ex-Confederate colonel could sit on his porch and look down the chimney of his colored colleague at the bar, Devotion L. F. Banks, whose house, on the flat below the bluff, was convenient to many of the clients that he defended so eloquently in Police Court.

At the foot of the bluff, emptying their waters into the creek, were the Old Government Springs. The earliest white travelers to come that way had learned of the springs from the Indians. A generation of cow outfits, following the Chisholm Trail, had camped beside them. In the early days of Enid, before wells were plentiful, the springs supplied drinking water to a great part of the population. A number of people still used them. The water was clear and cool and tasted of minerals, though not unpleasantly. The notion that it was good for the health had come down from the Indians. Of an evening you would see folks from the far West Side of town come in their buggies for water. This was about the only use West-Siders made of our Park, which they called Happy Hollow.

Mama had wanted to go to the West Side to live, especially after Mr. Ed Weatherly offered to deed Papa two lots in the Weatherly Addition if he would build a house on them. Ed Weatherly was doing all he could to boom his addition, and most of the people who were building new homes were building there or in Kenwood. It seemed that about all who could afford to do so were moving from East Hill to the West Side. Banker Fleming had been about the first to go, and the succeeding exodus took classmates I'd known since my days under Miss Edna. But Papa said no, the West Side was flat as a pancake: no view, no water. Someday our Park would be a garden spot and those tony West-Siders would come begging for lots where they could get a glimpse of it.

Our house afforded more than a glimpse. It surmounted a sort of mislaid portion of the bluff in the form of a knoll which rose twenty feet above Maine Street. From this elevation we could look all the way to the springs. It was not a new house, but an old one which Papa enlarged and fixed up quite tastefully the way Mama wanted. Though not so spacious as our crazy old house on the claim, the six rooms seemed like heaven to Mama after the cramped quarters in the Cogdal-McKee building. Papa had the knoll terraced, sown to Bermuda grass and dotted with locust trees. I could have done without the grass and the trees which fell to me to water from a pump, all my persuasions upon Papa to install a windmill being unavailing.

When these improvements were completed it developed that the west porch Papa had built stuck a foot or so out into Sixth Street. Papa saved the porch by annexing ten feet of the street which, like the Park, existed almost entirely in theory. Some years later, when sidewalks were laid, my father, not wishing to appear selfish, had the rectified line run through to Broadway, the next street over, so that the abutting property owner, a Mr.

Kelso, also got a present of ten feet of highway. That explains the jog in Sixth Street that exists to this day.

On the back end of our property was a cow stable, half of which Mama converted into a chicken house. It was understood that the rest was to be enlarged to shelter a horse and buggy when we should get Tom back. Since leaving the claim Mama had been without the use of a horse for the first time in her life. The buggy horse, Tom, had been sold to Mr. Dick Kennedy of Kennedy Brothers, Enid's only department store. Our grief at the parting was somewhat assuaged by our pride at seeing Tom in white harness drawing Mrs. Kennedy's rubber-tired trap. Then Mrs. Kennedy got lung trouble and had to go to New Mexico. Tom was transferred to the Kennedy delivery wagon and it nearly broke Mama's heart. That was no way to use a "fairly good" buggy horse. When Mama called a horse "fairly good" you may be sure he was all that.

2

I converted to my own uses the vacant portion of the cow stable. It became the headquarters of the secret society which I organized in all its ramifications. The ritual, passwords, and countersigns were secretly buried at night in the dark of the moon in a Silver Leaf lard can beneath two feet of earth in the southeast part of the chicken run. You arrived at the spot by reference to directions recorded in code and buried elsewhere. To find *them* was a secret of my memory.

The secret society was the fruit of ideas gathered from Tom Sawyer's robber band, the Oklahoma Anti-Horse Thief Association, and the Woodmen of the World. Claude Dixon's father belonged to the Woodmen and Claude looked forward to the day when he should become a Junior Woodman. I regarded it as unfortunate that my father belonged to no lodge.

Working up the ritual and the signs and the passwords by which members could recognize each other called for the creation of certain offices and titles. At the head of everything was the Grand Exalted Commander-in-Chief. The rank and file was composed of Exalted Citizens. In between were various dignitaries. The post of Grand Exalted Scribe and Keeper of the Secret Scrolls was the one designed for myself.

The outward sign of our invisible empire was the letters KN. That would be on our badge, like the Masons' square and compass. Innermost of our secrets was what KN stood for. The answer was Kid Nation: a self-governing republic of boys bound together, one for all and all for one, to help each other in connection with scrapes boys get into. To do this we pledged our lives, our fortunes, and our sacred honor.

It was only natural that I should have thought of Sherman Rooney, Jay Radcliffe, and Claude Dixon as charter members to start things going. Already we four formed a sort of society. It had grown out of these words from a song the Negroes sang:

Jig jog fo' butchah,
Butchah jig fo' you.

The words didn't mean anything but you know how Negro songs are. This is what we did with the words. Suppose I saw Jay coming. I'd yell:

"Jig jog"
and Jay'd yell back:
"fo' butchah"
and I'd yell:
"butchah jig"
and Jay'd yell:
"fo' you."

Sherman Rooney originated most of our projects. Those he didn't originate he took charge of and told the rest of us what to do. Sherman had bright blue eyes that bored right through you when he talked; and he had thick ears, freckles on the bridge of his nose, and a mop of black oily hair. My respect for Sherman Rooney went back to my first year at East Hill School. Some of the big boys had dirtied the floor of the outhouse. When the superintendent of schools—the "p'fesser"—discovered the muss the big boys blamed it on some of us small boys. We were set to cleaning the floor under the supervision of the big boys whose false testimony had convicted us. I was scrubbing away, feeling so disgraced and so nearly blind with anger that I could scarcely keep back tears, when Sherman snatched up a water bucket and swinging with all his might caught a big boy on the side of the head. The big boy went down and Sherman streaked for home. Another big boy started after Sherman who was lucky enough to hook onto a passing buggy and get away.

Next day he reappeared at school with his grown brother, who drove the yellow bus that met the railroad trains. The brother put in circulation the word that if anything should happen to Sherman by way of retaliation the consequences would be unpleasant for certain big boys.

With everything concerning KN letter-perfect, one day I joined my three companions back of the Radcliffe barn, busting to see the secret society under way right off. But Sherman had already introduced a matter for our consideration.

Previously we boys had rolled cigarettes of dried corn silk (which burned too fast) and of coffee (which spilled out at the ends). "Now," said Sherman, "I'm going to treat you all to a real smoke."

He produced a piece of buggy whip about as big around as your little finger. With his pocket knife Sherman cut the whip into two-inch lengths. To this day I don't know what a buggy whip was made of, but the porous inside was easy to draw through because of the nearly airtight covering. And it burned just about right. But the smoke was so hot and powerful that it stung my throat so that I could hardly speak. And had that not been the case it would have been tactless to mention KN just then—with Sherman's mind on something else.

At the next opportunity other doubts assailed me. Would Sherman and Jay and Claude *like* KN? Or would they make fun of it? Alone, once more I rehearsed the ritual. It was so grand and fine that I was sure *any* boy would be captivated. Especially

Claude, who wanted to be a Junior Woodman. That was an idea: Claude. Why not tell Claude first? He would be for it; then we could both tackle Sherman and Jay. But, come to think of it, Sherman didn't seem to care so much for other boys' suggestions. He liked to do the suggesting. No, I'd have to tell Sherman first and let him tell the others.

I tried to do so. But words simply failed me.

About this time I became acquainted with a new boy who lived down by the Rock Island track. I have forgotten his name, but his father was a house-mover and we played with his rollers and tackles. I let slip some phrases from the ritual. The boy was interested. I explained that the words were part of the affairs of a vast, secret boys' organization, spread over this whole town. The boy looked wonder-struck. Could he join? I said that would be a matter for the next secret conclave of the exalted officers. I went away feeling buoyant. KN had a member.

My enthusiasm subsided when it occurred to me that it had just one member besides myself. I had permitted this boy to get the impression that he was dealing with a numerous society. I felt I could hardly go back to him until I had some other members.

They were not forthcoming; but finally I returned to the boy's house. The house was empty. The family had moved. I sat on the front stoop, relieved.

3

When Mr. Vernon Whiting became postmaster of Enid I got the job of delivering special-delivery letters. Papa bought me a bicycle. The inside workings of the post office turned out to be so wonderful that I was surprised not to have found out about them before. To see the clerks sort and distribute mail was really something. I began to collect stamps. And there was so much to read—magazines a body had never heard of before. I would take them out of their wrappers and lie on a pile of mail sacks and read sometimes all day. Then I would put them back into the wrappers and they went to the people they were intended for. I don't think I lost a wrapper over once a week.

I liked all the post-office clerks except George Blue. George Blue complained of my reading, complained of my handwriting in the special book, and said just let a postal inspector catch me sorting mail. George Blue would open an incoming sack and if there was a special he'd yell:

"Where's that dam' boy?"

One day the funniest thing happened. It was Opening Week and Enid was celebrating the anniversary of the Run with a street carnival. George Blue gave me a quarter.

"Here, kid," he said, "have a good time."

I had never been more surprised in my life. I bought a bottle of pop, took two rides on the ferris wheel, and George Blue and I became the best of friends.

"Here y'are, kid," he'd call. "For Jo Barnabee. Scoot an' get that extra dime."

It was well known that Miss Josephine Barnabee always tipped the special boy a dime.

I suppose Miss Josephine Barnabee got more special-delivery letters than anyone else in town. Two Street as a whole was a good customer, though. The girls often gave you tips. I think the only other tip I received was from a traveling salesman at the Hubbard House.

"Wait a minute, son," he said gravely when I handed him the letter.

Opening it he read a little way and let out a whoop.

"You brought good news, bub! Here's four bits."

When a certain important politician of our town was in Guthrie, Josephine Barnabee got a special every day. Hers was the biggest house on Two Street: yellow and square, with a screened three-story porch in back. The house was set on a slope so that the back was three stories high and the front two stories. The dance hall was in the basement. The music never sounded so loud as the music at Jennie Hearn's, a few doors away. Josephine Barnabee was the only resident of Two Street who owned a carriage. There was seldom any trouble at her place and when there was nobody got arrested. On the other hand Jennie was often in hot water. I used to see her in Papa's office pouring out her troubles.

When Josephine Barnabee's politician friend was writing every day from Guthrie, I got so I would just say, "Here's your letter, Miss Josephine," or "Number 4 was late today, Miss Josephine." She would sign my book in a hand that was like a child's writing, say something pleasant and give me ten cents. By rights Josephine Barnabee should have signed with a flourish, like Colonel John C. Moore. A second-grade-kid signature was out of keeping with the magnificence of her person and her surroundings.

Another source of reading matter was the Enid Public Library which occupied a second-floor room on the south side of the Square. Jay Radcliffe and I would go there together on our bikes, returning books or calling for them for our mothers. Miss Jennie Kelso, the librarian, would suggest books which she thought might interest us personally. There were not many chairs in the library so usually we boys would sit on the floor and go over the books Miss Jennie had recommended. I don't know whether it was she or Mama who put me on the track of Froissart's *Chronicles* which did much to further my interest in history. My mother's favorite reading was history, historical novels, memoirs and biography. She would often tell me stories from what she read. In that way I had learned something of presidents other than James A. Garfield. My favorites were George Washington (though he seemed a little too good to be true, never having told a lie), Andrew Jackson (for his refusal to clean the British officer's boots), Abraham Lincoln (he was such a good wrestler), and Andrew Johnson (the runaway apprentice).

Abraham Lincoln was brought a little closer than the others because Mama had met him. Mr. Lincoln had not been elected President, though folks were talking about it. Mama's class at school got up a tableau in which girls took the parts of the different states. When they got ready to give the tableau, who should happen along but Abraham Lincoln in the tow of Congressman Shanks, whose daughter was Mama's closest friend in the class. Later they roomed together at college. After the tableau each little girl was presented to Mr. Lincoln. She curtsied and he shook hands with her. Mama said she would have forgotten all about it except that Mr. Lincoln went to the White House. During the Civil War the family used to speak of the time Rachel had shaken hands with President Lincoln.

I was anxious to get to the seventh grade in school so I could study Barnes's history of America, which began with Columbus. You used the same book in the eighth grade. There you began with the Revolutionary War. By the time I was in the fifth or sixth grade I had got hold of a very ragged copy of Barnes and read it all through. In high school they studied three Barnes's histories, as I recall. One was an ancient history, beginning with the Egyptians and ending with the Romans; another a European history; and the third an advanced history of the United States. I got copies of these from Harold Houston, who went to high school, and read the most interesting parts.

On a Fourth of July, Mr. Henry Sturgis came by in a carriage to take my parents and me to a barbecue in the country where Mr. Sturgis was going to deliver the oration of the day. While driving along, Papa and Mr. Sturgis got to discussing the battle of Waterloo. I spoke up to say that Napoleon would have won had not Blücher shown up.

"What was that, Marquis?" asked Mr. Sturgis.

I repeated what I had said and he corrected my pronunciation of Blücher's name. I thought that was all he wanted. In reading I ran on to so many names you seldom heard in ordinary talk and I was unsure of how to say many of them. Mr. Sturgis asked other questions about the battle and about Napoleon, some of which it seems that I was able to answer, Napoleon being a favorite of mine.

"How old are you, Marquis?" Mr. Sturgis asked.

"Nearly twelve," I said.

"Judge," Mr. Sturgis said to Papa, "not many twelve-year-olds could answer those questions."

It was pleasant to know that my reading of history constituted something out of the ordinary. Thereafter at the post office and about the lawyers' offices I would make a point of showing off my learning. On my twelfth birthday Papa gave me an eight-volume history of the United States by Edward S. Ellis, and, on the following Christmas, Ridpath's *History of the World* in nine volumes. I read Ellis all through, skipping only the dry parts about the tariff and such. In Ridpath I bogged down and wound up by using the pictures as guides to the good parts like the Gunpowder Plot, the massacre of St. Bartholomew, the voyages of Sir Francis Drake, and the gorier incidents of the French Revolution.

Mr. Temple Houston never came from Woodward without dropping in at Papa's office. Mr. Houston still wore his hair long and he wore high-heeled boots with his pants over them. You could see the bulge his gun made under his coat. Lawyers didn't usually carry guns any more. I was trying out my history on Mr. Temple Houston when Papa asked what I knew about General Sam Houston of Texas.

This must have been before I had finished Ellis for, beyond the fact that Mr. Howell had spoken of him favorably, I couldn't think of a thing about General Sam Houston of Texas.

"Temple, had you known our Mr. Howell, you'd esteem that as a compliment to your father," Papa said.

Pretty soon I got hold of a book that told about General Sam Houston of Texas; also Daniel Boone, Davy Crockett, James Bowie and others—all in the one book. Then something happened. Much in the way that tops succeed marbles and jacks succeed tops on a school playground, my passion for posing as a historical wizard gave way to something else. So I cannot recall ever having paraded my knowledge of the hero of San Jacinto before his son, whom I continued to see every now and then.

While we were living in the Cogdal-McKee building Papa bought a Hammond typewriter. I was the only person who ever learned to use it. For some reason the girls from the Business College were no good with it. Once I dropped the Hammond on the floor, but Jack McCutcheon fixed it. Papa's next typewriter was a Smith Premier and with it came Miss Knight. She wore peek-a-boo waists. The Smith Premier was a double-keyboard machine, one board for capitals and one for small letters—or caps and lower case as I would say, displaying a terminology picked up from printers.

I liked to hang around the office because I had a crush on Miss Knight and because I liked to hear lawyers talk, just as I liked to hear printers and railroad men and post office people talk. Each had a language of his own. Papa sometimes took me to Kingfisher or Medford when he had a deposition to take or a motion to argue.

Papa was emerging as the most interesting person of my experience, excepting Mr. Howell. About Mr. Howell I had known practically everything, which is too much. About my father I knew next to nothing, which is not enough.

There were those scars on his hand. Scars are always interesting. I had asked Papa how he got them.

"In a runaway," he said.

"Tell me about it."

"Team just too much for me, that's all."

I tried to imagine a team that could be too much for my father.

Mama told me how badly the hand had been mangled, and how, when a doctor set the bones, Papa wouldn't take anything for the pain.

And then there was the scar that went clear across Papa's forehead—so deep that I could lay a finger in it. You didn't see it because Papa's hair, which was dark brown and very thick, came just over it. As often as I wondered about the scar I never dared to ask of its origin.

One time a cousin named Stella James, who was visiting us, happened to see the scar.

"Uncle Houstin, for goodness' sake!" she said. "How ever did you get *that?*"

I listened, all ears. Papa took his pipe from his mouth and smiled.

"Stella," he said, "it's a kind of a secret. So, if I was to tell you and tomorrow someone was to ask you about it, would you tell him you didn't know?"

"Of course, Uncle Houstin," said Stella.

"Now, Stella, you always tell the truth, don't you?"

"I try to, Uncle Houstin."

"Well, I want to make it easy for you in this case. You just tell him you don't know."

I had heard enough lawyer talk to know how one became a lawyer. When you were young you "read law" in a lawyer's office. I'd heard Papa tell about reading law in Ohio. So I made up my mind to read law.

In the back room of Papa's office was a long table on which stood a shaded oil lamp of the kind known as a student's lamp and a bowl containing pipes and tobacco. Carelessly disposed about the table, as if people just got up out of them, were three or four low-backed chairs, a single piece of wood having been bent to form the back and the arms. You saw chairs like these in every lawyer's office and in every courthouse, but almost nowhere else. A small stove, gray from lack of polish, stood in one corner. The floor was covered by a black-figured red carpet which Mama called a disgrace, though under the table it was quite unsoiled and bright. The table was usually strewn with tan-covered law books, some open, some closed. Similar books lined the walls from floor to ceiling. There were other books, too: a thumbed volume of Shakespeare, which had belonged to Doctor Fairgrieve; Burns's poems; Darwin's *Descent of Man*; a Bible; a new book called *The Rhymes of Ironquill*; and I don't know what else. I had given Papa *The Rhymes of Ironquill* for his birthday, and was very proud that he liked them well enough to take the book to his office and read from it to Mr. Henry Sturgis. This volume of verse had been written by a man in Kansas who signed himself Ironquill. Mr. Parker, who ran the bookstore, said he thought Papa might like it.

Well, I started on the law books, and for all I understood of them they might have been arithmetic. I was tussling with a big book when I looked up and saw Papa standing beside me, feet apart and hands in his coat pockets, as he often stood. He smiled and asked what I thought of the *Revised Statutes*.

I told him my plan.

"Given up your ambition to be a printer?" he inquired with interest.

"Well, sort of; yes, sir," I said.

Papa asked if I didn't think that might be a mistake. After all, I *was* young to read law. Couldn't be admitted till I was twenty-one. Suppose I went on with my printing for a spell. Later on if I still wanted to read law there would be plenty of time.

4

This seemed a wonderful solution of my problems. I had really hated to give up being a printer, especially since I had such a good start.

Something about the art of printing, the production of the printed page, went to the core of my being. This may have been because the printed page had meant so much when I was a small child. Type was my only link with the world that lay beyond our prairie horizon. I had come to sense a satisfaction in the printed page which could not always be had from a closer acquaintance with persons and things. The printed page involved one in no embarrassing complications. Adventures encountered in type never sent you on a quest for a left-handed monkey wrench. The printed page let you look at life and shielded you from the rough edge of it. At times life was a little like Kid Nation, which had worked out only as a game of solitaire.

I could observe a printer at the least exciting form of composition known to the craft—a nonpareil "legal" on a solid slug—and watch him strike a galley proof, the very sight of which would thrill me.

From the day I had seen my first printer at work on a handbill for Colonel Joshua Mathis, the fascination of the craft tightened its hold. By degrees I learned how type was set and how printing was done. I learned the names of the things they did it with: stick, case, quad, lead, slug, rule, quoin, imposing stone, chase, planer. I learned the meaning of pi and offset and of bastard type and hell-box and devil. To say some of these words made me feel grown up. An even greater thrill came when I learned that "devil" went back to the medieval dawn of printing when superstitious minds associated the craft with the powers of evil.

You distinguish type according to the heights, the faces, and the styles of the letters. This proved a bewildering business. The point system for denoting height had come in too recently to be thoroughly assimilated by the craft. Veterans continued the ancient custom of saying nonpareil, minion, brevier, bourgeois, long primer, small pica, and pica, the new names for which were, respectively, 6 point, 7 point, 8 point, and so on to 12 point, which was pica. Eight point, or brevier, was the type in which the straight, or reading, matter in a newspaper was ordinarily set. The point system went beyond 150 point, which would be the great wooden studhorse type used in handbills and screaming page ads. Old-timers who held to the name system identified large type as being so-many picas. Eighteen point was pica-and-a-half, 24 point double pica, 36 point three-line pica. I had to learn both systems.

A type face refers to the design of the letter, each design being known by a name. In the job, or display, cases we had dozens of type faces, each called by a name such as Cheltenham, Caslon, Gothic, De Vinne, Copley, Clarendon, Janson, Century. A printer told me that some of these faces, like Caslon, had been in use a hundred or so years. On the other hand, new faces and new styles of old faces were coming in all the time. You could see that the city papers had styles that hadn't got to Enid yet. But when you had to learn them it seemed that we had enough. For instance: Caslon bold, Caslon compressed, Caslon extended, Caslon outline, Caslon shaded, Caslon backslope, Caslon eccentric. Backslope was a letter that leaned to the left, the opposite of italic; eccentric (also called ornamented), a letter adorned with loops and curlicues.

Until you caught on to a few of these things the talk in a print shop was so much jargon.

In the meantime, of course, it was necessary to "learn the case." To concentrate on this I abandoned the effort to master the telegraph key. A case is that assemblage of little open boxes in which a font of type is kept, with a separate compartment for each letter and character. There are two cases, really: the upper and the lower. The upper case is for capitals—the two sets of them that printers use, called caps and small caps. All boxes are the same size and they run A, B, C, and so on, except for the Js and Us which come after Z at the end. The lower case, for small letters, runs every which way. The largest and easiest-to-reach box contains the letter e because you use e oftener than any other letter. Other letters used frequently—t, i, a, s, o, n—are right in front of the typesetter, while the little z, x, and j boxes are over on the left-hand edge of the case with exclamation points and question marks.

I learned the case not in a printing office but at Jay Radcliffe's. Jay had a small printing press, a case, and the remnants of a font of type. They had once belonged to his brother Earle. I think that it was I who stimulated Jay's interest in printing—so I could use his things. In any event we set up together as printers in a small building which had been the summer kitchen of their house. I was by far the more active member of the firm. I made the rounds of the print shops, observed the operations of printers and tried to repeat them in our shop. A shortage of type was a great drawback. This I sought to remedy by sifting the sweepings at the back doors of the printing offices downtown. Type thus collected was of various fonts and sizes, but we made it do. My greatest finds were a cut of Theodore Roosevelt in his Rough Rider suit and a boilerplate advertisement of Doctor Miles's Nervine.

In this way I became familiar with all the print shops in Enid. The one in which I felt least at home was the *Wave* because that paper printed such mean things about Papa. I purely hated the sight of the editor, old J. L. Isenberg. In the early days he had been run out of town a time or so for printing mean things about people, and I could not see why Papa didn't do it now. One time on the claim Ad Poak had come to Mama fit to bust over a piece—something about politics—that was in the *Wave*.

"The judge ought to horsewhip old Isey for that," he said.

But Papa didn't do it and nowadays he and J. L. Isenberg even spoke on the street.

"'Lo, Judge," Isey would pipe up, big as you please.

"Evening, Mr. Isenberg," Papa would say in his bland way.

My favorite paper was the *Events*, which printed nice things about Papa.

Jay and I started printing a newspaper called the *Evening Squeak*, a name I had run across in Artemus Ward or Petroleum V. Nasby. The varied nature of our case of type would produce results something like this:

Mr. F. w. Buttrey, tHe pOpular grocEry, has got hiMself a new dElivery wagon.

The boiler-plate ad for Doctor Miles's patent medicine saved setting a lot of type, though.

Jay left to me most of the work of getting out the paper. His brother Earle was the champion high-school pole vaulter of the Territory. In the back yard he had a bar for pole vaulting and a trapeze. When Earle and the other big boys were not using these things, Jay would get a bunch of younger kids together and neglect the *Squeak*.

I got Papa to buy me a proof press of my own and I told Jay the time had come to dissolve the partnership. That seemed all right with him until I started to carry off the type I had collected and the cut of Teddy Roosevelt and the plate for Doctor Miles's Nervine. Jay said they were his. I said they were mine.

Mrs. Radcliffe came out and asked what were we boys quarreling about. I told her and she said that she had noticed how much harder I had worked at the printing than Jay. She told Jay that we ought to divide the things up.

About the time I got my share moved to our house, school let out for the summer and Papa asked if I wanted to go to Ohio. Of course I wanted to go. I had heard about Ohio all my life and had come to regard it, from what Mama said, as a kind of lost paradise.

My father gave me a quarter and said to go to Mr. Mills and have my hair cut. In his opinion I was getting too grown up for Mama to cut my hair. I could not help reflecting that it had been a long time since I had had twenty-five cents in my pocket; for Jay and I had tasted an experience, not rare among publishers, dealing with the difficulty of getting a newspaper on a paying basis. This as well as the trapeze had something to do with Jay's loss of interest in journalism. So it seemed a pure waste of good money to spend a quarter for a haircut.

With these thoughts running through my head I was walking up Broadway toward the Square when, a little past Mr. F. S. Kirk's feed store, a man standing beside some steps which led to a basement addressed me.

"How 'bout a haircut, bub?" he said.

Now wasn't that strange, considering the fact that a haircut was what I was on my way to get?

"Give you a free cut here," said the man. "This is the Barber College."

I wondered if I had heard the man rightly. "You mean you don't charge for cutting people's hair?"

"That's it, son," the man said. "This is the Barber College."

I didn't want to expose my ignorance by asking questions about the Barber College, which sounded superior to a barber shop. I followed the man down the steps.

"Here's a good head of hair, boys," said the man. "Joe, I'll take you first."

Joe started cutting my hair, my benefactor showing him how. Pretty soon it was all cut and combed. Then the man called another fellow, who cut it again. After the third cut there was hardly any hair left to get at. The last man who cut my hair put some elegant-smelling water on it and combed it nice. Then the man who ran the College said:

"There you are, son. Come back again when it grows out."

I gratefully assured him that I would.

Mama was rather scandalized because my hair was so short but Papa only said:

"I see you got your money's worth, Marquis."

For two or three years I patronized the Barber College. Between haircuts I would drop in and read the *Police Gazette*.

Papa and I went to Chicago first and then we went all over Ohio. We saw the house Papa was born in and we saw his mother who was ninety years old; also a great many other relations, some in towns and some in big cities. But mostly they lived on farms, like Grandma. Papa and I were walking along the sidewalk in the town of Waverly when a man said:

"As I live, if it isn't Cap'n James!"

I had never heard my father called captain before. It turned out that this man and Papa had been in the war together. They talked for quite a while. Papa told a great many wonderful things about Oklahoma which I had not thought wonderful at all until I heard Papa speak of them just then.

In Columbus we called on one of Papa's clients. He was in the Ohio State Penitentiary. While Papa talked to the client a guard took me and some other visitors all over the prison. The convicts wore striped suits. On the well-behaved convicts the stripes ran up and down and on the ones who disobeyed the rules or had tried to escape they ran across. The guard showed us one man with a ball and chain on his leg. He had tried to escape twice.

While in Columbus we stayed with my Aunt Ruhama who had fireplaces you didn't have to get any wood for. You just lit the gas. Though it was summer she lit one so I could see how it worked. Another reason for going to Columbus was to see the governor of Ohio and get him to pardon Papa's client who was in the pen. When we left the prison we got into a hack and went to see the governor. He wasn't in and Papa had to talk to someone else. This man was very polite and let me sit in the governor's big chair. After we had gone I could see that Papa thought it no way for the governor to do: not to see him when he wanted a pardon for his client. I told Papa I hoped the man escaped. I thought escaping a more manly way of getting out of prison than to be let out by any governor. That was how Jesse James would have done it.

CHAPTER SIX

The Tramp Printers

ALONG with learning a little about printing I began to learn about printers. This doubled the attractions of the trade, for I found printers every bit as interesting as the things they did. Theirs was more than a craft; it was a way of life. About one out of four of the printers who kept Enid's five little offices going were tramps. By dint of considerable effort at making myself useful and agreeable, I would strike up an acquaintance with a compositor at the *Events*. A couple of days later I would go back with the idea of pushing the budding friendship a little further and the compositor would be gone. He'd have "hit the road," and there would be a stranger in his place. I came to find this a normal state of affairs in printing offices.

"Tramp printer" was no term of derogation. It was the name the trade applied to its birds of passage. A tramp printer was nearly always a skilled and versatile workman, capable of hanging up his coat in a strange office and tackling any job that came up: straight or display composition; press work of any kind known to a country shop. Display composition called for a certain artistry in the matter of design and an instinct for emphasis. His mind a catalogue of hundreds of faces and styles of type, the tramp had to make his way without loss of motion among the fonts of an unfamiliar office. No country shop contained more than a small fraction of the type a much-traveled printer knew. Having imagined an effective display line of 36-point Gothic outline, and not finding the office equipped with that font, he must switch to something else. In a way it was like work on the *Evening Squeak* where we might not be able to say exactly what we had in mind on account of having run out of the letter h. Press work called for ingenuity in operating the antiquated and cranky machinery with which all the Enid offices, excepting possibly the *Eagle*, were equipped. Though a worn-out printing press can be a temperamental thing, I heard stories of tramp printers, on a one-day acquaintance, getting as good results as the editor himself.

The editors of Enid's three daily and two weekly newspapers were printers as well, though none worked in the "back room" more than he had to. But when money for the payroll ran short or a tramp hit the road in the middle of a rush job or any of the other plagues that can afflict a country print shop descended, the editor would pitch in and help get out his paper. I have even seen Mr. Hunter of the *Eagle* make up his front page. One vivid and satisfying picture of old Isey of the *Wave* I shall never forget. The press had broken down in the middle of the run. His white shirt and his hands smeared with ink, Mr. Isenberg was tying something in place with wire, and making the atmosphere blue with profanity while the rest of the office, and the waiting carrier boys, stood about grinning. In the *Democrat* office gentle old Mr. Moore must have set half his type as a regular thing. Scatter-brained Tom Hopley, his wife, and his wife's sister set most of it for the *Daily News*. At the *Events* Mr. Everett Purcell would get an idea for a powerful Republican editorial on press day, and to save time set it up out of his head.

Where tramps fell down was on the score of dependability. They were the freest creatures on the face of the earth; and many of them were hard drinkers. You never knew when a tramp would lay down his stick and ask for his "time," or when it would be necessary to fire him, though more quit than were fired. Tramp printers rarely went hungry. Printers who had jobs would stake them until something opened up.

Like all frontier communities, the Cherokee Strip was a pausing place for migrants of various kinds. Within ten years probably half of the hundred thousand persons who had made the Run had moved on. The far field was ever greener. Cowboys, barbers, telegraphers, bill posters, and railroad men were accepted as drifters as a matter of course. Carpenters, painters, and brick masons built one boom town and scattered to build another. There were lawyers in Enid who had practiced in half a dozen states; my father had done almost that well. Then of course there were the farmhands, the jacks of all trades, and the pure hoboes with their "jungle" beside the railroad track in every town. Enid's jungle was in a patch of willows beneath a bridge about half a mile north of the Broadway crossing.

Of them all, printers were the aristocrats of the road. No class of itinerants was better informed. The first copies I ever saw of Adam Smith's *The Wealth of Nations* and of Henry George's *Progress and Poverty* were in the hands of tramp printers. No journeymen stood higher in the councils of their craft. None roamed farther or faster. Theirs was a nationwide brotherhood.

The syllables of place-names that fell from their lips touched my ears with the enticing harmony of lines of Edgar Allan Poe: Wichita, Guthrie, Oklahoma City; Fort Smith, Coffeyville, Dallas; St. Louis, Denver, Mobile; Topeka, Cheyenne, Savannah. . . .

Chicago was Chi; Kansas City, K.C.; Cincinnati, Cincy; Jamestown, North Dakota, Jimtown; Jefferson City, Missouri, Jeff City.

You heard not only the names of cities but the names of the shops to be found there. In Chi it was the *Trib* and the *I.O.*; in New Orleans the *Pic*; in Fort Worth the *Record*; Wichita the *Eagle;* Topeka the *Capital*; Louisville the *C-J*; Denver the *Rocky Mountain News*; Frisco the *Bulletin*; Omaha the *Bee.*

During a noon hour some printers on the back porch of the *Events* had rushed the can and were drinking their beer. One would take the bucket in both hands, slosh the beer gently to work up a collar, drink, and pass the bucket to the next fellow.

"Natchez: there's a town—for a whistle stop."

"California for mine. Never intend to winter anywhere else."

"Don't get thrown off an S.P. freight in the middle of the desert. I got a look at the inside of the jail in Tucson."

"Always heard the S.P. about the toughest road in the West."

Someone mentioned Chillicothe.

"Chillicothe?" I said eagerly. "I been there, mister."

"You from Ohio, bub?"

"No, sir. Just boomed through."

Their conversation drove me to the maps and even to the *Encyclopedia Americana* which Papa had bought me. In this way it was that I began to pick up a non-resident acquaintance with another world—the second of my experience, Mr. Howell's having been the first.

And yet there was a cloud in the sky of the tramp printer's Elysium. It was the typesetting machine—what they called the linotype. The first time I heard of a typesetting machine I was sure someone was fixing to try a joke on me, like that one about type lice. For how could a machine set type? By that time I appreciated that there was more to the compositor's art than met the uninitiated eye. Type lay in the boxes in no orderly fashion, but topsy-turvy like jackstraws. With a motion so quick you could not follow it the compositor picked up a letter with his thumb and two fingers, spun it face up and right side front and clicked it into his stick. The spinning was done by sense of touch, a fraction of a second's feel of the "nicks." Nicks are little grooves in the belly of the type shank which enable a printer to insert his letter in the stick right end up and right side forward and also to detect a "wrong font"—a letter of another face which has strayed from its proper case. Nicks vary with each face of type. A printer can read them by instantaneous touch.

In view of all this, I would stand before a case trying to imagine what a machine would have to do to duplicate the skills of a compositor: it would have to think, that was all.

Finally I laid the matter before Mr. Moore on the *Democrat*. That courtly old gentleman would not fool a boy. Mr. Moore said yes, there were typesetting machines. No, he had never seen one; but he had read about them in the catalogues. "Let me see. Might have a picture of one somewhere around."

He justified his line and laid down the stick. I followed him into the little partitioned-off corner that was his office. Burrowing into a pile of papers he came at length on what he wanted.

"Yes, here it is. The Mergenthaler linotype."

Mr. Moore told me how the machine worked. There was a keyboard, on the order of a typewriter's. You touched the letter you wanted and a matrix fell down. When you completed a line, the mats somehow moved into a place where they were cast in molten lead and you had a line of type like a line of type in boiler plate.

One of these machines could set as much type as three or four compositors. I heard a man say that in the St. Louis *Globe* office where they used to employ twenty compositors on straight matter, six machines did the work. Only the heads were set by hand—unless too many of the machines broke down at once. There seemed some hope in the fact that linotypes were always breaking down and having to be fixed. And then they were too expensive for small offices. This tended to drive the tramps into the smaller towns—whistle stops they would not have thought of bothering with before the machines came along. Thus Enid was occasionally honored with a visit by a "swift."

A swift was the opposite of a "blacksmith," the name for a slow, clumsy printer. A swift could set eighteen hundred ems of 8 point an hour, and turn in a clean proof. His hand flying over a case was something to see.

2

On their travels printers rarely rode the cushions. A cushion was a seat one paid for on a passenger train. Blinds and decks were the facilities available to non-paying riders on passenger trains—the elite accommodations, the fastest free transportation known. A blind was the space between the baggage car and the locomotive tender. It was called blind because baggage cars did not have end doors. A rider was safe except from the fireman who might crawl over the tender and chunk coal at him. A twenty-five-cent piece would usually pacify the fireman. A deck was the top of a baggage car or passenger coach, reached by way of the blind. There one was safe from observation at night and hard to get at any time. But it was the most perilous form of tramp travel. The roofs sloped and all you had to hang on to was a grip-rod next to the stovepipe. The new steam-heated cars, which did not have stovepipes and grip-rods, could not be ridden.

Rods, bumpers, and empties were freight-train accommodations. The rods were iron bars which extended underneath the floors of freight cars to give them strength. At one point there was a space of possibly fifteen inches between the bars and the beds of the cars. A man could lie in there quite snugly. When a train was moving the noise was deafening, the dust almost unbearable, and the view rather hard on the nerves. Really, though, the only dangerous part about riding the rods was swinging on while a car was in motion. This was a favorite mode of travel for the out-and-out hobo devoid of pride in his personal appearance. Bumpers were a part of the coupling gear between freight cars. They were good for night travel only, when a brakeman passing over the tops of the cars could not see you. Empties were empty freight cars. This means of travel was for tourists who liked their comfort, and who had a quarter. Brakemen made it their business to find out when empties were occupied.

To take advantage of any of these traveling accommodations, it was necessary to be able to board and dismount from moving trains under a variety of conditions—an accomplishment which came only with practice. Among boys this was called hopping trains. To say of a boy, "He hops trains," was to confer a badge of distinction. As a qualification for manhood it ranked above smoking cigarettes or chewing tobacco. We must have lived in the Cogdal-McKee building for all of six months before I got up nerve enough to hop a train, though I played at it on cars that were standing still.

The sight of Vern McMillen and his crutch was a factor in my retarded education. Vern was just learning to use the crutch as a substitute for a leg. Eventually he got so that he could play baseball, fight and wrestle better than most boys who had two legs; but first he had to learn. While fleeing from a brakeman along a string of cars in the Rock Island yard, Vern McMillen had fallen between two cars. Half the train ran over his right leg.

Central School was not far from the Rock Island yard where boys played on freight cars that were standing on the sidings. Our game was called brakey and bums. The boy who was "it" was the brakeman. When he caught a bum and threw him off the train, the bum became the brakey and the brakey a bum. All this had to be done without touching the ground because we pretended the cars were in motion.

Once in a while the switch engine would pick up some of the cars on which we were playing and we would get a real ride. The next step was hopping trains proper. They were ballasting the roadbed near the school and work trains moved slowly up and down. They were easy to hop. Nevertheless, a brakey-and-bums playmate named Willie Pierce missed the step of a gravel car, slipped under the train and was cut in two. I was a pallbearer at the funeral—the first I ever attended.

Before long I was making Saturday excursions to Kingfisher and Pondcreek and Garber. These adventures constituted a needed claim to renown. I was no good as a fighter, just average as a wrestler, and nothing wonderful at baseball. Tobacco made me sick. But I could flip a freight going ten miles an hour. My ambition was to ride a blind.

3

Another magnet that drew boys to the railroad depot was the prospect of selling horny-toads. A gentleman in a Pullman might give you a quarter for a horny-toad, though the going price was ten cents. South-bound trains were better for customers. So many of the north-bound people came from Texas where horny-toads were not marketable commodities.

This was not my sole grievance against Texans, with their high and mighty ways. Though every part of the country contributed to the hundred thousand who had made the Run in '93, most of the Strip's first settlers hailed from neighboring Kansas, Arkansas, and Texas. In my earliest days I had learned a sort of rule of thumb to tell which was which. Kansans were people you felt sorry for. They had had such hard luck: grasshoppers, droughts, hot winds, Carry Nation. Kansas made me think of the plagues of Egypt. Arkansas was a place you joked about. They said that you could tell an Arkansawyer because one leg would be shorter than the other, from plowing around hills. But Texans—well, from the way they walked and talked you could see that they thought they owned the earth with a fence around it. In some law office or print shop I heard a verse about Texas which I liked to recite because it sounded uncomplimentary. As nearly as I can recall the verse went:

> Here's to the grand old State of Texas:
> Where there are more rivers and less water;
> More cows and less milk;
> Where you can see farther and see less
> Than in any other commonwealth in the Union.
> From the top of the City Hall in Fort Worth
> You can make out the International Bridge at El Paso—
> There is nothing to obstruct the view.

In the light of this attitude it may seem odd that my greatest hero among the older boys should have come from Texas. His name was Tell Daniels. I would repeat it over and over, entranced by the sound of the words. At first I associated the name in my mind with William Tell. When I discovered that in my hero's case Tell was short for Telemachus it made no difference. From what the encyclopedia said, this Telemachus had been quite a fellow, too.

Tell Daniels was small for his age, wiry and quick as a cat. He played third base on the high-school ball team. Although I never exchanged a word with Tell Daniels in my life, he filled me with a desire to go to high school and read the strange books, learn the strange ways and speak the strange tongue of high-school students. I would walk alongside a group of high-school boys just to hear what Tell Daniels was saying. I tried to copy his walk, his mannerisms, his speech. I was in ecstasy when Sister Zoe sent me a turtleneck sweater almost like Tell Daniels's.

Another example of adoration at a remote distance seems less difficult to account for. In this instance the cause of my affliction was a high-school girl named Blossom Fleming. I had known her brother Ed slightly at East Hill School. A little later Banker

Fleming built on West Pine the finest house in town and Ed moved out of my orbit. The talk that the Fleming mansion sheltered a bathtub was entirely true: Earle Radcliffe had seen it.

Though she had a good deal to live up to, Blossom Fleming did not disappoint my expectations. Not since my childhood glimpses of Miss Mabel Moore (who apparently had married and moved away long ago), had I seen anyone who reminded me so much of a princess in a fairy tale. Living away out in Kenwood, in the towered mansion with its spacious lawn, Blossom Fleming's exalted social position, her Kansas City clothes, her radiant beauty confounded reality, leaving only fantasy to cope with the emotions churning inside me.

To see her walking from high school, a boy carrying her books, filled me with rage and despair. Seeing her driving their buggy horse, I longed for the animal to run away so I could throw myself at its head, grasp the foaming bit and save the life of Blossom Fleming.

Sometimes these reveries were so satisfactory that momentarily I could ignore the distressing fact that Eva Britton, two seats removed from me in the sixth grade at Central, seemed to prefer Taylor Lyons.

4

When I was in the sixth grade Enid's schools were given an overhauling. Extra bright kids were advanced a grade and extra dumb ones put back. Grades were divided into A and B classes—A for the smart kids and B for the "retarded" pupils. I went in class B.

News of this degradation was withheld from my parents until the next monthly report card made further concealment impossible. Mama gave me a sure-enough scolding, rattling on at a great rate. I was really more pained by the way Papa took it. He just said, in his slow way, that he was "disappointed."

The trouble was arithmetic and grammar. My thick skull for

mathematics was a source of humiliation. For a year or two I slaved over the subject. As a spur I announced my intention of becoming a civil engineer. The results of these efforts were peculiar. Occasionally I would come up with the solution of a complicated problem—and then miss a string of simple ones. This created suspicions that I had been helped with the hard problem. So, in the end, I just gave up mathematics.

Grammar I wasn't obliged to give up, not having paid it any mind to begin with. I had no intention of doing so now. My position on grammar was that it served no useful purpose. This business of learning which words were verbs and which words nouns; what was the subject of a sentence and what the predicate; and that mumbo-jumbo about moods and tenses—there seemed no more sense to it than learning the alphabet backward (which one teacher required her kids to do). My teachers and my parents said grammar was necessary, to know how to speak and write properly. *Bushwa.* As often as any other kid I was asked to read my compositions before the class.

So I decided to haul off and be a poet. I wrote a poem and dropped it into the slot in the door of the *Democrat* office. At the end of the week when the paper came out there was my poem—printed!—with my name in caps and small caps at the bottom. How very kind of old Mr. Moore to have taken the extra trouble to reach into the upper case to set my name. I tried to repay him by going around and distributing a couple of sticks of type.

I watched Mr. Moore distribute the type in which my first published lines had been set. I cannot quite get into language my feeling on seeing my poem thus physically dispersed into its elements. There they lay in the case, the letters of lead which had spelled the words that had made my poem—their identities lost, their association in *my* poem gone the way of earthly things. Ah, but the letters were still there. Along with all the other 8 point in the whole *Democrat* office they awaited an opportunity to display to the world the very next thing I should write.

After I had reached the seventh grade, one evening my teacher, Miss Allen, asked if she could see me after school. This was a common enough occurrence. Usually it meant trouble.

This time Miss Allen began to speak of my verses. She said I had talent—a perception of the obvious I thought remarkable only because it came from a schoolteacher.

"On Monday morning," continued Miss Allen, "you may move your seat over into the A class."

Seven A! Gee!

CHAPTER SEVEN

Social Notes from East Hill

It is telling no more than the sober truth to admit that I was ahead of Miss Allen, my seventh-grade teacher, in recognizing the presence of talent which was to bring me fame as a poet, and that at no distant date. In point of fact preparations for this turn of affairs were already under way. You studied the lives of poets in school. It followed that some day kids would have to study my life. In order that the facts required might be on hand I began a diary, which opened with this entry:

"Nov. 25, 1904. Bright and fair my just one month until Christmas. Went up town this morning and got 2 doctor peppers. I did not have to go to school today. I painted Franklin's picture with Catherine's paints. When I went to write this a bottle of ink was sitting on the floor and Catherine tipped it over. I part my hair in the middle and Sister Nan wants me to part it on the side. I expect she will be here 2 months. This afternoon I got 9 horse redish bottles and sold them for 9¢."

Franklin and Katharine, as I should have spelled it, were Sister Nan's youngsters.

My Chicago sisters came to Enid more often now. I associate

their visits with all manner of costly gifts: a "graphaphone" from Sister Zoe; a Brownie camera from Sister Nan; a stamp album, pocket knives, a fountain pen, and no end of twenty-five-cent pieces from my brothers-in-law, who seemed to be made of money. Another thing I remember about their visits is that the extra bottle in the caster on the dining-room table was always filled. The caster held salt and pepper shakers and three bottles. One of these bottles contained vinegar and another horse radish, but the third was never used unless one of my sisters was with us. Then Mama filled it with olive oil, which was something Chicago people ate on their lettuce. I used it to grease my ball glove.

The diary continued:

"Nov. 26, cold this morning but at noon it was bright and fair. I got 2 jugs and they are worth 6¢ at Mr. Cooper's. [Mr. Cooper was an old man who put up horse radish to sell. I found my jugs and bottles in alleys about the Square.] Mama bought 1 at 5¢ and 1 of Franklin at 3¢. Brother Perry got his camera fixed and took 2 pictures. . . .

"No. 28, bright and fair. Papa was hunting yesterday and came home with 2 squirls 4 rabbits and 16 birds I have got the squirl skins drying. I started to wear my Sunday shoes for every day. . . .

"Dec. 3, cold. My little dynamo came today from Sears & Roebuck. It makes electricity come pretty thick. George Hendricks come over and we played with it a while then we went over to Georges and played with Georges Battery. I went to the theater. 'A Merchant of Venice.'"

Cold weather continued, bringing what was recalled for years to come as the Hard Winter. The Hard Winter was anything but hard on us boys. Most of us made sleds and acquired skates and enjoyed times the like of which we were not to know again, as boys, in Oklahoma. The only way farmers could get to town was by replacing the wheels of their wagons with runners. Out came one or two regular cutters which had stood unused in barns since their northern owners had brought them to the Strip. What a brave showing they made! We boys learned to hitch our sleds to these vehicles and ride for miles.

"February 16 [1905] Bright and fair. I read 'Ralph Raymond's Heir' and finished 'Cap Baileys Heir.' I wrote a fine poem about Harry. I was invited to attend a Surprise party for tomorrow evening. I don't think I will go. I want to read."

The implication that I preferred staying home and reading to going to any old party indicates that I was still under the spell of a bluff I had thrown for the benefit of Eva Britton. I wanted her to think me different from the run of boys who were crazy to go to parties. Eva Britton was the prettiest and the most popular girl in the seventh grade. Her father was one of the first early settlers to prosper sufficiently to move to town and give his children "advantages." The Brittons lived on Maine Street, a couple of blocks from us, in the house Banker Fleming had vacated to go to the West Side. Their porch had more scroll work on it than any other porch in Enid.

Naturally, I went to the party, which was at Maud Luther's. "Dan, Jay, Eugene, Wilk and I met down at the bridge. Then came the girls. We took them to Luther's house. We started to play Clap In and Clap Out and after we had played a while Mrs. Luther told us to come in the back parlor and there she gave each of us an orange and a piece of cake and a popcorn ball. When we finished eating we played Wink on the Sly. Eva would always wink at me and I would always wink at her. When the party broke up Dan and I and Eugene took the girls home. We took Ruby home and then we were going to take some of the rest of the girls home and we met Mr. Britton and he made Eva go home with him. What a shame."

When I wrote that we "took" the girls to Luther's and "took" them home, I was making conscious use of a word high-school boys employed in connection with their social activities. We Central kids discharged our functions as escorts in this manner. Bound for a mixed gathering, the boys would meet at some convenient spot, such as the Broadway bridge, which the girls would have to pass. The girls would get together somewhere else and all in a bunch approach our rendezvous, as if by accident. Then we would proceed together—the girls in one bunch walking ahead giggling mysteriously and the boys walking just behind shoving each other and saying things for the girls to overhear. In the same way we "took" girls home, the boys keeping together until the last girl had been trailed to her front gate.

Maud Luther's party touched off a stimulating social season, with a party about every other Saturday night. Never before had a Sunday suit of mine seen such service in Enid, and on party nights I would black my shoes and comb my hair without being told. I bought a high-standing celluloid collar, acknowledged the last word in elegance. The only trouble was I could hardly turn my head around. If my diary is reliable it was at Enos Shaw's that we first played post office. The girls shrieked and some of the older boys snickered knowingly at the mention of the name. Pretty soon I found out why. It was a kissing game. Well, it was neither so bad as you might think nor so wonderful as I'd heard it cracked up to be—this kissing a girl.

Not only did I grace these worldly affairs with my presence (and my celluloid collar); I took a hand in the promotion and the management of some of them. This was a devious and underhand business, with the particular object of keeping the company congenial by the exclusion of rivals. To this end old alliances were broken and fresh attachments formed for nearly every party. Sometimes I came out on top as a result of these manipulations; sometimes I fell the victim of another manager's artful schemes.

When Eugene Dwelle began talking of giving a party a problem of transportation arose, for Gene lived in the country. We found a hayrack that we could use. Now we needed two horses. Papa said he would pay for the hire of one if I could scare up the other. My deadly rival for Eva Britton's favor, Taylor Lyons, came forward with an offer of a second horse. This I considered an act of inexcusable presumption. Gene hadn't even sent out his invitations, and he had promised that should I get a second horse there would be no invitation for Taylor Lyons. But as I couldn't raise the extra horse Gene had to invite Taylor.

Then things took an unpredicted turn. Eva accepted the invitation of another boy to go to a church social on the night of Gene's party. That, I said to myself, sure leaves old Taylor in the soup. But it didn't leave me in the soup because my fancy had been caught by a new girl in our class whom I shall call Mary. I told my diary that Eva was just too fickle for any use.

On the ride out to Gene's I drove and Mary sat beside me. She asked if I could drive with one hand. "Why, sure," I said, thinking that a funny question. Mary took my free hand in hers. Playing pleased-and-displeased at the party Mary kissed me in a way that left no room for doubt that there were things about kissing I had undervalued until then. Not long before the party broke up Gene took some of us boys to the barn to look at a new colt. Going back to the house we passed Taylor Lyons and Mary under the grape arbor. "Oh, take that lantern away," she said. "The light hurts my eyes." On the way to town it was Taylor's turn to drive. Mary sat with him.

"Well I don't care," concludes my diary's account of the evening's events. "Taylor is going away next month. Tanned my cat hide today. Tattoed my name on my arm and my initials on my thumb."

My most spectacular social triumph came by accident. A bunch of us boys were on the Square after school trying to attract the attention of girls with whom we had been in the same classroom all day. In the midst of our showing off I became conscious that Josephine Barnabee was passing by. There was just time to snatch off my cap.

"Evenin', Miss Josephine," said I.

"Evenin', Markey," she said, smiling beneath her lacy parasol.

The first thing out of the ordinary I noticed was that the boys stopped talking and shoving. The girls were walking off, their noses in the air.

"Whillikers!" Jay Radcliffe said. "You know *her?*"

"Sure. Ever since the summer I carried specials."

2

By the time I had my party we had moved into the new house Papa built at Tenth and Maine, where he had acquired some lots in the Reed Addition. There was a bathroom. The only reason we didn't use it was because the city water didn't go to the Reed Addition. It was less trouble to bathe in the kitchen where the pump was. We had gas lights, though.

Perhaps I should mention that Papa built not only one house in the Reed Addition but two—one to live in and one to rent. And on the choicest of our lots he did not build at all. They were saved for the real fine house we intended to have as soon as Papa's oil well should come in. They had struck oil over near Tulsa, and Judge Garber and Papa and a lot of others were sure there was oil under the ground around Enid. They started to drill for it out near the town of Garber. Their money ran out before they struck any oil. Judge Garber and Papa were all for drilling deeper. They began to raise more money. To make up Papa's share our two new houses were mortgaged.

Sometimes I would speculate on the things I'd have when we were rich. I was pretty disappointed that all Mama wanted was "a fairly good horse" and buggy. I wanted a machine. Besides the Goltry's Oldsmobile there were a couple of Buicks and a Stanley Steamer in Enid now. Of course as a compromise I would have accepted a red Columbia racer with a coaster brake. For the most part just the hayseeds rode ponies now.

I continued to write poetry and, moreover, I changed publishers. The *Events* now printed my works. I think consideration for the sensibilities of my old friend Mr. Moore of the *Democrat* had something to do with this. Though on the other side of the fence politically from my father, Mr. Moore did not print hateful things about him, as old Isey did in the *Wave*. But the editor of the *Democrat* had been a Confederate soldier and, as some of my poems were of a historical nature, glorifying the deeds of the Boys in Blue, I felt that they belonged in a Republican paper.

Though Papa tried to help with my poems I got my main help from the works of other successful poets. The fact is Papa could be a positive hindrance, as when he would observe that Longfellow "seems to have anticipated you in the use of that wording." Finally I found a poet Papa hadn't read. His name was S. E. Kiser, and he had a poem every day on the editorial page of the Chicago *Record-Herald* which Sister Zoe took during her visits with us. They were very superior poems. Sometimes I would only have to change a few words.

It might be well for all poets to keep diaries and try to induce the public to read them. Then people would have a better idea of the everyday distractions that poets are up against. Take my own case:

"March 18 [1905] Rained last night but this morning was bright and fair. Dan bought my ball glove for 85¢. Cousin Maud is here from Kansas City. She has almost as many diamonds as Sister Nan. . . .

"March 21 Bright and fair. Jay paid me the dime he owes me and I went up to the skating rink and skated for 2½ hours. We had our old examination in arithmetic. I got 73. . . .

"March 24 Bright and Fair. Bessie White drew me a picture of a yellow rose. I wish it was Eva that drew it. I was clear up in the top of McQuilken's big wind mill. Then Dan and I got the rubber hose and squirted water on each other. My cap will hold water.

"March 25 Bright and windy. Right after breakfast I took some flowers down to Mrs. Houston. Harold was digging a hole to plant trees. I helped him and when he was done we went up to his room and washed and looked at some of his things. He gave me a pistol. I dassent tell papa or mamma. . . .

"March 30 Cooler. I got a box of cartridges for my pistol. I showed my pistol to papa and he said not to point it at anyone. . . .

"April 5 Cooler. Last night I wrote 2 poems, 'How Roosevelt Beat Parker,' and 'Oklahoma.' Today I wrote 'The Conflict of John Paul Jones,' a story of the battle between the Bonhomme Richard and the Serapis and 'The American Caesar' and 'Lincoln' and 'Why Oklahoma Should Become a State.' We had an examination in grammar. I think I failed.

"April 6 Almost hot. I wrote 2 poems today. I got only 10 on my grammar but I got 77 in physiology and 98 in geography.

"April 7 Hot. Lots of boys are going barefooted. We haven't seen the cat for two days.

"April 8 Hot. I played a game of ball today on Ray Ott's team. We got beat 13 to 11. I went out to get some kindling wood in my bare feet and ran a nail clear in my foot. Mamma is going to put some fat meat on it tonight. Jay went swimming today.

"April 10 Cooler. Yesterday after I wrote my diary I wrote this. A REWARD WILL BE PAYED FOR THE RETURN OF MY CAT TO MY RESIDENCE 1006 EAST MAIN ST. SHE IS THREE YEARS OLD AND BLACK AND WHITE SPOTTED. HOUSTIN JAMES. I signed papa's name for they would see my name and laugh. Then I looked under the porch and saw the cat stiff and dead. I was shocked. She had been with us 4 years and now had left us forever. I took her out in the back yard and put the lid of an old trunk over her. They told me to bury her. I didn't for I wanted to skin her. Well, I got up early this morning and skinned all but the head and fore feet. Then I put her under the trunk lid and went to school. I came home and finished skinning the cat and then I went up to Stephens hide house and asked Mr. Stephens how to tan a hide. He said to take pulverized allum and salt and put it on it and wet it and roll it up and put it in a cool place and turn it over every day for a week and then to scrape it. Gee I am neglecting my poetry. . . .

"April 20 Bright and Fair: Papa is going to Garber and make a speach to the Oil Company. There is a new oil company formed and they haven't dug their hole yet. Well they may not strike it. If they don't papa will go broke. I hope papa doesent loose his money in oil speculations for he lost some bucking the board of trade [playing the wheat market]. . . .

"April 28 Bright and hot. Oh say the wheat market went down to 84¢. My papa lost awful. He bought his at 1.14. I guess he will quit bucking the board of trade. . . .

"May 11 Bright and fair: Gee we got a piano. It is a Fisher. George came over and I learned him to play 'My Old Kentucky Home.' "

3

It fell out that the piano was not a sign of Papa's return to affluence, as I first imagined. The instrument came from Jennie Hearn's on Two Street and was for legal services rendered. Just the same Mama said that we were going to keep it and not give it away as we had the other piano. Papa gave that one to a neighbor because he said it would be played in their house and that there was no sense having a piano that was not played on. I wouldn't take lessons and Papa didn't count my efforts to learn the piano by ear from a colored boy named Clarence.

School let out in May and, weary of waiting for Papa to strike it rich in oil, I decided to get a new wheel on my own. A Columbia racer was out of the question, but in Frantz's window stood a bright orange Ranger which could be bought for twenty-five dollars. I had three dollars on hand and reckoned that I had thirteen dollars in the bank. I told Papa that with the wheel I could easily make up the balance during the summer running errands for people. I asked him to go with me, and vouch to Mr. Frantz that I would pay the balance as I earned it.

After adjusting the handlebars low as on a racer, for three days I tore all over the town and surrounding country, promising myself I'd settle down and organize a messenger and errand business as soon as I got my wheel broken in. Then the telephone rang and a man asked to speak to Marquis James. The man said that he was Mr. Kelley of the Garfield Exchange Bank. Mr. Kelley asked if I was the author of a check payable to the Frantz Hardware Company in the amount of twelve dollars. That was the first time I'd ever been called an author by anyone but myself. And I had never heard of anybody being the author of a check. But Mr. Kelley's tone was so earnest that I said, yes, sir, I had written a check for twelve dollars to help pay for my new wheel.

"Are you aware," he asked, "that your account shows a balance of only five dollars and ten cents?"

Mr. Kelley asked me to "step" down to the bank and try to identify the checks drawn against my account.

I flew down there, sure that someone had been forging my name. But it wasn't true. I had just forgotten about that check for five dollars to the building fund of the Methodist church, and another check for three dollars to the *Youth's Companion.*

Mr. Kelley asked what I intended to do about honoring the twelve-dollar check. The accusing document lay on his desk and he tapped it with his forefinger.

"If you'll let me go see my father I think he'll honor it."

A smile crept over Papa's face.

"Marquis, we're in the same boat. Both broke."

Somehow I didn't feel so bad being broke if Papa was broke, too. He didn't look worried.

I asked what I should do.

He said to go to Mr. Edmund Frantz, explain the whole transaction and ask if he would trust me to keep the wheel and work off the debt.

Mr. Frantz said he would.

My own press being disabled I went to the *Events* and had cards printed saying:

If You Want A
MESSENGER BOY
Call up
Phone, Day, 171, Night, 307 Grand

Those were the numbers at Papa's office and at our house. I took the cards all over town and asked people to put them by their telephones.

Business started off pretty good and the first week's earnings enabled me to enjoy the attractions of a street carnival which was in town. At a church social I met the girl I have called Mary. She ate forty cents' worth of ice cream and cake. My diary summarizes the matter: "Girls are awful cheats." Then came the

Fourth of July. But the greatest extravagance was my stamp collection. All in all, in five weeks' time only three dollars and five cents had been paid on the bicycle. I wrote out and signed the following:

"PLEDGE"

"I, Marquis James, on this 8 day of July in the year of 1905 do pledge myself on my honor to buy no more stamps further than ordered or to even open my stamp book unless by request until my wheel is paid for."

The vow was kept fairly well, and by the end of the summer I had added to my private business the long-distance telephone calls and the night messages of the Postal Telegraph. When a person not having a telephone received a long-distance call he was notified by a messenger who got ten cents for the service. Thus I came to have something approaching a monopoly of the messenger business in Enid. The proceeds paid for my wheel and to spare. Papa must have had a good summer, too, for in September I managed to persuade him to take me to the national encampment of the Grand Army of the Republic in Denver.

To my chagrin Papa was not an enthusiastic member of the G.A.R. He never marched in the Memorial Day parades. The only war stories I'd ever got out of him were about other people. My diary mentions Sam Slavens and Reuben James. Sam Slavens was one of the band of Union soldiers who captured a railroad train in Georgia and tried to run it through to the Federal lines. Sam was caught and hanged. "I knew him as well as you know Jay," Papa said. He bought me a book about the raid and I learned the story almost by heart. And just about as good was the story of how Reuben James saved Stephen Decatur's life in the war against the Barbary pirates. Papa said Reuben belonged to our family.

In Denver my father paid scant attention to the patriotic goings on and spent most of his time in the Brown Palace Hotel playing poker. But I didn't miss a thing. I must have collected a dozen badges. On parade day I went to the livery stable and brought the commander of the Oklahoma Department his horse.

After the encampment Papa and I took in the sights of Colorado. I wrote a big piece about our trips amid the splendors of the mountains and Mr. Purcell printed it in the *Events*.

CHAPTER EIGHT

The Reporter for the *Events*

THERE are ambitions that grow pale and disappear. My aspirations to become a stage driver, a bear hunter, and a railroad brakeman had gone that way. There are other ambitions that modify themselves—like my ambition to become a tramp printer. I had not given that up. But my zeal to set up as a poet consumed so much energy that there wasn't any left to go on improving myself in the printer's art. I intended to get back to it, though. Then someday I'd hit the road as a combination printer and poet.

There is still something else that can happen to an ambition. You may keep it bright, you may work at it like all get out, and then meet defeat and go through life tasting the flat brew of a dream unfulfilled: thinking all the time that except for perhaps one tiny thing, amounting to a miscarriage of justice, it would have been. That was the way with my musical career. That was how it was I never did become a member of the Enid Silver Cornet Band.

My acquaintance with the Enid Silver Cornet Band dated from the time of our residence in the Cogdal-McKee building. On Saturday nights the band gave concerts in the Square. On certain other nights there was band practice in the Old Post Office. I was a regular attendant at these functions. I made up my mind to become a member of the band, wear a blue uniform, a cap with a plume, and march in all the parades. Every time I heard the band practice or play I would think about it.

Well, when we moved to Sixth and Maine, Mama and Papa and I got to going over to the Houstons' to hear Harold and Hazel play duets. Harold played a mandolin and his twin sister a guitar. Harold belonged to the Mandolin Club and he told of what times they had, playing at church socials and all. So I got me a mandolin and began to take lessons from the lady who ran the Mandolin Club. She said it wouldn't be long before I'd be in the club.

Then we got our first piano, the one Papa gave away, and I got to know Clarence. The effect of knowing Clarence was fatal. He was the grandson of Aunty, the old Negress who lived in a squatter's shack in the Park and after the move to Sixth and Maine became a family retainer. She was "treasureman" of the African Primitive Baptist church and, as she could not write, Mama kept her accounts. Each Christmas Papa gave Aunty a prodigious plug of Battle Ax chewing tobacco. She was always entitled to fill her pipe from the brown bowl which held Papa's pipes and tobacco. She would sit on the pump platform, smoking and telling of old times in Tennessee.

Aunty bore the name of an honored family in Middle Tennessee and probably much of its blood: she must have been seven-eighths white. Aunty was proud of her "fam'ly," meaning the people who had owned her "b'fo' freedom." She said freedom hadn't made much difference at "ouah place." Mostly the hands went right on making crops. Aunty's troubles never started until her youngest girl took up with a triflin' nigger and went to Texas. Aunty followed and found her; begged her to come home; begged in vain. A procession of towns and places and a procession of sons-in-law was Aunty's history in Texas. Then came a time when the daughter died and left the child Clarence. Of course it took us years to learn all this.

Clarence must have been two or three years older than I—a thin-shanked, loosely put-together, timid, yellow youth with reddish wool, blue eyes, and negroid features. He was timid among the other Negro kids at the colored school, and the butt of their broad jests. When he passed a white person he got clear off the sidewalk and, of course, touched his cap. I think I became the only friend Clarence ever had. Aunty was always making excuses for him on the ground of delicate health. She wouldn't let him work except to help her a little with people's house cleaning or to tote wash to and from the shack.

When we got the piano I resolved to master that noble instrument and not waste my time monkeying with a mandolin. But I hadn't got around to starting when on one of Aunty's cleaning days I came home and heard someone playing the piano.

The performer was Clarence. He gave me a frightened look.

"Yuh don' min', does yuh, white boy?"

"Course not. But gosh, Clarence, where'd *you* learn to play like that?"

"Right heah, Ma'key. Plays d' o'gan down to d' chu'ch house, sometimes. Sneaks in an' plays when nobody lookin'. But nevah play no p'ana 'fo'."

Clarence could not read music. Except by sound he did not know one key from another. Yet he could play anything he could hum. I got my mandolin and tuned it. Clarence had never had a mandolin in his hands, though he said he could "hit a box"—play a guitar. In ten minutes he was getting more out of the mandolin than I could.

I decided to put my musical future in Clarence's hands. All I had to do was learn his way—and no more tedious lessons. Next day I was down at the shack. Clarence owned a mouth organ, a Jew's harp, and drum sticks. A washboard, a table top, a skillet or almost anything answered for a drum. Clarence could just about make those sticks speak. I told Clarence I'd learn the drum first. Although at one time or another every instrument in the band had captivated my fancy, I was rather partial to the snare drum. Moreover, in Enid was a G.A.R. veteran who had been a drummer in the war and could still beat a drum. In event of war I thought it would be nice to be a drummer boy and rally the retreating troops.

"Yuh jus' takes an' does lak dis," said Clarence.

He picked up the sticks and commenced a rat-tat so fast I could not follow the movements of his hands.

I asked him to go slower. I got him to show me how he held the sticks. Then I asked him how I should start.

"Yuh jus' catches d' beat an' sta'ts."

Pretty soon I just gave up and sat there and listened to Clarence.

I thought I'd try the mouth organ, and bought me one for fifty cents. As a mouth-organ instructor Clarence was a little more successful. In due course I could wheeze out a recognizable tune. Then Clarence would pick up his dented harmonica, catch the beat, throw his head back and cut loose. When Clarence made music his whole being fused into the bliss of creation. Somewhere I have read the phrase, "a Negro's appreciation of laughter and his acceptance of sadness." The words come to mind as I recall Clarence making music. Swelling harmonies seemed to banish for a moment the terrors that pressed about this gifted boy who was without race, being neither white nor black.

As music had the power to elevate Clarence's spirits, it depressed mine in proportion, for I simply couldn't get the hang of what Clarence did. And Clarence was no teacher. Nobody had taught him to play. I suppose that something you haven't been taught is pretty hard to pass on to another. The experience with Clarence gave me a feeling of futility about music. I hardly enjoyed the band concerts any more.

By and by Professor Mariger, who led the Enid Silver Cornet Band, got up the Boys' Band. When a boy could play good enough he would be promoted to the big band. Some of my friends joined, bought cornets or altos or French horns, and East Hill was noisy with their tooting. I offered various excuses. The truth is I was afraid to risk a repetition of the defeat I had suffered at the hands of Clarence.

The Boys' Band was a success. When I was in the eighth grade Jay Radcliffe and Dan McQuilken were admitted to the big band. There were openings for beginners in the kid band. I read in the Sears-Roebuck catalogue that anyone could learn to play a fife in a few days. Instructions went with the instrument, and the price was seventy-nine cents. There was no fife in the Boys' Band, but I didn't see why there shouldn't be one. So I sent off for the fife. After a while I could play little things. I began to feel better. I went and saw Professor Mariger. The result of that audition is painful to relate. The crusty old bandmaster ridiculed my fife and my mail-order style of execution. He said to get a piccolo and take proper lessons.

I had given my mandolin to Clarence. I could not give him the fife because by then Clarence was dead of galloping consumption. He went so fast that I saw him only once after he was taken down. But Clarence had lived long enough to leave his mark on my life. Had it not been for the accident of exposure to his devastating talent, I should like to believe that I, too, might have made the Silver Cornet Band, like Dan and Jay.

2

The summer after I had finished the eighth grade I went to work for the *Events* as a reporter. It wasn't the job I wanted; merely the one I got after a talk with Mr. Everett Purcell. I wanted a job as printer's apprentice. That would be an official connection with the fellowship to which I had dedicated my future. I wanted to keep up my poetry, too. The proposal I made was to be taken on as a devil, and that a "Poet's Corner" be established in the paper. At no extra charge I guaranteed to fill the Corner each week, composing the poetry and setting the type after hours. I don't think a recognized poet ever made a more reasonable proposition to a publisher.

I say recognized poet because that's what I was now. As sometimes happens, recognition had come unexpectedly. A few weeks before I had written a number of verses entitled "Satire, a Criticism of the Local Authorities," and left them on Mr. Purcell's desk. As he had printed occasional offerings of mine all winter, Mr. Purcell, who may have been up late with brother Elks the night before, stuck this one on the copy hook without reading it. On Thursday when the paper reached its subscribers there was the dickens to pay. The more sensitive of our officialdom were on the editor's neck, and, what was more, on my father's neck.

This is what they complained of:

Listen to a bold satire
About the officers of this town
For already I have begun to tire
Of hearing their praises all around.

First I mention our mayor, Peter Bowers,
Who can see a joke but it quickly sours. . . .

There were several lines more on His Honor's negative sense of humor.

Next we mention City Attorney Walker
Who says very little but is a furious talker. . . .

Sam Campbell, who draws our sheriff's pay,
Cares little for chasing crooks but loves display. . . .

Frank Hamilton, our register of deeds,
Has one fault, his ravenous greeds. . . .

And so on, touching the weak spots, as I conceived them, of Republicans and Democrats without distinction. That was part of the trouble. The *Events* was a party organ which held that a Republican could do no wrong and a Democrat could do no good. Though my father was a Republican, more or less involved in Territorial politics, he was by no means an uncritical party man. The fact that he failed to see eye to eye with the party organization in our county had brought about his defeat for a vacancy appointment to the probate judgeship only a few days before the "Satire" appeared. His successful rival was James B. Cullison.

When my verses came out it was said, in certain quarters, that my father had inspired them to get even with the Republican county committee. Really, he had known nothing about them. Nor had I been inspired by the contest for the judgeship, but by something I had come across in the *Biglow Papers*. True enough, ideas for my characterizations were obtained from discussions of local affairs heard in our home and in my father's law office. Whatever his disappointment over the judgeship, I had heard Papa answer a criticism of his adversary in these words: "Let's wait and see. Cullison may do all right." This thought I had appropriated:

> The Commissioners made no mistake
> In electing a judge of probate court
> And there is no reason for knockers to kick and snort.
> Although Mr. Cullison may seem queer for a while
> We can at least give him a trial.

Everett Purcell suggested that Papa meet the charge of poor sportsmanship by publicly dissociating himself from my doggerel. He declined to do so. I suppose he must have figured that a disclaimer wouldn't put him in a much better light. What Papa could have done, though, was give me Hail Columbia. He didn't even do that, beyond saying the verses were in shocking taste and offering a suggestion. "Hereafter suppose you confine yourself to the statehood fight and leave little matters of local politics to me." Oklahoma's effort to become a state was our overshadowing issue, which I had supported from the inception of my literary career.

The truth is I enjoyed the notoriety flowing from the "Satire," and was disappointed in Mr. Purcell when he vetoed the printer-poet proposal and put me to work as a reporter for a dollar and a half a week. (The summer before I had made twice that as a messenger boy.) My feelings were further trampled on when the editor said that all he expected me to get were personals. He asked me to look at an item:

"H. H. Edmundson drove in from his fine farm in Patterson Township on Saturday with a load of early vegetables. He says Black Bear Creek is low for this time of year and they could stand a rain out there."

"Markey, that's the perfect personal. I wish I could fill the paper with 'em. Now take this one." Mr. Purcell read:

" 'S. E. Carrier of Carrier was at the courthouse Thursday.'

"See what it leaves out? Why was he at the courthouse? To petition for a bridge, or what? And how are the crops up his way? It hails a lot around Carrier. Anybody been hailed out yet this year? Get the idea, Markey? Now rustle me a whole column of personals for this week's paper."

Although this was Monday and press day was Wednesday, I got more than a column of personals, though some of them were left out when, unfortunately, Kennedy Brothers brought in an ad just before they locked the forms. I got my items by making the rounds of the stores and the farm-implement dealers, and at the St. Joe and the Curtis hotels where a lot of farmers ate their dinners. Of course many farmers brought their own grub and ate under the trees which had been planted in the Square. In a day or so I got over my bashfulness and rather enjoyed going up to a farmer and saying, "I'm the reporter for the *Events,* sir, and would like to print an item about your trip to town."

A lot of those country jakes had never heard of a newspaper reporter. "Don't care to subscribe, son," one would say. When I'd tell him (a bit loftily) that I wasn't soliciting subscriptions, it would generally be all right. Of course I ran into people who didn't like the *Events.* "Don't put *my* name in your nigger-Republican sheet."

3

The second week I got two columns of personals and Mr. Purcell raised my pay to two dollars a week. I discovered the advantage of interviewing the rural mail carriers at the post office. A barn painted, a baby born, a threshing accident, husking bee, fish fry or funeral: they knew the news of their routes.

Still, I could not escape the conviction that the emphasis Mr. Purcell laid on personals was a mark of provincialism. Above this I aspired to rise. I wanted to produce items with headlines to them, and I did so, writing the heads myself. A good many of these came from Police Court.

Shooting Scrape
Drunk and Disorderly
10 Days For a Chicken Thief

were examples of this kind of news.

I thought the typography of the *Events* suffered by comparison with the big city dailies which came to the exchange table from Guthrie and Wichita. Mr. Purcell would put a measly one-line head over an item a column long. The metropolitan press ran to attractive heads with several banks. Moreover it gave the news of the world. I sought to improve the *Events* along these lines, and in the second issue with which I had to do the following headlines appeared:

BIG NAVAL REVIEW
Oyster Bay Will be the Scene of
the Biggest Naval Review
Ever Held in Ameri-
can Waters

YALE WINS
Yale is Again Victorious Over
Harvard in Two Races

I myself had set these heads—without consulting Mr. Purcell. Once he saw how they elevated the tone of his paper I was sure it would be all right. Again, I had overestimated my employer. Not only did he disapprove the heads. He said to never mind Yale-Harvard boat races unless held on Boggy Creek; the Cimarron would be too far away. Apparently Mr. Purcell wasn't a follower of Frank and Dick Merriwell.

I wrote that Mr. J. P. Jack, the popular real-estate and insurance man, had gone to Waterloo, Iowa, to be united by the bonds of matrimony to "Miss Susy P. Jackman, a bright, educated young lady and the society leader of that city." It seems that Mr. J. P. Jack hadn't gone anywhere and hadn't got married. Some of the lawyers at the courthouse had given me the item as a joke. Himself a convivial bachelor, Mr. Purcell could appreciate the outraged feelings of Mr. Jack. He said never to print anything about a marriage unless I had it from the family of one of the "victims."

I described a big country wedding. The particulars came from an R.F.D. carrier, a brother of the groom. There was a whole-hog barbecue and a square dance. Mr. Purcell looked up from my copy and said:

"Markey, I want to congratulate you."

I thanked him.

"You've done something I've never seen before in my years in the newspaper business."

That sounded wonderful.

"You've written up a wedding and omitted the name of the bride. It deserves publication as an inspiration to American men."

All the same he put her name in.

Though my pay was boosted to two-fifty a week I was not so important in my own eyes as I liked to let on when making my rounds of the Square. I could not but regard John Bass and Sam Godfrey as boys who had succeeded where I had failed. John and Sam were the ink-smeared apprentices in the *Events* office—members of the fabled hierarchy of printers—I, a mere front-office hand.

The irony of it was that they didn't appreciate their good fortune. Neither intended to become a printer. Sam was rather noteworthy nevertheless, being an orphan from Brooklyn, New York, and a cosmopolitan personage. He wanted to become an actor and he hung out backstage at the Opera House. With John Bass it was simply a case of insensibility to the finer things of life. The trait ran in the family. John's father was Mr. Dan C. Bass, a building contractor, who, as a carpenter getting his start, had made Dick Yeager's coffin. Mind you, Dick Yeager's coffin.

When we first moved to town I had made Mr. Bass's acquaintance at the Methodist Sunday school where he taught a class of boys older than I. One day I asked him:

"Mr. Bass, they say you made Dick Yeager's coffin."

"Believe I did, son."

"Well, tell me, please, Mr. Bass, *how'd* you make it? How'd you *feel* when you made it?"

Mr. Bass sent a puzzled look down his long nose. "Why, felt all right—far as I recall. They wanted to bury him by sunup. So I slapped the box together in the nighttime. A rush job by lantern light."

I did what I could to efface the front-office stigma and make myself a part of the back-room establishment—a sort of apprentice without portfolio. Owing to the amount of job printing it did, the *Events* was a busy shop, ranking next to the *Eagle* in the size of its force. The straight-matter compositors were two jolly, black-aproned girls, Gussie and Delia. On the display side was a seasoned printer, Jennings, a keen young fellow named Byron Demonbrun, and one or two tramps, as the tide of work required. The foreman was Cliff Dull, a thin, nervous, driving man with the fastest and most dexterous hands in the shop. He never stopped work for a second, even when giving orders. The veins in his temples throbbed perpetually. Noon hours made him miserable. He would wolf down his meal, fidget about for a while, and, unable to tolerate idleness any longer, fly back to work before it was time.

Dull was very deaf and he talked to himself. The first I knew of this I was setting one of my items at the case when Dull's tense rapid voice behind me almost caused me to drop my stick.

"God-damn that boy. That front-office boy, messing around my shop. Have to speak to old Everett. Or Miss Ethel. Why don't they keep him the hell out of here? Pi a galley the first thing. God-damn that boy."

Miss Ethel was Mr. Purcell's sister who had the title of business manager. That summer, after her brother became postmaster, she practically ran the paper.

I saw the foreman bending over, and apparently speaking to, an imposing stone. The girl compositors told me not to take it to heart. The fact is, Dull's habit of thinking aloud afforded the shop a great deal of merriment. Fortunately he led a life of monastic rectitude, without friends or associates. His ideas of women—especially the sloe-eyed Miss Ethel—were exalted. For a while he worried about the intentions of a young man with whom she was keeping company but to our disappointment dropped the subject before his speculations became particularly interesting. Although Dull's language was a little forthright (as in the privacy of one's mind whose isn't?), the foreman's sentiments concerning drinking and other lapses would have been applauded by any clergyman in town.

Of course the tramps interested me most. They came and went pretty fast, for Dull was a hard taskmaster. Some of them, resenting the frank characterizations in Dull's soliloquies, laid down their sticks and called for their time in the middle of a job. This independence was fascinating, and when the editor told me to chase out to Denton's and get an obit of the old man I said:

"I can't do that, Mr. Purcell."

He was speaking of Scott Denton, a distinguished pioneer lawyer who had just died. Though my father and Scott Denton had been the reverse of friends, the thought of intruding on a widow's grief to get a newspaper item appalled me.

"What can you do, then?" asked Mr. Purcell.

"I can quit," I said.

I thought the scene approached tramp-printer standards of independence. But after a week wielding a hoe at Lopeman's nursery I was glad to accept the editor's invitation to return to the paper.

4

The epochal event of the summer was not my debut as a professional journalist. It was this, recorded in my diary under date of June 25, 1906:

"Hoop-ee. I am a Real Real Soldier in a Real Real army. Yes, sir. I have enlisted as a private in Oklahoma National Guards 1st Regiment Co. K. I have the honor of being the youngest soldier in Oklahoma."

That is, I had joined the militia. The protestations of reality were to distinguish this affiliation from my connection with a company of boys who drilled with sticks.

At home was a "Military Record" of the James family going back to the Colonial wars. I got it out and at the bottom of the last page inscribed my name, rank, and organization.

Then, with a sinking feeling, I saw that it didn't rightly belong there. The "Record" was arranged by wars and campaigns. Peacetime soldiers were not included. I prayed for a war to come quick, and scanned the city papers for signs of hostilities. The Philippines seemed to afford a glimmer of hope. The pacification of the islands was incomplete and a fresh insurrection had broken out. Gee, if Teddy Roosevelt would only call on the First Oklahoma!

Enthusiastic would be a weak word to describe the ardor with which I went about my military duties. The youngest soldier in Oklahoma was one of the busiest. We drilled in the streets on the Square two nights a week because the annual encampment of the regiment was only a short while away. I would be on hand an hour before time, furbishing my equipment and rehearsing the manual of arms. Every few days one of the non-coms would take a detachment to the edge of town for rifle practice. I managed to be in every detachment. Those Krag-Jorgensens kicked like mules and my shoulder was black and blue.

I pored over the *Infantry Drill Regulations* and the *Field Service Regulations*, committing passages to memory. I could rattle off a sentry's general orders as fast as any man in the company. By special permission I attended the non-commissioned officers' school conducted by First Sergeant Jim Cullison. In the *Events* I printed appeals for recruits. The company needing a bugler, I provided one in the person of Jay Radcliffe. Offering myself as a volunteer to sweep the Armory, I was given the custody of a set of keys.

It was the keys that got me into that trouble. There was a key to the orderly room where the officers had their desks. The captain's desk was open, and while dusting the papers I happened to see, along toward the bottom of the pile, the questions for the non-commissioned officers' annual examination. My interest in these questions was purely academic. I did not intend to take the test, knowing that the officers fatuously considered me too young to be a non-com.

Nevertheless, I copied out the hard questions and after looking up the answers felt very important indeed. I could take that examination and get 100. The thought was tantalizing.

But having the demerit of total impracticability, it was put aside. Then a perfectly marvelous inspiration laid hold of me. I was in a position to help some of my friends among the non-coms and aspirants to chevrons. If this was done unbeknownst to them, what could be the harm? None, certainly; but on the other hand it would be a regular boon to K Company.

Take Jim Cullison. Certainly he deserved to retain his rank as first sergeant. Not only did Jim, who was clerk of his father's court, give me news items every day, but he had been one of the most active sponsors of my effort to enlist. And there was Mr. Otjen, a private surely entitled to promotion. Mr. Otjen was a new lawyer in Enid whose office had become one of my special hangouts. He kept company with Jim Cullison's sister, Miss June, whom I liked. He was one of eleven survivors of the Catubig massacre in the Philippines, and he had been a policeman in Chicago. A shame if he shouldn't get to be a sergeant.

On my reportorial rounds I made the customary calls at Jim's and Mr. Otjen's offices. With elaborate casualness I brought up the subject of the forthcoming exam. I speculated as to what the questions might be, observing that, naturally, if such-and-such was asked thus-and-so would be the answer.

The result of this nobly motivated stratagem was not altogether happy. Especially did I leave Mr. Otjen with a feeling of discomfort. It takes a lawyer to ask the darnedest questions.

Next day I met Lieutenant Scott on the street. He, too, was a lawyer, and he it was who had persuaded Captain Lewis to take me into the company.

"Captain Lewis says the non-com examination questions are missing. You haven't seen them around when you were cleaning up, have you, James?"

My knees turned to water.

"Questions missing?" I stammered. "No, sir."

I flew to the courthouse and confessed to Jim Cullison. Jim was a tall, red-haired, freckled fellow with a smile that looked as if it never came off. But it came off then.

Jim said I had committed a military offense of which the Articles of War took a serious view. New questions, naturally, would have to be prepared. The first sergeant suggested that I make a clean breast of everything to Lieutenant Scott.

The next day was Sunday, and a long Sunday. I went to church, but it didn't do much good.

On Monday I saw the lieutenant. He gave me a proper dressing down but said he'd get up new questions and say nothing to Captain Lewis.

The lieutenant's leniency eased but did not lift the weight of disgrace bearing upon my spirit. A Navy recruiting officer made periodical visits to Enid. On his next trip I applied for enlistment.

"How old are you, young man?" asked the officer, pleasantly enough.

"Seventeen, sir."

Seventeen was the minimum age stated on the recruiting poster.

"Live with your parents?"

"Yes, sir."

The officer handed me a paper. "If you can get one of them to sign this, come back."

My father was in Guthrie. Mama refused to sign the consent form. When Papa returned he wouldn't sign either.

In September came the event of the year in the life of a National Guardsman: "camp." The regiment mobilized at Guthrie and went to Fort Riley, Kansas, for maneuvers with the Regular Army which included a sham battle that lasted days and days. I returned a nonchalant veteran, rolling soldier slang on my tongue.

CHAPTER NINE

High School

THE high school was on Broadway next to Stephens's hide house where I had learned to tan the catskin—and make a passable job of it, too. Only the end of the tail got soft and came off; I hadn't scraped it enough. The pelt supplied my room with a rug which was a nice thing to stand on getting dressed of a cold morning.

Our high school possessed advantages not duplicated in any educational institution I have come across since. I believe the building was the largest in Enid, excepting one of the flour mills or the Alton Mercantile Company. Only the top floor was devoted to school purposes, though. The rest was the Opera House and the acoustics were such that you could hear the stage troupes rehearsing below. To hear distinctly it was necessary to pay strict attention. The best way was to put one ear to a desk and plug up the other. Amid the distractions of a Latin class this tended to develop powers of concentration.

Out of school hours closer contact with the drama was possible by hanging about the stage door. As a result the Opera House was practically staffed by high-school students, serving as stage hands, ushers, ticket takers, property men and supers. As a rule these positions of privilege went to upperclassmen. Some of them actually got to talk to members of the troupes, usually stock companies playing a week's stand. In this way wisps of the mysterious erudition of the theater filtered through to us freshmen.

The back end of our building, where the history and English rooms were, overlooked the hollow filled with the Negro shacks and the other establishments which made up Two Street. Two Street was really at its best after sundown, but daylight afforded an occasional sight worth tearing your attention from history or English. "A nigger killing back of the school," my diary notes. "Shot with a shotgun at close range & it made a big hole in his side."

A hundred yards away the Rock Island went by, affording the means by which, at small expense to myself, I accompanied the football team on its travels.

From the first I did not find high school dull, as I had feared on my return from army maneuvers. But too much went on that was new and strange. I felt out of it and uncomfortable. I came from the least fashionable of Enid's three grade schools, for the social tone of East Hill continued to decline.

My initial triumph was one of reflected glory in connection with Sam Godfrey, the ex-printer's apprentice. During the summer Sam and I had struck up such a friendship that I induced Mama to let him live with us. Lively, intelligent, good-looking, and, as Mama pointed out, well-mannered, Sam was the kind of boy who made friends everywhere. As the end of the summer drew near and other boys were making ready for school, we could see how dearly Sam wished to attend. But as Papa was going through the most acute financial crisis since icehouse days, we could not afford to keep another boy.

My father mentioned Sam to a member of the Board of Education and the boy's winning personality did the rest. He was employed as janitor of the high school with the privilege of attending classes. The pay was handsome: forty dollars a month and a cot under the stairs to sleep on.

Sam captivated the Enid High School. A corps of volunteers shared his janitorial duties, which were considerable. Four classrooms, the science lab, the assembly hall, and the principal's office were swept daily and heated by means of soft-coal-burning stoves. All the fuel was toted, a scuttle at a time, up two long flights of stairs. You have to know how fast soft coal burns to appreciate that part of the job. As it won't bank overnight very well, each fire usually had to be started fresh from kindling in the morning. Despite the support of admiring friends, Sam was at work at 6 A.M. and the only chance to study came after the night show was out in the Opera House below. While still on the *Events* Sam had ingratiated himself into an enviable position at the Opera House. He shifted scenery, rustled props, and suped in the plays.

At the freshman class election I nominated Sam for president and looked to the Central henchmen, with whom I had been in caucus, to see that our candidate's merits received their due. As a result Sam got more votes than there were voters. On the second ballot he was merely elected unanimously.

Another piece of good fortune came my way during the "flag fight." The annual flag fight was a high-school institution that began on Hallowe'en. In these contests seniors and sophomores opposed an alliance of juniors and freshmen for the honor of flying their colors from the staff on top of the school. This year Hallowe'en was on Wednesday, and the contest was to end at 4:15 Friday afternoon. Theoretically all students were eligible to participate, but actually the fights were carried on by selected teams. The selection of the junior-freshman team was in the hands of Ed Fleming. It did not occur to me to feel slighted at being passed over.

So on Hallowe'en I went quietly about my own business, joining a tough East Side gang which overturned eighteen privies, made off with two buggies and one hayrack, and committed minor depredations. Once we were shot at and to my consternation a member of our gang whipped out a pistol and fired back. As I walked home from the night's work I saw the junior-freshman colors afloat over the Opera House.

But next morning the senior-soph flags were there. Ed Fleming put in motion a counterstroke. While classes were changing, a picked squad rushed the laboratory, I joining in uninvited. Someone boosted me through the trapdoor in the ceiling. Just then the seniors and sophs broke down a door opening into the lab and began to clear the place of our people. By that time I was on the roof hauling down the senior-soph standards and running ours up.

The contest had two more days to run. Inasmuch as I was accepted as a member of the junior-freshie team, they were wonderful days despite the fact that victory ultimately perched on the banners of our rivals.

2

The fact that I imagined I had made an impression on Ed Fleming helped to compensate for the unhappy issue of the flag fight. Nearly any freshman would have welcomed the good opinion of Ed Fleming, who in addition to having the richest father in Enid was a school leader in his own right. To me, there was still another reason: Ed was Blossom Fleming's brother.

That Blossom Fleming was now Mrs. Harry Alton made little difference, really. The secret life of the secret world I maintained for myself was impervious to the issue of the dashing courtship, the most widely advertised courtship in the history of Enid in my time, by which Harry Alton had carried off Blossom Fleming. I had to confess that in ways he seemed worthy of her.

Our town was growing. There were four railroads, which the Chamber of Commerce said made Enid an "unrivaled distributing center." An evidence of our facilities for distribution was the Alton Mercantile Company, a wholesale grocery house, established on South Grand Avenue by Mr. S. T. Alton, a citified-looking gentleman from the East, which to us might mean anything the other side of Indianapolis.

Each tin or package sponsored by the Alton Mercantile Company bore the hallmark of the house in bold red caps:

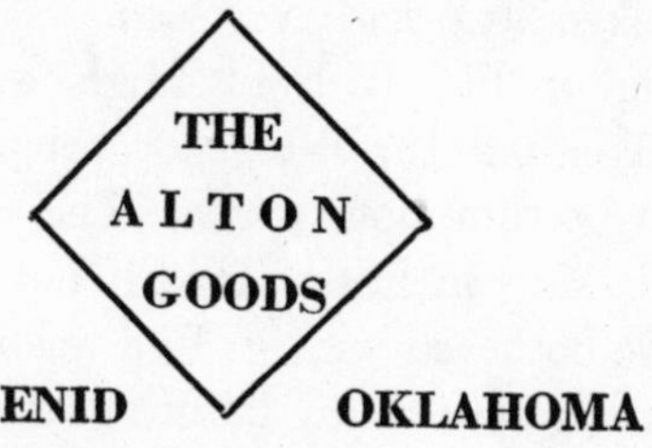

It swelled our hearts with pride to see on the shelves of Mr. Buttrey or Mr. Byerley rows of THE ALTON GOODS with ENID, OKLAHOMA, on each and every article. Moreover, it was important to realize that THE ALTON GOODS were sold not in Enid only, but all over the Cherokee Strip and maybe in Old Oklahoma and Kansas as well. As the Chamber of Commerce said, it marked the beginning of Enid's march to greatness: the future Queen City of the Plains.

With his close-cropped gray mustache and his urban air, Mr. S. T. Alton seemed to me a most unapproachable man. And as for his son Harry—he looked like a city dude out of the pages of a magazine. It is one thing to stand in awe of a man's clothes and another to stand in awe of a man. Harry Alton was tall and broad-shouldered; and he carried himself well. His features were handsome, decisive and cold. But what really made Enid look beyond Harry's wardrobe was his ability as a horseman. The loungers at Randolph & Mehew's livery stable would tell you that a better team of driving horses than Harry Alton's sorrels had never been seen on our streets. They were like coiled steel springs, those horses.

Though flashy, Harry's yellow-wheeled rig was in good taste, because my mother said so. How her eyes would sparkle to see Harry Alton, the sorrels and the yellow-wheeled rig spin by, sending up a rolling cloud of brown dust. Whenever he went for a drive Harry's outfit was appraised, admired, and talked about. That was what made his courtship of Blossom Fleming public property. On what foundation I haven't the slightest idea, Enid assumed that the Fleming family opposed the romance. If that was so in the end they gave in, and threw the grandest wedding the Cherokee Strip had ever seen.

Another side of life at Enid High was less satisfactory. I aspired to be taken into the West Side young people's set, which I understood gave scrumptious parties. The social existence of East Hill I found lacking in luster. Had it not been for Eva Britton I wouldn't have bothered with it. Eva was no social climber. East Hill suited her. In view of my failure to make a dent in the West Side barriers I was secretly glad of this. "Sent off for a ring with 125 soap wrappers tonight." "My new ring came today. It is a peach with a pretty tiger eye stone." Eva wore that ring and I wore a pin of hers in my tie.

My classroom work was almost uniformly poor. To remedy this, I stooped to homework. The sacrifice brought me barely up to passing averages in all subjects except history and Latin. In history I did better than passing, but Latin I couldn't get the hang of. One trouble seems to have been my ignorance of the structure of English. I belonged to one of the school's two "literary" societies. This honor was compulsory. Every Friday afternoon one of the societies gave a program which the whole school had to listen to. I found the programs boring and would play hookey and take a train ride. When, at length, I was assigned to a program, an unprecedented thing happened. A week in advance I became petrified with stage fright.

My assignment was an "original poem." With the consent of the society officers, I got a sophomore to read it for me. But I knew this a mere postponement of the evil day. I got so that I would shake like a leaf when I had to give a recitation in class. There were times when I would say I did not know the answer to a question rather than rise and address the class. The affliction grew worse. I would tremble if spoken to by a teacher. Suffused with shame, I began to feel that something terrible was wrong inside of me.

3

The next thing anybody knew was that the world was coming to an end. Some religious sect had made this discovery and the idea spread all over our part of the country. The signs were in the heavens that sometime along about the coming of warm weather everything would just go to smash and we'd all be up for Judgment. Though most people laughed when they mentioned the subject, churches were filled as never before and all sorts of revival meetings started to prepare sinners to meet their Maker.

An itinerant apostle of the shoutin' Baptist creed threw up a "tabernacle" on the edge of Happy Hollow and carried on for a month. His wife helped him, and they had a man who played a banjo and a pretty, well-formed girl who strummed a guitar. For a spectacle it was as good as a Negro baptizing. Some of us kids used to go, I, for one, professing a degree of levity which in my bones I did not feel. You heard that it was possible to date up the guitar player and steer her emotions into secular channels. The bare notion sent a shiver through me. That would be a sure way to wind up in hell: fooling around with one of God's legates on earth.

The tabernacle was lighted by smoking kerosene flares. Fidgeting shadows cast an eerie something over the singing and shouting throngs and over the confessing sinners whose self-revelations were encouraged by supplications from their hearers. "Pra-a-ise the Lord!" "A-a-a-men!" "Out with it, Sister!" A wonderful night was when a fat old slattern with a greasy smile who told fortunes and dispensed love philters confessed her sins and made a profession of faith. Arms lifted toward heaven, she waddled, shouting, to the mourners' bench to be received into the fold of the "saved." The saved. What would not I have given to join that blessed and tranquil company? Almost anything, it seems, but the price required at the tabernacle. I couldn't, just couldn't, get up before all those folks, swaying and clapping and stomping in rhythm, and turn my life inside out.

I felt so bum that half the time I wished the world *would* come to an end and take me with it. This feeling did not diminish when the time came to prepare to participate in a "literary" program. No pretext sufficed to get me off. I was just about as miserable and scared as a boy could be when an unseasonably warm wave came along which the end-of-the-world people fitted into their prognostications. Though only the middle of March, it got warmer and warmer. Well, if the world was coming to an end, I hoped it would do so before the day for me to say that piece.

On the nineteenth of the month the thermometer reached 96. I shucked my underwear. To cool the apprehensions of my spirit was not so easy. On March 20 I read in the paper that a comet was headed for the earth. "If it hits the earth," my diary reports, "it will kill all the people and if it does not we will pass through its tail & burn up anyway." On March 27, with the crisis at hand, I affected a tone of nonchalance not wholly fictitious. "Tomorrow is the day that comet is due to strike. I guess there is a comet alright because you can see it right off in the southeast at about 1 A.M. The newspapers say that the thermometer will go up to 140° tomorrow! Well, if it's coming let her came. so long!"

"Mar 28 Thu. Aw there was nothing to that old comet for it was even cooler than usual today. Well there was some people pretty scared about it and even some people went crazy."

I came near going crazy when I realized that with the world still a going concern I would have to make my appearance on the literary program. The week was one of indescribable misery. When Friday came my mind had ceased to function. My legs were in working order, however, and they carried me down the stairs and to the Rock Island track.

On Monday I was in for it. Mr. Wright, the principal, said I would have to say my piece that day at chapel before I could attend a class. When the hour came Mr. Wright began to address the school. I knew he was saying that I would speak my piece but a giddy roaring in my head drowned his words. At length he stopped. I struggled to my feet. A new sound assailed my ears: cheering from the freshman section. I managed to get to the platform and mumble my lines.

4

The fact that Papa was desperately hard up contributed to the depression of my spirits. Hitherto my small world had rested on the bedrock of my father, in whom my confidence was axiomatic. The summer I paid for the bike I had worried only for myself. I knew Papa'd pull through. Now this unquestioning faith of childhood was shaken.

Had not my brother-in-law, Perry, advanced two thousand dollars we would have lost two of the three houses we owned. I shared the humiliation I was sure my father felt at accepting this assistance. Although exceedingly fond of Brother Perry, I found it embarrassing to be in his presence. Moreover, I understood my father's reluctance to oust non-paying tenants of our rental houses, notwithstanding Mama's more practical view of real-estate management. Since we had lived on the claim, Papa had always owned a house or so in Enid which was nominally rented. When tenants learned that a hard-luck story would do about as well as cash, many of their payments were in that coin. The family living in our former home at Sixth and Maine was so consistently the victim of misfortune that in order to get more benefit from the place we moved back there ourselves.

The cause of our money troubles was assumed to be the non-producing nature of the oil well at Garber. There is this about an oil well, though. As long as the drill is going there is hope. Every other week ours would rise; and then subside. The economies effected by the move into the smaller house, and the punctual collection of rents (which Mama saw to), helped some but not enough. We owed a three months' grocery bill to Mr. Buttrey when one morning Papa was informed that the Republican caucus, meeting the night before, had nominated him for the office of city attorney.

Mama received the news joyfully. "What does it pay?" was her first question.

"Why, I believe a thousand a year," Papa said.

She smiled wryly. "Little enough; but right now it's a godsend. It'll save our properties."

"Rachel," said Papa, "I did not seek this nomination. I was not consulted. The organization put me on the ticket to try to save its skin. Something to offset those paving contracts and the street-railway franchise. I can't let them use me that way."

My father's scruples were overcome. He consented to let his name stand, with the stipulation that he should make no campaign, but if elected would serve.

The building boom which was changing the face of Enid made the coming municipal election important. Arthur E. Stephenson's five-story skyscraper had been finished. People flocked to ride in the elevator and to take in the view from the top floor. Papa's office was only on the third floor. A block away Albert Loewen's five-story skyscraper was almost complete. Nor was that all this public-spirited citizen was doing to prove his faith in Enid. The finishing touches were being put to the splendid four-story Loewen Hotel and Loewen Theater. This would be the knell of the old Opera House. Next fall the high school was to have a building of its own on North Independence.

The Square and the principal streets leading from it were being paved with asphalt. Street-car tracks were going down.

The emergence of modern Enid imposed new responsibilities on its governing authorities. But there were the complaints about the paving contracts, involving sums which seemed astronomical. As to the street-railway franchise, Enid wanted street cars, certainly, but couldn't she have bargained to a little better advantage? My father was one who thought so.

The Republicans were on the defensive, their hold on the local government threatened. The head of the ticket, the candidate for mayor, was an excellent tactical choice—Art Stephenson, the skyscraper builder. My father had been named to attract the independent vote and, as I learned later, because Everett Purcell knew him to be broke.

The campaign was a warm one. All persuasions to move my father to take part failed, and I tried as hard as anybody. His Democratic opponent, O. D. Hubbell, was an old frontier lawyer and a good man. He spoke to large crowds in every ward in the city. He was for cheaper paving.

Never before had I taken such interest in an election, for the reason that, according to Mama, never before had we so much at stake. Mr. Buttrey's grocery bill loomed larger as an issue than paving or street cars.

As soon as the polls closed on election day I was at the bottling works, the polling place of the Fourth Ward. Papa stayed home. For the first election night that I could recall he was not at Republican headquarters paying off or collecting bets. I got inside the bottling works and watched the tellers count the ballots. My heart leaped, for Papa was running ahead of everybody. Ballot after ballot was solidly Democratic except for Papa. I rushed home breathless with the news.

"That's our home ward, boy. Go over on the West Side and you'll find Republicans who've scratched me for Mr. Hubbell."

I snorted that it wasn't necessary to go to the West Side to find one such stinker. Right here in the Fourth Ward *somebody* had voted every name in the Republican column except Papa's. Oh, but I'd just like to get my hands on him!

"You wouldn't commit any great violence, I hope," smiled Papa.

Papa squeaked in by thirty-eight votes. Art Stephenson and three other Republicans won. Four Republicans were defeated.

Papa was enormously pleased at his election.

"I can't help it," he said, "though I think it was wrong to accept the nomination and do nothing for the ticket. That's why when I got in the booth I couldn't vote for myself."

5

I squeaked through the freshman year at high school in everything except Latin and began my second summer on the *Events*. The oil well was abandoned as a duster.

Mama said the end of the uncertainty was a relief. "Your father will pay some attention to his law practice now. He can always make us a good living at that."

This was the nearest to a criticism of Papa I'd ever heard Mama utter. Though I felt the implication true I wished she hadn't said it.

I wished she hadn't said it because enough was wrong as it was that summer. My world was clear out of joint. I was frightened all the time. In all seriousness I felt that *had* a comet with a long tail put the world out of business on March 28, 1907, it would have ended my present troubles. For the fears which dogged my wretched steps I despised myself. Distilled from the yeasty vapors of adolescence, my turmoiled thoughts formed an accusing pattern in which every youthful lapse became a crime.

The activities of K Company aroused in me more resistance to the forces of melancholy than everything else put together. The regiment had received two Colt machine guns. They were mounted on wheels for transportation and fired from tripods. They used .30-caliber ammunition like a Springfield and fired up to four hundred rounds a minute. A spirited contest for the guns ensued among the different companies. L Company of Alva, M Company of Oklahoma City, and K Company were the chief contenders. These were the best outfits in the regiment. Simply because Oklahoma City seemed to get anything it wanted, we of K Company hardly dared to hope that we should beat out M Company. But Oklahoma City didn't get the machine guns. We got them.

Lieutenant Scott was detailed to organize a battery. I begged to be taken in. From the day I first laid eyes on them I was in love with those guns. Jim Cullison and I had opened the boxes, removed and cleaned the parts of their heavy coatings of grease, and by a study of the instructions put the guns together. I would slip into the Armory alone and spend hours with them. Though I had never had anything to do with a piece of machinery before, and have no special bent for mechanics, I learned to strip and assemble those guns and to recite the nomenclature as quickly as anyone in the company, excepting Jim. Moreover I learned what made them work: how a portion of the force which sent a bullet from the barrel was harnessed and made to eject the empty shell, thrust a fresh cartridge into the breech, lock the breech and fire that cartridge. As I recall, some fifty moving parts were brought into play.

Lieutenant Scott took me into the battery.

He had no more devoted machine-gunner. Those primitive Colts were tricky affairs. There were half a dozen ways a cartridge could jam or the mechanism fail. I learned the remedy for each. I could relieve a stoppage as dexterously as anyone.

On the Fourth of July we paraded in Guthrie. It was certainly something to see the men from the other companies crowd around the machine guns and gape while I showed how they worked.

The September maneuvers, at Fort Reno, opened with a series of personal triumphs. I had mastered the rudiments of firing a Colt—using short bursts so as not to waste ammunition or overheat the barrel. I could direct the fire somewhere near a target. This was not easy, for the agitation of those moving parts, particularly a thing called the gas lever, set up an awful vibration. Once while firing I nearly bit my tongue off.

One of the two coveted posts of gunner was given to me. Lieutenant Scott had been promoted to captain and given the command of K Company and of the battery which comprised a platoon of K Company. My friend Jim Cullison was made the lieutenant in charge of the battery. K Company took the play from M Company as the smartest outfit in the regiment. The smartest part of K Company was the battery.

Maneuvers were brought to an end by a prairie fire which imparted a momentary touch of realism to our amateur soldiering. We had fallen in for an overnight hike when someone noticed smoke over the rise in the pasture to the south—a part of the unpeopled military reservation. A twenty-five-mile wind was blowing and in no time the fire came over a crest a little better than a mile away. The terrain intervening was level and covered with grass waist high—ready to cut for hay for the cavalry mounts. A creek lay between our camp and the fire. Regimental headquarters apparently didn't think the fire would jump the creek, for no orders to backfire were given.

But it did jump the creek and came at us faster than a man could run. Our battalion deployed along a narrow road south of camp and started a backfire. The wall of flame roaring toward us was the scariest thing I'd ever seen. I glanced toward the company on our left. One or two men furtively dropped back and after a few steps started for camp on the run. Then one or two more. Next the whole line broke pell-mell. Jay Radcliffe's post was beside Captain Scott. He blew his bugle and the captain signaled us to make interval to the left and take over the abandoned sector. By this time the scorching breath of the oncoming flames was in our faces. In another moment they had met the backfire, which we had started too late. But as tongues of flame licked across the burned gap we were on them, flailing away with blankets and blouses. Had other companies done as well the fire might have been arrested there. But we were spread too thin. I heard men shouting and, looking to the left, saw where the flames had broken through and were in the M Company street. Our company street was next but one. Jay blew a blast and Captain Scott passed the word to fall back and strike the tents.

It was not an orderly retreat. Flying ashes and smoke were blinding. Ammunition, reached by the fire, began to go off. My legs carried me right on through our company street. I was by no means alone. Finding myself abreast of regimental headquarters, I helped load the colonel's baggage. Then I stood by protectively while the colors were furled and hurried toward the fort—an old frontier post built for protection against Indians.

I looked down the slope at the camp. All over, tents were afire and men struggling among them. But more men were running for the fort. I started back the other way. Ammunition was popping here and there.

In K Company's street I found Jim Cullison and a dozen others. Sweat streaking their blackened faces, they worked like demons to save our stuff. Tents were down, some of them afire. The sergeants' tent was on fire. I crawled under the burning canvas and dragged out the first sergeant's field desk.

The regiment was burned out. Having left Jay Radcliffe and two others in the hospital on account of injuries, K Company reached home next morning. Although only my hair had been singed, I was not disagreeably surprised to find my name on the published casualty list. In the afternoon I was at high school making responses to admiring questions. Life seemed pretty good, after all.

CHAPTER TEN

The Hand of Change

"NOV 16 1907 Bright & Fair. Well the great state of Oklahoma is now a fact. As long as I can remember people have been talking about statehood and I have thought a little about it myself. The president signed the proclamation making Oklahoma a state at 9:15 A. M. central time he signed it with an eagle quill which will become the possession of the Okla Historical Society. The Governor was installed in office at high noon on the steps of the Carnegie library. He made his speech very short and in it criticized Pres. Roosevelt. Yes just like a Democrat."

It was in my capacity as a private in K Company that I witnessed the installation of Governor Haskell, which took place in Guthrie. On display were flags with forty-six stars, the forty-sixth being for Oklahoma, one of the United States at last. For me the fruits of this success had rather soured on the vine because Oklahoma came into the Union under the auspices of the Democratic party, with a constitution modeled after the state constitutions of the Solid South, plus innovations like the initiative and referendum inspired by William Jennings Bryan.

I had inherited my politics from my father and multiplied it by two, not believing him a sufficiently staunch supporter of the G.O.P. Although he had voted against the adoption of the constitution, against the prohibition rider and against Haskell, his pronounced opposition had been to Haskell. In his early days in the Indian Territory my father had acquired fixed ideas concerning a type of lawyer who achieved sudden wealth and political power in an Indian constituency. Mr. Haskell had come to the Creek Nation from Ohio. He changed his politics from Republican to Democratic and, in seven years' time, crowned a series of triumphs among the Creeks by becoming the first governor of the State of Oklahoma, which had been formed by throwing the Indian and Oklahoma territories together.

Papa belonged to the minority wing of the Republicans, called by their adversaries the Lily Whites. Among other things, the Lily Whites opposed the blanket enfranchisement of Negroes. In my father's case this was not because they were Negroes. It was because they were ignorant. He believed suffrage should be restricted by an educational qualification which would have denied the ballot to most Negroes and Indians and some whites. On this item of political doctrine my father and I were at variance. I thought Negroes should vote. I assumed that they would vote Republican.

2

The hand of change had touched the high school. A new building which struck us as the last word in modernity, a rejuvenated and enlarged faculty, new courses and more up-to-date ways of doing things all around made for a little more civilized school spirit without loss of native vitality. This was largely the work of the principal, whose first year with us had been our last in the Opera House.

As I look back, Milton Wright bordered on the ideal as an educator, the time and place considered. The product of a Nebraska homestead, he knew the plains West and spoke its vernacular, unlike so much of the Strip's imported teaching talent. Wright set out to develop an Oklahoma school, not to copy something else. He was a middle-sized man in his early thirties with an intelligent poker face and humorous blue eyes. A natural leader of young people, he was so adroit at modifying their impulses that usually they thought they'd done it themselves.

Mr. Wright announced the abolition of the traditional flag fight on the ground that the new building and new equipment were too nice to smash up. Surprisingly, he carried a majority of the school with him. In place of the flag fight activities galore were provided to absorb our surplus energies.

New faces were present and old faces gone. Sam Godfrey was playing with a stock company in Brooklyn. Jay Radcliffe was studying art at the University—Oklahoma Christian University which had opened for business a mile east of town: another sign of the swelling tide of Enid's fortunes. Two newcomers whose paths I crossed early in the day were Horace Copple and Russel McKinley Crouse, whose presence was further proof that things were booming out our way.

Horace Copple's father was an energetic printer who had set up a shop over Byerley's grocery and established a weekly newspaper called the *Square Deal*, which he distributed free and got enough advertising to make it pay.

As for Russel McKinley Crouse, his connection with metropolitan journalism justified the high-sounding name he bore. Nevertheless we shortened it to Mike, and this distressed Mike considerably. Circumstances came to his rescue in a measure, however, for that was the year we young men began to press our pants and to lay aside the childish habit of calling each other by first names. Except when we forgot, it was Crouse, Copple, Byerley, Frantz, Herrick, Francisco, Kendrick, Fleming, Snodgrass. Crouse's father was the editor of the Enid *Morning News*, our new daily, whose smooth and citified appearance I definitely approved. For two summers I had tried to enhance the tone of the *Events*. It would serve Enid's poky old editors right if Mr. H. P. Crouse, of Toledo, Ohio, just put their hick sheets out of business.

I thought I saw where Crouse and Copple would fit into a scheme to revive the *Evening Squeak* as a high-school newspaper. The difficulties confronting me were purely mechanical. Merwyn Byerley had consented to be business manager. That would mean ads and subscriptions. His father's position as a merchant gave Merwyn entrée among potential advertisers. As for the editorial management of the paper, I felt my own talents equal to that and to spare. The matter of getting access to a print shop made it advisable to seek other partners, however.

Crouse was all for it. He exhibited copies of the high-school paper published in Toledo. He had a lot of ideas, editorial ideas. I listened to his editorial ideas and said that what we needed right now was someone to set our straight matter. Could Crouse get his father to have it done on one of the *News'* linotypes at a pretty reasonable figure? The ads could be set at Copple's father's shop and the paper run off on his press. Crouse's father's answer was no and this placed my relations with Russel McKinley Crouse on a less intimate footing.

Copple and I decided to set the paper ourselves, working at night. This for the first few issues, at any rate; after that we would be in a position to hire a compositor. Things moved swimmingly. Byerley lined up a batch of ads and when I offered a draft of the masthead with myself as editor-in-chief and Copple associate, Copple offered no objection, proving that he was certainly a wonderful fellow.

We were all set to get out the first issue when we decided we'd better speak to Mr. Wright. Wright was enthusiastic. He praised our initiative and made us feel fine. But, he said, why didn't we do the *big* thing: let the whole school in on our enterprise? This line of talk carried the day, but no sooner had we closed the door on Wright's office than doubts began to trouble our minds. We had agreed to submit the matter to the School Cabinet composed of representatives of each class. The Cabinet was one of Wright's innovations. What would that bunch of laymen know about getting out a newspaper?

The Cabinet fulfilled our worst expectations. They talked and talked and adjourned to reconsider. In the end, disgusted and jealous, we pioneers transferred our interest to other things. Copple went out for the debating team and Byerley and I joined a basketball team called the Kenwoods which got five dollars a game, win or lose, for playing at the roller-skating rink. There was no paper.

Mr. Wright introduced organized yelling and singing in the school, his deputy being the new history teacher, Mr. Deming. Deming and I had hit it off from the first. If I didn't know the day's lesson, he'd let me spout away on my general knowledge of the subject. Up to this year the high school had had but two yells that I know of. One you said so fast that it sounded like three long words:

"Nigger-nigger-hoe-potater-half-past-alligator-rum-bum-bully-nigger-ricka-chow-chow! Enid-High-School! Row-row-row!"

The other was directed at our adversaries:

Chaw tobaccer, chaw tobaccer
Spit, spit, spit!
Pondcreek, Pondcreek,
Nit, nit, nit!

For girls to yell was considered unladylike. Mr. Deming changed this. He held a contest for the selection of new yells and songs. The yell and song sessions were real fun. Grace Goltry was chosen song leader. Deming spread such a spirit of hilarity through the noisy proceedings that my terrors at facing an audience fell away to the extent that I entered the contest for yell leader and won. This effected almost a complete cure of my stage fright.

I went out for dramatics and landed in the chorus of a sumptuous production of *The Mikado*. For a fellow who had difficulty carrying a tune that wasn't doing badly.

I began to make the grade with the West Side social set. This came in the nick of time to stem a rising resentment against my parents because we lived on the East Side and because they were so unsocially inclined. My father's idea of a social pastime was the lawyers' poker game in the back room of the National saloon. After prohibition it moved to the rooms of the Bar Association. Though I had been told what a good dancer she was as a girl, I had never known the time when Mama cared for society in Enid. She preferred a book or a side-door visit among a few old East Hill neighbors like Mrs. Houston and Mrs. Radcliffe. Within recent years a slew of new people had come in, all living on the West Side or the far East Side by the University. My parents knew none of them socially. I imagined that this placed me at a disadvantage with their sons and daughters. In some respects I suppose it did.

The first new girl to trouble my emotions is described in my diary as "the late sensation from Philadelphia—the peach with brown eyes." I didn't get to first base. Her eastern speech and ways had me buffaloed. Fortunately, with another new girl—a sure-enough Easterner, too—I had better luck. She was a tumultuous, extravagantly beautiful blonde from a place called Asbury Park, New Jersey. She carried a breeze of good nature wherever she went and always had a fine noisy time. That kind of person melts reserve, but you could have knocked me down with a feather when she invited me to a Leap Year party.

At a Leap Year party the girls ask the boys. The party was given by Lily Bass, John Bass's sister, whose home was the first West Side home I entered on a formal occasion. The evening passed off pleasantly enough, I winning eleven of fifteen games of progressive dominoes. I tried to be careful of my manners, laughed heartily at everybody's witticisms, and went home wondering whether I'd been sufficiently amusing. Would I be asked to another West Side party? As it happened, I was. In addition to my time-honored Saturday chores I would set up the ironing board in the kitchen and press my two suits so that you could have sharpened a pencil on them.

Along toward the end of the school year you began to hear wisps of talk about Lula Jacoby's forthcoming party. Lula's annual party seemed an established affair in the glittering life of the West Side and, man, it was supposed to be a darb. West Side boys spoke confidently of the girls they'd take, the time they'd have. This made me vaguely uncomfortable. But a day came when I received, *through the mail*, an invitation which had at the bottom:

"R. S. V. P. Miss Helen Oldham."

I thought I knew what that meant (boy!) but I wasn't going to pull any boner. So I asked Mama. She said it meant what I thought. But then Mama's ideas of social usage might be obsolete, and this was a time when there mustn't be any mistake. Without (I hoped) permitting him to penetrate my design, I learned from Mike Crouse that Mama was right.

For all of two months I had been trying to commend myself to the favorable notice of Miss Helen Oldham.

3

Family fortunes were mending decidedly. Papa's office was a busy place. He had two young lawyers helping him: Blaine Acuff and M. A. Dennis. They were full of fun and I liked them immensely. Mr. Acuff came from Memphis, Tennessee, and Mr. Dennis from Massachusetts, I believe Boston. He was the first real New England Yankee I ever knew. His accent amused me. The boom-brought increase in Papa's practice concerned civil matters mostly, a branch of law in which my father had not hitherto been very active in Oklahoma. His latest big criminal case had been a year before, in 1907. With the courthouse hangers-on betting even money on first-degree murder, he got a second-degree manslaughter verdict, and was destined never to defend another killer. Killings were getting rare. Still, I heard Papa say he was so rusty on civil procedure that he didn't know what he would do without Acuff and Dennis.

The sight of those jovial young attorneys with piles of books before them on the long oak table in the back office being so helpful to my father recalled with momentary regret the disappearance of my aspiration to do that very thing. In the last couple of years, however, a new ambition had crept up on me. I was going to be a newspaperman, a big city newspaperman. One day I mentioned it to Papa.

"Well," he said, "if that's what you want."

"It's exciting, Papa. Those big city reporters, they go everywhere and see everything. They help the detectives unravel murder mysteries."

"You know," my father said, "there's lots of time to make up your mind, but I've always been in hope that you'd want to be a doctor."

In his slow voice Papa spoke as casually as if telling the time of day. I was plumb surprised. It was the first intimation I'd had that he didn't expect me to be a lawyer.

"A doctor, Papa? An ol' sawbones?"

"A doctor like your Grandfather Marquis. You bear his name and I'm the one who named you." I knew that: Mama had wanted to call me Houstin. "Your grandfather was a great man and a great gentleman: an ornament to the noblest of professions."

Papa could read my disappointment.

"Plenty of time yet, boy; plenty of time to decide."

I don't believe he mentioned the subject again.

My father and I were drawing closer together, closer than ever before. That winter I was made a corporal in K Company. Papa seemed to like to listen to my babblings about K Company. He would smile and look up from his reading, through the cloud of smoke from his pipe.

Congratulating me on the promotion, he made one of his infrequent allusions to himself.

"A corporal at sixteen: you're ahead of me, boy. I wasn't a private until I was seventeen, and then just in the home-guard company."

"But you went off to the war very soon, didn't you, Papa? And then you were a captain."

"A year later. And I was a first lieutenant."

"But you commanded your company in the battle of Nashville on your twentieth birthday."

"Yes; the captain was sick."

"He was drunk, Mama says."

Papa chuckled. "You're not going to involve me in an argument with your mother about the Civil War." After a moment he added, "It seems like a dream, the war. My recollections have no sense of reality at all."

He sat with his pipe in one hand and the evening paper in the other, which had dropped to his side, letting the paper rest on the floor. For an instant he seemed to be trying to fortify that dream with the substance of actuality. Then he restored the pipe to his mouth and resumed his perusal of the *Eagle*.

To Pap Crosslin, who lived in the next block, the war was no dream. Old Pap still had the Yanks on the run. When I was little I had listened to him with a mixture of fascination and dread.

He made it so lifelike I was sure the war was still going on and that the Rebs would win every battle. Sometimes I wished that Papa could be a little more like Pap. Other times I liked him the way he was.

I spent a good deal of time on the rifle range, trying to make the company rifle team. Once Papa and I got to talking about frontier shooting habits. Our growing camaraderie made me bold.

"You never carried a gun in the early days, did you Papa?"

"Yes; I carried a gun in Old Oklahoma and the Indian nations —even here in the Strip, for a while after the Opening."

"Ever need it?"

Papa paused. "Well, there was one time I thought I needed it, and I didn't have it. That was the luckiest day of my life. I'd have killed a man if I'd had my gun that day. I never wore a firearm after that."

"Gee, Papa. Was that the trouble in El Reno?"

No sooner were they out of my mouth than I wished I had the words back. In Oklahoma you didn't inquire into the particulars of a man's past. "Trouble" in those days meant shooting and often killing. I knew no detail of the "trouble in El Reno" except that Papa was supposed to have been involved. It was just one of those fragments of early-day gossip you picked up. I could see that the mention of the trouble in El Reno surprised my father. He said:

"No, that wasn't it."

"It was right here in Enid," Papa went on, "the year of the Opening. A certain coolness had sprung up between me and another citizen of this place. One day it came to my notice that he had circulated a lie, a rather scandalous lie, about me. I just saw red and started to find the slanderer. I came on him in the street in front of the Monarch. I called to him to defend himself and reached for my gun. It wasn't there. By this time my adversary was going for his gun. I took it away from him and knocked him down. He got up and I knocked him down again. By that time Marshal Williams came up and I tossed him the gun. My adversary was prone in the street. My foot was on his neck. I said to Williams, 'Get this carcass out of here before you have to bury it.' When I got into the Monarch my hand was trembling so that I could hardly lift a glass of whiskey."

That was the story: without adornment and without apology. I felt strangely mature, and enriched.

Other intimate talks followed. Although they were rarely in the form of direct reminiscence—and there was never anything else so memorable as the incident in front of the Monarch saloon —I knew them to be distillations from a varied life. My father spoke on such topics as courtesy, truth-telling, duty, honor. I doubt if many parents have been able to get home the values of those shopworn virtues better than Papa did. In this he was reaping the reward of a consistent course of conduct toward his son—how much of which was deliberate and how much merely natural to my father's temperament I do not know. I don't believe Papa spoke sharply to me a half dozen times in his life. And he never laid a hand on me by way of punishment. I heard him say that a father who struck his child degraded himself. This was in a discussion of the case of a nearly grown boy who had run off from home after a whaling by his father. Nevertheless, the lickings Mama used to give me had Papa's entire approval; but that was somehow different. All the same I would disobey Mama twice as quickly as I would my father.

"Papa, how can you tell when a witness is lying?" I asked one time.

"Can't always tell," he said, "but here are a couple of things to watch out for. There's the glib witness you half suspect from the start. Watch for him to get precise over unimportant details, so as to give the appearance of striving for scrupulous accuracy. Doesn't quite want to say whether it was a roan or a sorrel horse. Quibbles whether the distance was six or eight feet. Well, that man may be throwing dust in your eyes and the eyes of the jury to cover the fact that everything he is saying is untrue.

"Then again: study a man's language. Try to figure whether he is speaking from the remembrance of a mental image of events or trying to remember merely words. Lead him back and forth over the same ground. The man speaking from the remembrance of an image will not pay much attention to words and will vary his words every time he tells his story. The man who is speaking from remembered words with no image to back them up will try to use the same words every time."

I liked to slip into a courtroom and take a seat in the very back row and listen to Papa make a jury plea. It wasn't a thing I did often because I knew Papa didn't like it. Years before, he had ceased taking me to neighboring county seats where he had court business.

Papa didn't "address" a jury. He talked to it. Sometimes he would stand with his arms outstretched so that his hands rested on the rail of the jury box, his broad shoulders hunched a little. If it had been a long trial he would be tired and as anxious as anyone to get it over. Papa'd stand there, his feet a little apart, his shoulders drooping slightly and his hands on the rail, sharing the jurymen's weariness. Patiently, shred by shred, he'd brush away the cobwebs of error by which the opposition lawyer had endeavored to obscure the bright jewels of fact.

Most of all I liked to hear Papa examine and cross-examine. Here again he was patience on a monument, never raising his slow voice, never railing at a witness no matter how destructive to Papa's side might be his story. But how he could get at the truth and set it on display: that is to say, make anything his witnesses had to tell seem to be the truth embodied and anything a hostile witness had to offer just the contrary. Instead of flaring up, like Mr. Henry Sturgis when an unfriendly witness clung to a damaging story, Papa seemed moved by a deep disappointment that this man, this witness, should lower himself in the esteem of the jury by persisting in such an unlikely tale.

Papa's cross-examining had something to do with making up my mind rarely to lie—to him. Thus on the one hand I became a fairly frank and truthful kid, and on the other a rather subtle one.

In my father's code, honor touched matters likely to involve women—"ladies," as he said. One time after a good deal of circumlocution, he made his main point, and I was there ahead of him. This beating about the bush was unusual. For all his quietly discursive manner he generally talked straight to a point, or straight away from it. But this time he looped around quite a bit before coming out with the proposition that it was possible for a gentleman to give his affection where he did not give his respect.

Though my father had recently joined the Methodist church, I was not aware of the circumstances until thirty-odd years later when I was in Oklahoma trying to get some of the statements in this book in the same general neighborhood as the facts. The Reverend Mr. Barnes, then retired, told me about Papa's joining the church. Mr. Barnes said that he and my father had become warm friends, drawn together by a common love for the writings of Shakespeare. When they met religion was mentioned only casually. Mr. Barnes had heard of the failures of other clergymen in that direction.

Nevertheless, one day Mr. Barnes invited Papa to attend a service. A visiting minister was going to preach. He was a man of learning and Mr. Barnes thought Papa might enjoy him.

The sermon turned out to be an exhortation to join the church. Had Mr. Barnes known this he would not have asked Papa to attend. The sermon lined the altar with petitioners. To Mr. Barnes's surprise someone said that Judge James was among them.

"I knelt beside him and said how happy I was. I said that I would be glad to receive him at once into the church. 'No, no,' your father said. 'I know the procedure of the Methodist church: six months probation. I wish to be taken in that way.' Your father asked if he might say a few words to the congregation. Standing before the altar he told them that the step he was taking was not without deep reflection; that he knew he had much to live down; that he hoped that during his period of probation he might prove himself worthy, in the eyes of the Lord and of this congregation, to receive the sacrament."

4

I made the rifle team and in June (1908) went to Chandler, the home of Colonel Hoffman, to compete with other company teams for the selection of the State team. Though I had no expectation of making the State team, which always stood high in the national matches, I didn't expect to be dropped on the first elimination, as I was. Actually, my rifle went out of order, after which I never touched the target. I managed, however, to worm onto the pit detail and stay for the rest of the shoot.

One day Colonel Hoffman, noticing the K on my insignia, said: "You're from Enid. What's your name, Corporal?"

It was the first time I had ever been addressed by the regimental commander. When I told my name the colonel asked:

"By any chance are you related to Houstin James?"

"Yes, sir; he is my father."

"That so! Well, give the judge my regards. Used to see a good deal of him in the old days."

A note from Papa contained the barest allusion to my pride-swollen account of the meeting with Colonel Hoffman. "Yes! Chandler is a queer city on a hill, all long and no wide. Be careful and don't fall off. I know many pleasant people there." No mention of the colonel. Gentlemen do not boast.

Long letters came from Mama but from Papa only a few hurried lines at a time. He was so dreadfully busy; working at his office "by electric light." But he hoped that I would continue to write often. "Your letter most eagerly gob'l'd up. What is home without a boy? 'I would rather be a toad &c &c' than be without a boy." "Sorry your gun was crippled & hope you will have better fortune further up the creek." "Well Taft made the heat in fine shape. All Enid threw up their hats. I mean all the faithful." (Some irony in that. Papa had hoped the Republican convention would jump the traces and nominate Roosevelt.) "At no time forget to be a *gentleman*. Consider well the rights of others whether high or low."

Back home I went to work at the bottling works, where they made soda pop. The job paid six dollars a week, nearly twice what I could have got on the *Events*. The income was needed for the program of extra-curricular activity I saw before me at high school.

"Camp" was early that year—in August instead of September. Joyfully exchanging my bottling-works overalls for the uniform of my country, I took off to Guthrie with K Company. The regiment mobilized just outside of town and settled down for a few days of exercises before leaving for the maneuvers at Fort Riley.

One morning we were in formation for battalion drill when an orderly came up. I was called from ranks to answer the telephone at regimental headquarters. At the other end of the wire I heard the kindly Tennessee voice of Doctor McKenzie.

"Marquis," he said, "I have sad news for you. Your father died at 8:05 this morning."

CHAPTER ELEVEN

Background of an Oklahoman

THE clearest recollection that I retain of my father's funeral is of something I saw from the hack window between the house and the church. We were on Broadway, passing Second Street. Lining the walks was a collection of inhabitants of Two Street and of what was left of Happy Hollow after the Park had been cleared of squatters' shacks: Enid's poor people and its outcasts, half of them colored. In honest working clothes, in rags and in Two Street finery, they had assembled to pay tribute to one who had been their disinterested friend.

As for the rest of our community, more appeared at the church than could get in. From what had happened in Guthrie, I must have been prepared for something beyond the ordinary. During the wait at the depot a few people came and spoke to me. That this should have happened in a strange place like Guthrie, and that regimental headquarters should have sent a horse for me to ride to the train—these considerate and unexpected acts made the world seem a friendlier place than I had imagined. Later on, when Mama and I were acknowledging the letters of condolence, resolutions of bar associations, and the action of the City Council (which had named a street for Papa), that feeling gave me something I stood in need of: strength. Particularly I needed it when we began to go into financial matters.

We knew that for better than a year past Papa had been taking in a good deal of money. The night before his death, Mama said, they had been for a drive with a client. Afterwards Mama and Papa sat on the front porch for an hour, talking. It was a satisfactory talk. Papa was going to take Acuff into partnership, and dig no more oil wells. "Rachel, before we know it the boy will be on his own." A nice little law practice, just enough to keep a man reasonably busy, was all Papa'd need to take care of him and Mama the rest of their days. My father done with risking and daring. . . .

The next morning the end of it all came, peacefully, of a heart attack, while Mama was fixing breakfast.

2

Except for one vacant lot, all the real estate we owned turned out to be mortgaged. Interest and taxes were in arrears. There was a note for four hundred and fifty dollars at a bank. In the only bank account my mother knew of there was a balance of twenty-eight dollars. Mr. Acuff said there must be other deposits or investments. My Chicago brother-in-law, Perry, who was an attorney, assumed the obligations against the two houses we rented, said he would sell them and pay Mama the balance. He must have known there would be no balance. It would have taken a lawyer to involve those properties as deeply as Papa had done. That left us with the home place which had only four hundred dollars against it, the note at the bank and miscellaneous debts, footing up to eleven or twelve hundred dollars.

Reckoning my earnings at a dollar a day this seemed a large sum to work off.

Papa's law books and office furniture reduced the home mortgage, settled back taxes and other bills. The odd part was the wrench I felt at seeing those calf-bound volumes go. A few persons who owed for legal services paid up, and that was what we lived on. When voluntary payments ceased Mr. Acuff and Mr. Carl Kruse, a former partner, made a few collections, though efforts in this direction were impeded by the fact that my father had kept his accounts receivable in his head. I worked on Saturdays and after school—at Earle's grocery, at the bottling works, at a candy stand. Using mathematics seriously for the first time in my life, I calculated that my earnings less than paid the interest on what we owed and the taxes on what we owned. These computations were not shown to my mother. As income from collections began to dry up I started to look for a steady job. Mama learned of it and would not hear of my leaving school.

So we decided to sell the piano. Before we could do anything, however, a professional money-lender appeared at the door. He exhibited a chattel mortgage, executed by Jennie Hearn with "our" piano as security. Mr. Acuff found the mortgage valid: something that had slipped Jennie's mind when she turned the instrument over to Papa for a debt. The money-lender was decent. He offered to sell us the mortgage for less than its face value. But I failed in my effort to make a spot sale of the piano for enough to take up the mortgage, and a dray came and hauled the instrument away.

Within a few months I learned more about practical affairs than I had learned in the sum total of my life until then. Certain words in the language assumed the tangibility of things: tax, penalty, interest, discount, attachment, replevin, renewal, grace period, extension. At the bank that held our mortgage I arranged to pay carrying charges and something on the principal each month. The interest was 8 per cent. The bank which held Papa's unsecured note for four hundred and fifty dollars proved harder to deal with. This obligation matured shortly after I took over. Reluctantly the banker consented to renew for ninety days, taking interest in advance at 10 per cent per annum. Mama hoped to sell her lot to take care of the note and have a few hundred dollars over, for Enid real estate was bringing high prices.

At the end of ninety days I had found no buyer—at our figure. Again the banker renewed, still more reluctantly. We were asking too much for the lot, he said. Ninety days later he said he couldn't renew again. We had the assets and should pay. But I managed to persuade him; and three months later to persuade him again. That was the most I could do. When the note came due again he said he'd have to have his money. Mama talked to the banker but she had no luck either. He said real-estate prices would go no higher. They would go the other way. He gave her ten days to take up the note. The lot was sold for six hundred dollars.

Going back to the first winter after my father's death, the thing that kept me in school was the coming of Mr. Frederick. He was a widower with a thirteen-year-old son named Leo. Mr. Frederick offered nine dollars a week for a room and board. Mama said it wasn't much but she'd see how we made out. We made out all right. Father and son were small eaters and more than pleased with our table. A bespectacled carpenter about fifty years of age, Mr. Frederick was a sensible, modest man. He had worked over a good part of the Middle and Mountain West, but he wasn't much of a talker. Of an evening we'd sit about the dining-room stove (to save coal the living room was rarely heated) and try to draw him out. It was a cold winter, with snow and sleet and howling northers. When the weather was too bad for work Mr. Frederick would go through our house with his tools, fixing doors that did not close right and windows that let in the cold.

A carpenter can sense the tapering of a boom as quickly as anyone. Even before our banker had uttered his lugubrious warnings Mr. Frederick and Leo pulled out and we regretted to see them go.

By that time they were enlarging the Rock Island's Maine Street underpass. The boss man came to stay and board with us. He liked it so well that he brought three others. These men ate like horses and Mama raised her prices sharply. We could accommodate no more lodgers, but the reputation of Mama's table spread so that we fed four or five in addition to the roomers.

Aunty came to help and money just rolled in. The bridge finished, this windfall stopped as suddenly as it had started. I was not sorry. It was then summer and I had my first job on a daily newspaper. We drew the line at boarders. We'd be glad to rent out a room but my mother was through standing over a kitchen stove for strangers.

One of the bridge-builders, a hulking shifty-eyed fellow, skipped owing six dollars. He left behind a cardboard suitcase containing a dirty shirt and an Enders Dollar Razor. I had begun to shave, either patronizing a barber every fortnight or using the razor of a schoolmate named Karl Green. (Papa had left no razor. He was shaved at barber shops.) The Enders did me for several years.

3

No other bank account or investments were found. But gradually it came out—at any rate Mr. Acuff broke the news gradually—where so much of Papa's money had been going of late years. It had been going to satisfy obligations contracted in Missouri about the time I was born. "Debts of honor," said Mr. Acuff, explaining that the statute of limitations had long outlawed them. "Blackmail, let's call it to be plain," said Mama when Mr. Acuff mentioned the name of the man to whom the money was paid.

Mama never said what Papa'd done to have been "blackmailed" and I never asked her. But the word and the idea of blackmail made a powerful impression. I could have killed that man had it not been for my father's account of what had taken place in front of the Monarch saloon. My ideas of homicide had been formed when in our part of the country men were killed with impunity for less; that is, taking Mama's spirited assertion at full value. The question would have been important, for what an Oklahoma jury wanted to know in those days was: Did the deceased deserve what he got?

Aside from the lessons anyone can learn from adversity, other benefits flowed from that first hard year. I got to know my mother better: her pluck and energy and common sense. And it is pleasant to note that Mama's humor did not desert her. We found lots to laugh about, really. Mama would laugh over Mr. Frederick's homely expressions until tears came in her eyes. Wiping them with a corner of her apron she would say, "I ought to be ashamed of myself, I reckon."

Once Mama said:

"Marquis, you get right outside and clean up the yard. I won't have this place looking like a widow's."

After that I was always doing things "so this place won't look like a widow's."

Our second winter alone found Mama and me in easier circumstances. Though I was working hard and not home much except to sleep, it seems that most of the time Mama and I did have together was devoted to a protracted serial story I drew from her about my forebears. It began with a letter Mama got—from the president of a little mountain college in the border South. I think he had just heard of Papa's death. Mama went on to tell how she came to know the writer of the letter.

The year after the Civil War Mama was eighteen years old and teaching school in Osceola, Missouri. The countryside had been overrun by partisans of both armies and nearly everyone was poor. One evening when school was out she saw a strange young man crossing the school ground. He wore an obviously new and cheap suit of clothes that was too small (Mama illustrated where the sleeves and trouser legs came), but no shoes. The young man introduced himself. After three years in the army he was working on a farm to save for college. Producing an algebra book he asked if Miss Rachel would be so kind as to help with some problems.

Something about that recital may have brought home to me the last time we had been really close—when I was a child on the claim. Then Mama's stories, largely drawn from her own experience, had meant a great deal to me. On leaving the claim I had found Enid so rich in interests that, as a source of entertainment and enlightenment, Mama had been neglected. I'm pretty sure I didn't think all this out consciously at the time. Most likely, right now, I'm just fishing for a plausible explanation for what happened, which was this: I started Mama on a vein of reminiscence and family chronicle which lasted all winter long and left me with some notion of my predecessors from the time of their arrival in the Colonies to our coming to Oklahoma. The whole thing seemed to make an inexorable kind of sense—even our coming to the Strip.

Having grown up in an ancestorless country I felt none of the prejudices and passions of clanship for the people Mama told about. But I did feel what you might call a sympathetic historical kinship. Otherwise I viewed them with detachment and neutrality. That was true even of my father and mother in their younger years. Except for Papa's financial adventures they weren't the parents I knew. But the sum of what my mother said tended to bring closer the epic of the Westward Movement—in which, after all, I had my own minute place—and to make it more real than all my reading. Or so it seems from this distance.

4

The James family from which my father was descended reached upland Virginia about 1730. Like most early settlers above the "fall line" they were Scotch-Irish, which usually meant people of predominantly Scottish blood who had immigrated to this country from the North of Ireland. Before I knew what or where Virginia was I remember hearing my father say that yes, the Jameses were one of the second or third families of Virginia. I thought that placed us pretty far up the ladder. When old enough to understand that below the F.F.V.s there is only a void I recognized this to be a sample of Papa's way of putting things. Like all new countries the Cherokee Strip was settled by people who for one reason or another had lost out, been run out or weren't doing well enough to suit themselves in the places they came from. It often helps such persons to brag of what they used to have and be. You will appreciate, then, the reason for so little concealment of the fact that First Families, from Virginia and elsewhere, were pretty well represented in our neck of the woods.

My father's allusion to the social standing of his sires had the merit of accuracy. The Jameses were farmers, plain ones, and farmers they remained beyond Papa's day. As nearly as I can learn Papa was the second of our name and strain to break away from the land and adopt a profession. The first to do this would seem to have been Robert James of Logan County, Kentucky, a clergyman with a college education. Two of his sons likewise were able to gain their livelihoods apart from the soil. These were Alexander Franklin and Jesse Woodson James of Missouri. (See how the family was filtering westward?)

At this point, however, I am going back for a moment to Reuben James, of whose exploit in Tripoli Harbor my father told me more than once when I was a small boy. Before writing these pages I decided to dig a little into Reuben's feat, with the object of contributing historical luster to the James name.

I found Reuben and his exploit to be celebrated in song and story—literally. They are mentioned in authoritative naval histories as well as more readable accounts. All the naval immortals of the day—Decatur, Preble, Rodgers, Porter—knew the brave tar, Reuben James. Eventually a destroyer was named for the hero. While en route to Iceland in the autumn of 1941, five weeks before Pearl Harbor, the *Reuben James* was sunk by a German submarine with the loss of ninety-eight lives.

The events which gave Reuben his footnote in history occurred on the night of August 3, 1804. He was one of a picked gunboat crew of twenty-three with which Captain Decatur boarded and captured an enemy vessel. While the prize was being towed away Decatur learned that his brother, commanding another gunboat, had been treacherously killed. Re-entering the harbor Decatur led his men aboard a second enemy craft. In the fight that followed Decatur was knocked down and would have been run through by a Tripolitanian wielding a pike had not a seaman, wounded in both hands, thrust his head between the point of the spear and Decatur's body. In the opinion of chroniclers without number, and of the Navy Department, that seaman was Reuben James.

The gunboat action was neither the first nor the last bloody enterprise in which James risked his life at the side of his reckless commander. Reuben was one of a group of remarkable seamen who followed their adored captain from ship to ship—the *Constitution*, the *Congress*, the *United States*, the *President*.

After Decatur was killed in a duel in 1820 Reuben James stayed on in the Navy. A privileged old sea dog, his fondness for liquor was notorious in a service that took hard drinking for granted. On one occasion he fell ill at sea, and his life was despaired of. The naval historian Maclay recounts that a surgeon decided to ease the veteran's passage into the next world. He asked the old sailor which he'd prefer, brown stout or brandy toddy. The question rekindled Reuben James's interest in life. "Doctor, suppose you give me both."

Whatever the doctor gave him, the tough old salt lived to enter the Naval Hospital in Washington in 1836 where, as a result of an old wound, one of his legs was amputated. He was sixty-one years of age and a bosun's mate. On his recovery, Reuben James's name was stricken from the active list of the Navy and he was awarded a pension of nine dollars and fifty cents a month for "long, faithful and gallant service" in which the action at Tripoli Harbor was mentioned.

In 1875 Admiral Porter, writing his memoirs, remembered that his father, Commodore Porter, had spun many a yarn about Reuben. "The troublesome old rascal," relates the admiral, quoting his father, "had a favorite excuse for tippling. 'I was only celebrating the day I saved Captain Decatur's life.' "

Captain A. S. Mackenzie, who entered the Navy five years before Decatur died, wrote a biography of the great commander which is accepted as standard. After relating the incident of August 3, 1804, he adds that Reuben James's feat "sometimes is ascribed to Daniel Frazier." "After examining all the testimony on the subject," the author concluded that the "real hero" was James.

In 1923 Professor Charles L. Lewis of the history department of the United States Naval Academy brought to light the original manuscript of the surgeon's report of the action in question. It showed that Daniel Frazier had been treated for serious wounds in both hands and for a wound in the head. Reuben James's name did not appear on the list of casualties. Daniel Frazier was retired on a pension soon after the incident in Tripoli Harbor. On this evidence Lewis concludes that Frazier was the real hero.

It is better evidence than Mackenzie produces in favor of James. Officers interviewed by Mackenzie forty years after the event said they had seen a scar on James's head; but it appears that they had merely James's word that he received the scar as a result of the gunboat fight. It seems established that James used to tell that story pretty often—not to make a hero of himself so much as to counteract official consequences of a glass too many.

5

In early-day Virginia the Jameses appear to have been fairly typical settlers of the Piedmont, which is the strip lying between Tidewater and the mountains. They cleared wilderness farms and tilled them—in time, perhaps, with the help of indentured white hands and a few black slaves. They were political followers of Thomas Jefferson with his accent on the rights of man; political adversaries of the Tidewater nabobs with their accent on the rights of property. This got to be such a habit that later on when a few Jameses had laid up something in the way of property they were still shouting for the common man and his current champion, Andrew Jackson.

Jameses joined the west-going tide which followed the Revolution. Threading the green Allegheny passes they spread into Tennessee, Kentucky, and southern Ohio, to begin the pioneering cycle over again. Canvas-covered emigrant wagons were in use in that day, too. And sometimes settlers labeled them. "To Marietta on the Ohio" read a wagon-sheet in 1787.

My father's grandfather, John James, got to the Scioto Valley, in Ohio, around 1815 with a wife and six children. A son, also named John, made an early start at perpetuating the family line in Ohio by marrying when he was nineteen. The bride, aged sixteen, was Cynthia Shoemaker, of real Scioto Valley pioneer stock. Her mother had been born there, when the place was untamed to be sure. She could have seen the 1787 wagon arrive. A letter written by Cynthia in her eightieth year suggests that she could express herself with fair ease on paper and spell correctly—uncommon accomplishments for a Scioto Valley farmer's daughter born in 1813 and making no pretensions to intellectual pursuits. My mother never saw her read anything except the Bible.

The union of John and Cynthia James was blessed by eleven children, all of whom lived to maturity—an extraordinary thing in those days. They must have been tough and Cynthia a good, strong mother. Of this brood my father was the seventh, born December 18, 1844. He was named for Houston Westfall, a tall and adventuresome Blue Ridge Virginian who had appeared in the Valley a few years before and married Cynthia's sister Betsy. Houston Westfall's mother was a Houston—of the Virginia clan, one of whose members, General Sam Houston of the Texas Republic, was much in the public eye at the time of my father's birth.

Writing his son's name in the Bible, John James spelled it "Houstin." John James didn't tamper with what was written in a Bible: "Houstin" the baby was, for life. Papa used to say this was a convenience he wouldn't take a good deal for. A letter addressed to "Houston" James could be read at leisure, because it couldn't be from anyone who knew him very well. When my sister Nan's third baby was named Houstin there was a confab on the spelling. The "i" was retained. So those things go.

After the birth of her eleventh child, in 1859, Cynthia James announced that she was going to take it easy the rest of her days. She could afford it, her husband being one of Pike County's rich men. Cynthia was then forty-six. Church work and knitting were her sole occupations nine years later when my mother went to Pike County as a bride. A visit or two with her daughter Ruhama, who lived in Columbus at the head of the valley, were the only occasions to take Cynthia more than a day's horseback ride from her birthplace. This scheme of life agreed with Cynthia James, who died on January 1, 1915, ten days short of a hundred and two. She was the only grandparent of mine I ever saw to remember; that in 1903.

The Jameses advertised their religion and their politics. My father had brothers named Charles Wesley and Thomas Jefferson and an uncle named Andrew Jackson. When the currents which led to the Civil War were reshuffling political parties, the family, like many northern Jackson Democrats, became Republicans. On the ticket which Lincoln headed in 1860 John James was elected county auditor.

My mother was struck by the abundance amid which the Jameses lived, and on that score Mama would not have been so easy to bowl over. When a child of his married, John James's practice was to stake the couple to living expenses for one year. This was a big help to my father who had not completed his legal education. John James's farms were scattered up and down his part of the fertile valley. He would ride on horseback from one to another, looking things over. Mama often rode with him. The pleasant old farmer and his new daughter-in-law, regarded as a little overly fashionable by some of her James connections, hit it off from the first. John James had a humorous streak in him, and that was one of the things Mama liked.

When hymns were sung his baritone voice could be heard all over the little Beaver Chapel in which services were held by a circuit-rider every other Sunday. John James and his father-in-law, Peter Shoemaker, had defrayed the cost of building this house of worship. The preacher nearly always had dinner and spent the night at the James homestead. An assortment of sons and daughters and other kin and connections would be there. I have heard my mother say that fifty persons have been fed at "Father" James's on Sunday. In the busy seasons of a farmer's year there would be a "hired girl" or two, treated exactly as members of the family. At other times John's daughters, daughters-in-law and granddaughters cooked and served these feasts.

On Christmas John James's children came home with their broods. I have listened to Mama describe those reunions in detail but the thing that still sticks out in my mind was the presence of a *barrel* of candy for the kids.

6

My mother's people, too, came from Virginia: Tidewater and mountain stock, mixed. They owned land, naturally, but in the Tidewater branch was a sprinkling of physicians and clergymen. Though the name Marquis is French the pronunciation was anglicized long before I had anything to do with it. The couple who transplanted the name to these shores were Huguenots, though religion was not the reason for their departure from France. According to the story my mother heard, they left because the young fellow wished to marry a daughter of a Parisian silk merchant. His high-flying family did not approve because her folks were "in trade." He married her anyhow and with her money they went to the British Isles and then to Virginia, arriving about 1720. On the flight from France the young people traveled under the name "Marquis," which was not their real name. On this side of the water they stuck to it.

My mother's father, James Marquis, was born in Westmoreland County in 1806. His father had a stable of fast horses and a wine cellar, which seemed to him enough to occupy the time of a Tidewater squire. The youth, James, didn't care for that kind of life. He was critical of the institution of slavery and interested in the thriving young free states of the West. After taking a medical degree at the University of Pennsylvania, James married a girl he had met on a summer visit to the home of a classmate.

Her name was Mary Cosner, but she was always called Polly; and Hardy County was her home. The Westmoreland Marquises thought poorly of this match—with a mountain girl who didn't know how to enter a drawing room. Notwithstanding that the Marquises were running short of ready cash, the satisfactory size of Polly's dot seems not to have altered their opinion.

Polly Cosner's father, Jacob, was born in Vermont. His parents had come from Germany before the Revolution. About 1795 Jacob appeared in Hardy County, where he worked for seven years (it sounds like an indenture) for a farmer named Conrad

Hawk and then married his employer's daughter Barbara. This Conrad Hawk (who must have spelled it Hauck, originally) and his wife Hannah had been born and married in one of the German states. They came here on a wave of "Pennsylvania Dutch" immigration which spilled over into the part of Virginia where, under a series of local names, the Allegheny Mountains have their beginning in the ridges that form the western wall of the fruitful Shenandoah Valley. In Hardy County the lesser valleys between the ridges were likewise fruitful. Jacob and Barbara Cosner prospered—in a region where wealth on the Tidewater scale was unknown and which was developing the independent type of life peculiar to the mountain Southerner. The unprofitable nature of slave labor on their rugged farms gave hill Virginians little in common with their lowland countrymen. For all his prosperity, if Jacob Cosner owned many Negroes he was a rarity among his neighbors.

But his Tidewater son-in-law owned several slaves, which he freed in return for their promise to go west and work for him a while. The young couple settled on the western border of Ohio and a few years later, in 1834, pushed on to northeastern Indiana, which was the jumping-off place from civilization.

The Marquises' first residence in Indiana was a split-log cabin, their second a five-room house of lumber cut at a water-power mill which the doctor had erected. It was the only sawmill within thirty miles. About the same time he set up a gristmill. Those little industries must have made measurable contributions to the development of a frontier where civilized comforts were the products of an evolution achieved on the spot from the materials at hand rather than moved in ready-made from the outside as soon as the settlers could afford them—as largely happened in the Cherokee Strip, which went from the wigwam and sod-house era to the chamber-of-commerce era within one boy's memory.

In the five-room house, a mile from the village of West Liberty, my mother, Rachel Leo Marquis, was born July 14, 1848. She was the ninth of ten children, seven of whom grew up. By that time James Marquis was pretty much a part of the countryside, which was filling up and developing fast. He knew it as only a doctor, living in the saddle, could know any country. James Marquis bred and rode the best horses on that part of the border. Sometimes he filled the pulpits in log churches. He helped to organize Jay County. During a yellow-fever epidemic he answered a call from New Orleans for physicians. He was active in the temperance crusade and the anti-slavery movement in whose interest he made trips through the South, lecturing. The national leader of the anti-slavery forces was another southern-born man, James G. Birney, for whom Doctor Marquis named a son.

When my mother was eight, money troubles overtook another Virginia immigrant who had started to build in West Liberty a residence that was to be the wonder of that frontier. The house stood unfinished. Back in Hardy County Jacob Cosner had lately breathed his last. A large inheritance passed to Polly Marquis who bought and completed the busted Virginian's mansion—a pillared southern-style affair of sixteen rooms. Wagonload after wagonload of furnishings made the long land-and-water journey from the East. It was as if such a house had appeared on our claim a couple of years after the Run.

There being no inn in West Liberty, the house became a stopping place for travelers, notable and otherwise. My mother especially remembered a white-bearded, buckskin-clad old French trapper, the last survivor thereabouts of the *voyageurs* who were the first white men in the region. He would venture no farther inside the awesome abode than the kitchen, and there await the return of the doctor. The old man was sick only for someone to talk French to.

Another Jay County character was Johnny Appleseed—in the flesh. One of his famous nurseries flourished in the Wabash bottom fifteen miles from James Marquis's farm. This strange man, whose name was John Chapman, had appeared in Indiana with two bushels of apple seeds on the back of an ox. He planted a string of clearings which was an extension of a string already established in Ohio. He spent his time ranging on foot over the two or three hundred miles the clearings covered. Though these nurseries represented a considerable value in money, Johnny Appleseed never slept in a bed, ate at a table, wore a sound garment or called any particular spot his home. Sagas were gathering about him already. It was said that Johnny could walk up to wild animals and that snakes would not bite him. Indians and poor whites had faith in his ability to effect cures with roots and herbs. Johnny sold his seedlings to those who could pay. To others he gave them. Hundreds of orchards resulted. I am not aware whether the apple trees on James Marquis's place were of Johnny's planting but it's nice to know that they might have been.

The last three years of the Civil War my mother spent at Liber College, of which her father was one of the founders. Doctor Marquis, aged fifty-six, and Birney, seventeen, had ridden away in a cavalry regiment. The father returned first, emaciated by dysentery which he suffered from the rest of his life. Hoping to benefit by a milder climate, he sold most of the Indiana holdings and the family departed for Missouri in February 1866. A farm was purchased near the village of Eldorado Springs, in Cedar County, and five brood mares and a stallion were brought from Indiana to stock it. Two venerable Negroes, Uncle Abe and Aunt Ida, who had been Marquis slaves in Virginia, accompanied the family on the migration.

James Marquis's eldest son, Adonijah, was practicing medicine in near-by Osceola, Missouri, where he had settled before the war. That part of Missouri had got a head start on the rest of the country in the matter of hurrying up the Civil War. There were clashes between northern and southern partisans a year before Sumter. The band championing the cause of the Union to which Nige Marquis attached himself was led by a Virginian named Houston Westfall, who, on his way west, had taken a wife in Ohio. After one foray Houston Westfall and a sixteen-year-old son contracted pneumonia while hiding out and died within a week of each other. Doctor Nige Marquis married Sarah Ellen Westfall, a daughter of the late night-rider. About then the war started in earnest and the young husband joined the Army.

With the best of the menfolks away in the army of their choice, home guards of both persuasions in Missouri degenerated into marauding parties. Their bushwhacking conflicts were still going on when the real soldiers returned after Appomattox. Before long former Yanks and former Rebs were riding together in pursuit of bushwhackers who were becoming frankly outlaws.

This was the state of affairs when my mother arrived in Missouri at the age of seventeen. The life was so exhilarating that she decided not to return to Indiana for her last few months of college. A good many of the young men she met at dances had been in the Confederate Army. Rather to her surprise she found herself liking some of them almost as well as those who had worn the blue. The only disappointing feature about the dances was the fact that Mama's prettiest frocks, bought in St. Louis as the family passed through, were not worn that winter. None of the Missouri girls had new dresses. Some of the young men wore the jackets of their uniforms.

To be nearer the center of things Mama got herself a job teaching school in Osceola, where her brother practiced. The next year James Marquis insisted she turn over the position to the widow of a Confederate soldier, thinking this would bring his daughter home. But she obtained a place conducting the rural Brush Creek School, within riding distance of Osceola's parties.

7

Along Brush Creek there was plenty to talk about. Lately freed Negroes camped in a thicket where it was said the Samuels and the Younger Negroes hid the James boys and the Younger brothers when pursuit got too hot. The Samuels Negroes were former slaves of Doctor Reuben Samuels, stepfather of Frank and Jesse James. The Reverend Robert James, father of these young men, had died in California in 1855, whither he had gone in a composite search for gold and sinners. He seems to have been the first James to cross the continent.

In 1867 it was hard to catalogue the James and the Younger brothers. Although fugitives, they were not outlaws in the minds of most Missourians of southern sympathies. Their prolongation of the War Between the States found sincere apologists: that conflict could have no satisfactory end until the James brothers had caught up with the northern rogues in uniform who had visited the Samuels farm on a certain occasion. Mrs. Samuels had been carried off by the intruders, Jesse, fifteen, flogged with a rope end, and Doctor Samuels hanged by the neck but cut down when only half dead. His back still sore, Jesse James joined his brother Frank with Quantrill's guerrillas, who had no more regard for the amenities of warfare than the Union band which had raided the Samuels place. After the war Quantrill hadn't even a Confederate flag to wave over his depredations.

On Saint Valentine's Day in 1867 twelve mounted men drifted into Liberty, Missouri, by several roads. Two dismounted and entered the Clay County Savings Institution. Three sat on their horses outside. The other seven patrolled near-by streets. When the two rushed from the bank and leaped into their saddles all pulled out six-shooters and began blazing away over people's heads as they tore for open country giving the Rebel yell: "Yip! Yip! Yaw-aw-aw!" The few shots that went after them missed. By an accident of marksmanship on the part of one of the riders a student on his way to classes at William Jewell College was killed. The brief visit cost the bank seventy-two thousand dollars.

Within the next three months similar scenes were enacted at Lexington, Savannah, and Richmond, Missouri. These events raised the curtain on an important chapter of criminal history in the United States: bank robbery in the daytime. To this was presently added train robbery. The forty years during which daylight bank robbery and train robbery ranked as the West's most respected crimes of violence brought few alterations of the technique displayed by the Missouri innovators. This is not because train and bank robbers were more conservative than other people. It is because the Missourians set a pattern difficult to improve.

It seems impossible that Frank or Jesse James could have been present during the episode at Liberty; and an impartial historian must cast some doubt on the stories which make them parties to the other banking transactions alluded to. It appears certain, however, that all these were the work of old Quantrill men, of whom Jesse presently became the leader. Nevertheless, the Jameses were accused at the time and, as these affairs had resulted in the deaths of several citizens, the stepsons of Doctor Samuels had the discretion to depart from home and keep their itineraries reasonably confidential.

The Brush Creek School was twenty-five miles from her father's farm, and Mama had not been home for five weeks. A Saturday came when she said she was going, whether or no. As the Sac River was high her brother said he would see her across the ford, six miles from Osceola. At the last moment a sick call prevented Nige from accompanying his sister. She promised to turn back should she find no one at the ford to lead her mare across.

At the river Mama waited for some little time. The stream was a torrent, filled with driftwood. At length a horseman arrived by a woodland path which joined the main road at the ford. His mount was a fine black, with silver on the martingale. My mother did not give a second thought to the pistols on either side of the rider's saddle horn; her father and her brother carried arms on their professional visits. Her glance was for the stranger—an attractive, slender young man of a little more than middle height. When he removed his hat she saw that dark hair went with his intent blue eyes. His accent was southern. Mama was glad that she, too, was well mounted, and, moreover, was wearing a new riding habit.

The stranger assured her that he knew the ford and would be honored to lead her mare across. Mama passed over her hitching strap. The stranger removed his feet from his stirrups and crossed them on his horse's neck. Mama gathered up her skirts and perched on the top of her sidesaddle. The mare started to frisk but the stranger's soft, authoritative voice quieted the animal. In the middle of the river was a shoal where they paused for a moment to survey the flood, my mother enjoying a delightful sensation of security in the midst of danger.

For a mile or so on the yonder side of the river the road wound through woodland, trees towering on either side. The stranger set the pace, which was a canter almost too brisk for conversation. Then came open, rolling country with long views in every direction. The stranger slackened the gait of his mount. Mama found herself chatting gaily. She spoke enthusiastically of her school and mentioned her brother in Osceola.

The stranger said he had heard the Young Doctor highly spoken of; and, of course, the Old Doctor, too. His regret at not knowing them personally was the keener now that he had had the pleasure of this chance meeting with their sister and daughter.

Mama took this as a pretty little Missouri compliment and said, "Thank you, sir."

In no time, it seemed, they were passing through the hamlet of Roscoe, ten miles from the river. The stranger reined up.

"My horse needs shoeing," he said, removing his hat.

They said good-by and with a bound the black horse was off toward the blacksmith shop which stood a piece down a side road.

Mama rode on. She had told the attractive stranger she hoped they might meet again. A little disappointed that even this hint should have failed to elicit his name, Mama wondered if she had behaved too boldly, and decided not to mention the incident at home.

Next morning my mother breakfasted late with her father who had been absent most of the night.

His news of the countryside included the fact that Jesse James had had his horse shod at Roscoe yesterday, where a posse missed him by an hour. In a small voice Mama asked what Jesse James and his horse looked like. Amid blushes—Mama blushed easily—she told of the fording of the Sac.

The Old Doctor looked rather grave. He was particular of the company his daughters kept. At length he said:

"Under the circumstances, Sis, you were as safe with Jesse James as with any man in these parts."

8

The man who disturbed the Old Doctor at the moment was named Houstin James.

Home from the war, Captain Houstin James, twenty years old,

had announced his intention to prepare for the bar. A pleased father saw the young man on his way to law school in Cincinnati. At the end of the first term, instead of returning to Pike County, the student rode to Osceola, Missouri, to visit his Aunt Betsy, widow of the late Houston Westfall. Betsy Westfall introduced her nephew to her son-in-law, Doctor Nige Marquis, at whose home Rachel Marquis was staying. That was how my mother and my father met.

When autumn came Captain James—as they still called him—did not return to Cincinnati. He was more interested in the mistress of the Brush Creek School than in the law. He, himself, got a job teaching a neighboring school, and declared that he would remain in Missouri until accepted or rejected as a suitor. The reason he was not accepted, after a polite interval, was that James Marquis had sized up Captain James as too irresponsible for a daughter of his. Despite the fact that Nige Marquis took the captain's part the old gentleman would not budge—that is, for several weeks.

Various stratagems to get his daughter to return to college, to go traveling, etc., having failed, the Old Doctor obtained her promise that she would not marry for a year. The captain stayed in Missouri and made good use of that year. At the end of twelve months James Marquis gave his reluctant consent and in October 1868 my mother and my father were married.

Four years later it seemed as if the Old Doctor had misjudged his son-in-law. Rachel was the happy mother of two baby girls and her husband the busiest attorney in Piketon, Ohio. Old John James had been able to throw his son business from the start and, best of all, to show him how to invest money in land. The family moved to Waverly where Houstin James became counsel for James Emmitt, banker, distiller, canal boat and railroad owner—Pike County's only millionaire. The young lawyer ran for county judge and despite a Democratic landslide came so near to election that he was called "judge" the rest of his life.

When John James was buried in the yard of Beaver Chapel my father became his own adviser in the matter of investment. It was a time of economic depression and financial chaos. For a while he appeared to do well on those troubled waters. Then losses came. Good money went after bad. Ten years after his marriage he was penniless. Though law practice had been neglected in the interest of disastrous finance, Papa was among friends—in the county where he had been born and reared. Jim Emmitt's business alone amounted to a living. But there was something in my father that made it difficult for him to maintain a stand on a field where he had been beaten. Against every persuasion he moved to Hamilton, near Cincinnati, a larger place where he said he would recoup his fortunes more quickly.

He did recoup them. In the presidential campaign of 1880 he bore a local part in support of a fellow-Ohioan, James A. Garfield, which called for reward. The reward President Garfield suggested was a handsome one for a country lawyer thirty-six years of age. It was that Papa should be minister to China. Four months after taking office James A. Garfield was shot by a demented crank. His successor in the White House had political obligations of his own.

Shortly Papa was in financial hot water again. James Marquis died and my mother's inheritance came in time to be swallowed up.

My father accepted Doctor Nige Marquis's invitation to start anew in Osceola, Missouri. When Papa decided he had gone as far as a lawyer could go in Osceola, another local attorney, named John H. Lucas, proposed that they move to Kansas City and set up together. The project fell through because each lawyer wanted to be the senior partner. Mr. Lucas went alone to Kansas City and became a leader of its bar. Papa went to Springfield, Missouri, in the heart of the beautiful Ozarks, and did rather well. But not well enough to suit himself. Oklahoma was a word that gripped the imagination of the Southwest. In the Choctaw tongue Okla-homa means "the red people." Indians believed in the power of names to foster the ideas they expressed. Possibly Oklahoma was designed as a weapon against paleface intrusion. But by the eighties the land-hungry whites regarded it as another word for alchemy. In the spring of '89 a part of the cluster of counties called in my day Old Oklahoma was carved out of the Indian

Territory and thrown open to white settlement by means of a Run similar, though smaller, to that in the Cherokee Strip four years later. Papa went down. He returned without a fortune.

I was born in Springfield in 1891, the fifth child and the third surviving. Rumblings of fresh money troubles arrived about the time I did: Papa had invested in a lead mine. The crash came seven months later. This time it was complete. The family and the home disintegrated. My father went back to Oklahoma. My eldest sister, Zoe, got married. Nan lit out and landed a job in Chicago. Mama and I were taken under the roof of a second cousin, Isaac Marquis of Louisiana, Missouri. A quirk of fate saved this from an act of pure charity. Doctor Isaac Marquis was Mama's brother-in-law as well as her cousin. His wife, my mother's youngest sister, had died leaving three small children. Doc Ike needed someone to superintend his household. Nevertheless it was humiliating enough. What James Marquis feared had come to pass.

Polly Marquis died at the age of eighty. On occasions the old lady had not spared the feelings of her homeless daughter; nor had some of the other Marquises. She left a will in which Mama's name did not appear.

9

Of my father's year and a half in Old Oklahoma and the Indian Territory I know almost nothing except that he didn't get rich. That was not altogether to his discredit. In the Indian country available clients were outlaws and Indians. Indian business was by a long shot the more profitable. Trace the histories of some of the lawyers who enriched themselves caring for the interests of Indian clients and your opinion of outlaws is apt to go up.

Mama and I arrived in the Cherokee Strip six months after the Run. It had been a wearisome, roundabout journey, involving two or three changes of cars and tedious waits in wretched weather.

We reached North Town in the nighttime. In a buoyant mood Papa met us, his pockets stuffed with trinkets and candy. Mama said I went after the candy but otherwise seemed in awe of the tall, weatherbeaten stranger in a western Stetson who bounced me on his knee and sang "Old Dan Tucker" while the stage creaked to South Town.

As something had delayed the completion of our residence, it would be necessary to tarry at a hotel in Enid. Papa had written so expansively of Enid that Mama was a trifle let down to find that half of its edifices were tents. Papa grandly pointed out the Rex Hotel—not habitable owing to its unfinished state—but then our accommodations were at the Montezuma. Nor was the Montezuma altogether finished, because of difficulties experienced in freighting lumber from North Town. "Rooms" had been created by hanging calico curtains from ropes stretched a little higher than a man's head. After a few nights Mama said it was good to get a glimpse of the house under the bare branches of the mammoth cottonwood on the claim. The absence of a stairway—a deficiency of the moment only, as Papa made clear—was not hard to overlook.

Among the things I read in the newspaper accounts of my father's death was that he had saved the day for Enid at one stage of the North Town War by averting the loss of the county seat, which was South Town's principal asset. A bond issue having failed, my father induced a number of South Town men of means to build privately a two-story brick courthouse and rent it to the county for enough to reimburse themselves over a term of years. The structure was ready in time to forestall the removal of the county offices to the rival settlement. The rental was less than the county was paying at the time for makeshift quarters. It is pleasant to record that one of Papa's financial strokes panned out.

Counties in the Cherokee Strip originally were designated by letters of the alphabet, it being understood that the settlers would choose permanent names. Ours was O County. As chairman of the Board of Commissioners my father shared the labors of making the county a going concern. These included christening it. He suggested the name Garfield. Other proposals were offered but Papa stuck to Garfield. This was a little surprising. In naming the townships he had displayed no such pride of opinion except when he called one for Jack Jones's little girl Garland.

The county-name issue brought on a controversy which threatened to obscure more important matters. Papa was asked to recede from his stand on Garfield. He declined. The question went on the ballot at the next general election and Garfield won by a small margin.

CHAPTER TWELVE

The Gang at Waumpie Washburn's

FOR a boy working all the spare time he could find work to do and so poor that it looked as if he would have to leave school, my junior year at Enid High was a mess of contradictions. I was in every form of school doings except athletics, and that was given up largely because I was not good enough for the football or baseball team. Clothes became increasingly important and I managed to dress almost as conspicuously as any boy in school. Gambling began and I would drop as much as a dollar at a session of kelly pool, a big loss even for Horace Copple, the showiest plunger in Enid High's fast set. My position in West Side society was so well established that I ceased to think of it.

All this took mazuma: tin, spondoolix, shekels; a roll, a wad, the rhino, the do-re-mi. It was money that talked at Waumpie

Washburn's, where balls clicked, nickels and dimes spun on the green cloth, and so many of our in-and-out-of-school plans were hatched.

Provision for these activities became the *sine qua non* of my financial management. This made for certain ambiguities in the fiscal statements which from time to time I exhibited to my mother. Bookkeeping fictions were of two kinds, which about canceled each other. We had on hand approximately the amounts the books showed, though not in the way they showed. I kept to one side a secret fund of eight or ten dollars earmarked for the business of holding up my end with the high steppers at school. To our acknowledged assets I would add ten or fifteen nonexistent dollars to keep Mama from worrying. Should the acknowledged assets get down to where nothing remained except the fictitious part, I intended to leave school. At length this happened. The only cash in our possession was a ten-dollar bill belonging to my secret fund. A show came to the Loewen which all our crowd was taking in. Orchestra seats were a dollar and a quarter. Sometimes I could bum tickets off Mike Crouse but on this occasion Crouse had other uses for his comps. Including street-car fares and sodas at Weisenburger's after the show, that evening set me back exactly three bucks.

From the home of the girl I had taken on this round of pleasure it was a mile and a half to our house. Probably I would have hoofed it anyhow to save a nickel but this time I wanted time to think. The night was raw and blustery. With my hands in my pockets (Crouse was about the only boy who sported gloves) and my head scrooched down in order to get my ears inside the collar of my thin overcoat, I stumped past the dark houses on West Randolph trying to decide what to do. After all, hadn't I possibly been a shade ridiculous—blowing three bucks of the only ten Mama and I had in the world?

With an involuntary shrug I banished the discreditable thought. I could hold up my end. Heck, what was I learning at school, anyhow?

A few days before—just in case—I'd dropped around to the *Eagle*. Mr. Harrison, the city editor, couldn't promise anything right away. Well, I had to have something right away. That meant working for Mr. Earle full time, driving the grocery wagon. OK; but first I'd wait two or three days. Something might turn up.

Mr. Fredericks came and there was a windfall from Papa's office.

2

The year's towering landmark was the establishment of the school paper, the *Quill*, by Crouse, Copple and me. The three of us came forward with a good plan and had things pretty much our way. But not entirely. Mr. Wright, the principal, insisted that as a matter of fixed policy the editor-in-chief should be a senior. His choice was "the illustrious and ever present Mr. Greene." Or so my diary characterized Karl Green, the outstanding member of the senior class. Determined to make his job "a senacure," I cooked up a plot for ignoring my superior in the production of the paper.

Though Green presided at staff meetings, Crouse, Copple and I did all the talking. We issued orders right and left, filling the air with print-shop and newspaper-office jargon. The staff was thoroughly cowed—all but Green, who, darn it all, just sat there with a detached, pleasant grin on his mug, and went through the motions of running the meetings. In his distinct, agreeable voice Green would say: "Shall we consider as ratified all that McKinley has so expeditiously done for us?" Green called us old newspapermen by our first names—our full first names—as if we were strange little boys. "I am sure that we are in Marquis's and Horace's debt for their patient professional criticism."

After the final meeting before putting the first issue to bed, Karl invited the three of us to his house, which contained the only billiard table in Enid not in a public pool hall. As none of his guests played billiards, Karl arranged the table for pool and relieved us of our spare change at a few games of kelly. The little session made for better acquaintance. First names were dropped. Walking home I observed judicially:

"You know, we might make a newspaperman out of him yet."

I had heard of Karl Green when I was a small boy on the claim. Mrs. Ackerman described him as an "infant prodigy" and a "genius." Mrs. Ackerman also spoke the first good word I ever heard for Karl's father, Godless Green, the atheist. Mr. Green had bought up claims near hers until he was perhaps the largest landowner in the county. No claims were better stocked with animals and farm machinery and none better managed. Mr. Green was generous with what he had, always helping his less fortunate neighbors, which meant all his neighbors. "Kind of another Jim Utsler," was Mama's comment on Mrs. Ackerman's recital.

In only one thing did Mr. Green resemble Jim Utsler: his liberality. Godless Green did not use tobacco, liquor or profanity. He wore good clothes, but even after he moved to Enid and built the big house on West Oak he wore them with the air of a dressed-up farmer. The expression on Mr. Green's face I have never seen quite duplicated. He inclined his head a little to one side, giving his countenance an inquiring expression. There was also a look of abstraction and simplicity. He spoke in a low, soft, deliberate voice. His language was scholarly and his manner courteous. But while he was talking to you, you got the idea that Mr. Green was thinking of something miles away.

I wondered how the name "Godless" got hitched on to him: hardly because he did not go to church; my father had rarely gone to church. Could it have been the consequence of envy—of his learning, his unobtrusive ability to make money, or his generosity, coupled with the uncomfortable feeling his politely distant manner gave you? Many years later Karl told me that after studying the Bible until he knew it as well as many preachers and after informing himself on all the great religions, his father had simply come to the conclusion that there was no God and no heaven and no hell.

People blamed "Gran'ma" Green more than they did Mr. Green. They said that she was an infidel and had poisoned the mind of her son.

I didn't know what to make of this, either. Gran'ma Green—"Grandmother," I called her, as Karl did—was one of the remarkable old women of my experience. She must have been in her eighties, and she read Latin and Greek. I got to know Grandmother Green as well as any outsider. She was born in Connecticut and had been educated in New York City; and she lived like a hermit with her son, her grandson, and her books. Whether she believed in God I do not know. How the town came by its convictions was hard to figure out, unless from the fact that Gran'ma wore black satin dresses at home on weekdays.

With subsequent issues of the *Quill* the editor-in-chief had more to do. "I told you fellows we'd make a newspaperman of him."

Karl Green and I became inseparable. He was the only boy I knew whose reading was more extensive than mine. It was much more extensive. His knowledge of Greek mythology amazed me—though on that score I wasn't hard to amaze. Green was more at home with the dwellers on Olympus than with the dwellers of Enid.

Lounging in his room one day, rolling and smoking brown-paper cigarettes with a window open so the smell would go out, we fell to talking about poetry. I had assumed that Green was familiar with my published works. But he didn't seem to be. I said nothing and let him go on talking. It was instructive talk, interspersed with quotations from poets who were just names to me. As I say, I let him talk and at length he got around to the fact that he himself had dashed off a bit of verse. I asked to see some of it. Finally he got it out. With the air of a person competent to judge, I took the sheaf of manuscripts and began to read. Why, there were even verses written in Latin. Original? "Oh, sure," drawled Karl, "something I tossed off by way of an experiment in meter." I confined myself to those written in English. Enthralled, I read until Green took the sheets from my hands.

"Let's go shoot a little pool," he said.

Was I lucky not to have mentioned that drivel of mine in the *Events!*

In the springtime Green and I would walk to the edge of town, lie in a pasture, think thoughts too big for our heads, and talk about everything under the sun. Karl disclaimed any intention of ever having a poem published. I could not get him to put one in the *Quill*. He aimed to be a farmer, like his father.

Until he began to get thick with me, Karl's only intimate was Kendall Webb. They made a curious combination. Green was below average height, slender and strong: the only schoolboy of my acquaintance who knew much about the science of boxing as opposed to slugging. And he was handsome: straight black hair and gray-green eyes; a trace of his father's dreamy, withdrawn look; more than a trace of his father's low, distinct, correct speech. He dressed well, though not in the flashy mode most of us affected. Kendall Webb was a house painter, six feet tall and so powerfully built he seemed about to burst from his clothes. He had a short neck and a large flat face to which a broken nose imparted a battered look. I was jealous of Webb and could not make out what Green saw in him.

3

A salutary result of the association with Karl Green was the improvement of my pool game. The practice I got on his table made me a winner at Waumpie Washburn's. The time was when I had had no more ambition to become a pool shark than I had to become a saloon loafer. When the saloons went with the coming of statehood, the church people continued to agitate for the closing of the pool halls. I had been brought up with the notion that a pool hall was a sinkhole of sin. After prohibition some of them became blind tigers. But there were at least two pool halls in Enid which were neither blind tigers nor, so far as I could see, sinkholes of sin.

One was the Salty Dog, owned by Bill Kimmell who also managed the Railroaders, Enid's professional baseball club. The ball players who hung out there were, of course, drawing cards for the Salty Dog. Scores of all the games in the Western Association were posted by innings. The last summer that Papa was alive I got to going there to watch the score board. One afternoon Papa came in. He sat down beside me and asked how the games were going. He didn't say a thing about finding me in a pool hall. A few afternoons later I was at his office. Pushing aside the papers on his desk he removed his spectacles and said: "Boy, let's walk over to the Salty Dog, have a Dr. Pepper and watch the games for a while."

Another pool hall where you couldn't buy whiskey was Waumpie Washburn's, the hangout of the high-school boys. A stock greeting to the proprietor was, "Anything for me, Waumpie?" for Mr. Washburn served as a medium of communication, always carrying in his head half a dozen messages: Kendrick wants Francisco to leave the catcher's mitt; Harp wants his Cicero pony back from whoever took it; Counts wants to know if Goltry can get the auto for the Congenial dance.

The *Quill* was practically edited at Waumpie Washburn's. Dates were made over his telephone. We rolled poker dice for boxes of candy for our girls, to see whether we paid double or nothing. Suppose a fellow'd been stung three or four times running. Waumpie'd slide a pound of chocolates across the top of the glass case. "On the house," he'd say. Days before an important dance we'd carry our girls' programs to Waumpie's and swap them around and fill them out.

Now and then something outside the orbits of our personal concerns would be worthy of attention—as when Claude, who played for the house, was taking on an out-of-town shark or maybe some home product who played a good-enough game of pool to make it interesting. Claude had the most desirable wardrobe of any person of my immediate acquaintance: three or four Klassy Kut suits and a different fancy vest with pearl buttons for every day in the week. Claude took his opposition over more often than it took him over. One night a member of the Dirty Dozen from a bootlegging hall down the street took Claude over, though. Waumpie was sore—not because Claude'd lost but because Waumpie's orders were that you couldn't play a Dirty

Dozener in his hall. Several of us remonstrated. Claude ought to have a chance to get even.

"Nope," said Waumpie. "I run a decent joint. Haven't had a kick from any of you boys' folks yet." He knocked wood. "But I will have if the Dozen gets to flocking here."

Waumpie wouldn't let Claude play any of us kids for money: only practice, loser paying for the game. Claude would take endless pains demonstrating complicated shots. The last time I saw one of our old crowd he was playing for the house in a hall on Olive Street in St. Louis.

A good many of us aspired to a wardrobe like Claude's, but Horace Copple was the only one who realized that aspiration. This was because Copple's father took out in trade the cost of a good deal of advertising in his throw-away newspaper, the *Square Deal*. I can recall no other year of my life when clothes filled so prominent a niche in the scheme of things. Originating in the colleges, if my memory serves, the overnight transformation of young men's suits was like that from grub to butterfly. What had been coat, pants and vest, undeserving of more detailed mention, bloomed into a gorgeous ensemble. The pants were peg top: they stood out from the hip on either side as if you had a couple of summer squash, small ends down, in your pockets. From this extensive circumference the legs tapered to three-inch cuffs worn high enough to show about two inches of socks. The cuffs were so snug that you had to put your pants on before your box-toed shoes. The coats were more intricate works of art: long and dipped in front almost to the knees. Pockets had ornamental flaps, and there were other trimmings. And if you could set this off with a fancy vest—

Boys who had never given a clothing-store window a second glance would hang out in front of Meibergen & Godschalk's and Harry B. Woolf's discussing the relative merits of Hart, Schaffner and Marx, Kuppenheimer Clothes, and Society Brand. It was generally conceded, however, that the epitome of refinement was achieved by Klassy Kut alone.

Luck was with me or the financial stringency at home would have made it impossible to keep up with the real swell dressers.

In the first place Sister Zoe sent me a suit from Chicago—a Society Brand costing more than most Enid boys' suits cost. It offered in richness what Klassy Kut had in style. Along in the spring I needed another suit, and calculated my chances to acquire a Klassy Kut. They were twenty fish and up. All I could scrape together was nine dollars, for which I managed, in a little store off the Square, to bag a pretty fair imitation, the merchant taking my overcoat in trade. That handsome garment had been purchased from Jay Radcliffe for five dollars. As his brother Earle had worn it for four years at the University of Oklahoma, you can see that it was saturated in campus tradition. In my day a young fellow with a healthy circulation didn't have much use for an overcoat in Oklahoma.

One did come in handy, though, when you took a spin in an automobile. That old plains wind would sure go through you. A lap robe over your knees wasn't enough. The important thing, naturally, was to see that none of the girls got a chill. Yes, the motor car was sure changing things; it was going to change our whole civilization, Herschel Goltry said oracularly.

When he began asking me to go to parties and dances in his father's automobile, I reviewed my long-standing dislike for Herk Goltry and decided that it was without solid basis. The Goltrys, who brought the first automobile to the Cherokee Strip in 1901, had owned one ever since. Now they had a mammoth red Silent Northern, and was it a darb! Herk was the best motor mechanic in the county. He made piles of money fixing stalled cars. It was nothing for someone to get stuck ten miles in the country and telephone for Herk Goltry. He would jump on his motorcycle and have the disabled machine running in no time. He fixed Doctor Baker's Buick after two adult mechanics working on it half a day had failed. It is difficult to convey an idea of the prestige that his knowledge of the mystery of motor cars gained for Herschel Goltry in a day when not one person in a hundred had ever cranked one of the blamed things.

Herk Goltry got his dad's car just about whenever he wanted it because Banker Goltry knew the car'd come back, and with no horse dragging it, either. Other fathers who owned automobiles would let their sons take them out if Herk was to be in the party. Once Herk Goltry, Roy Athey, and Rich Richardson got their dads' cars and this cavalcade of three automobiles containing six girls and six boys went all the way to Carrier to see the high-school team play football. I guess Carrier had never laid eyes on the like of that before. Two of the boys in the party had been among a gang of high-school hoboes who bummed to Carrier and back on freights to see a game less than two years before.

III: Newspapers

1909-1911

CHAPTER THIRTEEN

The *Wave-Democrat* and the *Morning News*

ALL winter long I kept my eyes peeled for a summer opening on a daily paper. I would hurry through my grocery route to enjoy the privilege of helping Mike Crouse, who on Saturdays worked for his father on the *Morning News.* Getting out the *Quill* and hanging around the *News* office with Mike aroused an enthusiasm for editorial work which I had not known in the everlasting pursuit of personals for the *Events.*

Enid's papers were fat with advertising. Itinerant reporters drifted in, worked a few weeks and drifted on—times being easy and jobs plentiful all over the Southwest. In the course of the winter I drummed up a hint of an acquaintance with two of these tourists. They exerted on me the same effect that tramp printers exerted. One was a spruce-looking fellow lately out of the University of Chicago; the other a shaggy old man with dandruff on his coat collar, watery eyes, and a whiskey breath you could have hung your hat on. I learned that these personages were called road artists, or tramp reporters, and that they were an accredited part of the journalistic fellowship. Before that the only tramps I had heard of about a newspaper shop were printers. Road artists had no place in the front-office scheme of rural weeklies like the *Events.*

The first choice as a beneficiary of my services was the *Morning News,* which I regarded as the most up-to-date paper in town. Mr. H. P. Crouse was an extremely affable man and so fat he couldn't see his feet. He would lace his fingers on his paunch and be vague so agreeably that it took some time to get on to the fact that he had no place for me on the *News*. My next choice was the *Eagle*, always the most prosperous paper in Enid and to me the dullest. Personals, personals, columns of personals, was Pete Drummond's idea of what people wanted to read. He covered Enid as the *Events* covered Garfield County. I saw Cod Harrison, Mr. Drummond's city editor. He came to the point more quickly than Mr. Crouse: nothing doing. That left the *Wave*. I was wrestling with the prospect of putting my pride in my pocket and seeing Mr. Isenberg when all at once the curse was lifted from the *Wave*. It was purchased by Doctor M. A. Kelso. At the same time Doctor Kelso bought the weekly *Democrat* from my old friend Mr. Moore and called his new paper the *Wave-Democrat*. I lost no time asking for a job and was promised one as soon as school let out.

I believe Doctor Kelso had come to Enid with the Run. At any rate I'd always known him—a thick-set, hurried figure with a tuft of black chin whiskers, unpressed clothes and a dusty derby hat. In the early days when Stetsons were the rule, Doctor Kelso's derby was notable. His office was a clutter of books and periodicals, few of which pertained to his profession. On my rounds of the Square, while working for the *Events*, I would find him hunched over a book. With a gesture of annoyance he'd whisk the gold-rimmed specs from the end of his nose—and look a little relieved. At least I was not a patient. Once or twice we had had little talks. He told me he had worked in a country-newspaper office as a boy and had never got the printers' ink out of his system.

Doctor Kelso could afford to neglect his practice. Real estate acquired cheap in the early days had made him a wealthy man, as we measured wealth. The Kelsos had no children. Originally the household had consisted of the doctor; his wife, a power in the ladies' Shakespeare Club; and a spinster sister, Miss Jennie, who was Enid's first librarian. Miss Jennie also opened, in one of the churches, the first kindergarten in Enid. Everybody loved her, the kids most of all. Imagine, then, the shock to the sensibilities of some of our citizens when plump, cheerful Miss Jennie, good Christian that she was, up and married Godless Green, widowed father of my bosom friend Karl. A year later when she died in childbirth some of our citizenry may have seen the hand of Jehovah in the matter. If they did they were close-mouthed about it. The town wouldn't have stood for any throw-off on Miss Jennie. Also, you heard less of Godless Green these days. People were more apt to speak, and respectfully, of "F. I. Green, the capitalist," whose oil interests in Louisiana were supposed to be worth a quarter of a million dollars.

Getting back to Doctor Kelso, shortly after statehood a fresh field of activity had unexpectedly opened before him. While attending a meeting of some medical body Doctor Kelso had, in a hotel lobby, given expression to his opinion of Governor Haskell. It was not flattering. The remarks were overheard by a newspaper reporter who obtained the doctor's permission to print them. The reporter built up the doctor as a Democrat who had never sought party favors. The astonished physician received a number of letters from independent Democrats who were ashamed of the governor's shenanigans and believed the doctor might be the man to succeed Haskell and restore the reputation of the party in Oklahoma. Doctor Kelso thought well enough of the suggestion to close his medical office and buy the two newspapers.

Everett Purcell greeted the venture with a whimsical editorial. He spoke as highly of the new editor as the *Events* could be expected to speak of a Democrat: His courageous opposition to Boss Haskell was beyond all praise. And yet the doctor, so skillful in ministering to the ills of others, had fallen victim to two of the most devastating maladies that can afflict the human system. He had been bitten by the political bug and the newspaper bug at one swipe. As to politics, the doctor was too innocent a man to tackle Haskell and his gang and come out with a whole skin. As to running a newspaper, he would find that more than lofty intentions were essential to success.

The editorial made me sad. Somehow I feared that Everett Purcell had written the inevitable obituary of the *Wave-Democrat*, toward which already I had begun to develop a loyalty characteristic of western newspaper reporters of that era. You might work for a paper only a week. It might be demonstrably the shoddiest example of journalism in town. But while you drew its pay you gave absolute fidelity. You would relentlessly scoop your best friend if he was on the staff of an opposition sheet. During the years I was to work for western and southern newspapers I never witnessed a breach of that rule. We looked down on the East where reporters worked on a "syndicate" basis—each taking a different angle of a complicated story or leg of a long beat and swapping information. It is still my opinion that the cutthroat system developed the better newspapermen.

I say that we Westerners looked down on our eastern colleagues and their methods, and that is true. Another truth is that I never knew a Westerner who didn't long to work in the East, if only so he could return and run down the place. New York was a reporter's dream of Valhalla.

2

On Monday, June 7, 1909, I went on the payroll of the *Wave-Democrat*. I could not resist, however, covering the ball game the day before. I wanted to be seen at the press bench. Although Crouse had coached me on keeping a box score, I got mixed up when, amid a flurry of hits and errors, Enid scored six runs in one inning.

Had I asked him, Crouse would have straightened me out because he was present only in his capacity as official scorer for the Enid club. Having no Monday edition, the *News* did not cover Sunday games. But my imagination had ordered things otherwise. Once the umpire had called "Play ball!" Mike became my professional rival. By the journalistic code personal relationships were at an end. I refused to break the spell with an appeal to Mike to verify my score.

Consequently I had a time with it. The body of the story came easier, thanks to my study of the sports pages of the Chicago *Record-Herald*. The *Herald* had a baseball writer whose command of slang fascinated me. Having festooned my narrative with borrowed gems, I compared the result with Crouse's recent efforts in the *Morning News*. Mike's language appeared flat and undistinguished. I could hardly wait for him to see my masterpiece.

After Monday's game Mike and I dropped into the Salty Dog. By that time the *Wave-Democrat*, an evening paper, was out. Taking a copy from the collection of literature Mr. Kimmell kept for the edification of his patrons, Crouse turned to my story. When he had finished reading he suggested a game of pool.

Never had I seen Mike handle a cue with such confidence and address. When he ran out his string for game I tossed a dime on the table and said I'd have to be getting along and work up my box score.

"By—the—way," said Crouse, spacing his words significantly. "Speaking of box scores, who read proof on yours today?"

That seemed a funny way to bring up the masterpiece. "Why, I did," I replied.

"See anything wrong?" said Mike.

I consulted the paper, and saw nothing wrong.

"Look at the putouts."

"What's the matter with 'em?"

"You've got twenty-five putouts for Enid and twenty-nine for Pittsburg.

"Well, that's what I made it," said I.

A pained expression marred the not altogether Apollonian symmetry of the countenance of Russel McKinley Crouse. "Look," he said, distinctly, "Pittsburg batted nine times and Enid eight. See? It takes three putouts to retire a side in an inning. Right? Three times nine are how many?" Mike let that sink in. "Three times eight are how many?"

If the "battleship" linoleum on the floor of the Salty Dog could have opened and swallowed me it would have been an act of mercy.

"Well, thanks, old man; white of you to put me wise."

Baseball formed a small part of my daily grist for the *Wave-Democrat*. Aside from the girl who wrote society there was only one other reporter to cover the town. My beat was the heavier of the two: county offices, city offices, courts, *and* personals. "Rather have a half column of personals than a column on the City Council any day," said the city editor. His name was Mr. Harrison, the same as the city editor of the *Eagle,* though our Mr. Harrison was a stranger to Enid whom Doctor Kelso had caught passing through. The reference to personals was a sharp disappointment. It marked Mr. Harrison as another one-horse editor.

Though he'd never even learned to use a typewriter, you couldn't really dislike Mr. Harrison—a portly, graying man who shaved every other day, wore silver-rimmed glasses, and sucked a pipe that gurgled. His manner was patient and friendly. "Son," he said, "I'm giving you this beat because the other fellow isn't up to it. The Old Man says you were raised here and know all the officials. Take it and do what you can until someone with more experience comes along. Then we'll find something else for you."

Though awed by the responsibility, I resolved to do my level best to hold the beat which was the logical property of the best reporter on a paper. The competition was fearsome. Humphrey of the *Morning News* had acquired the reputation of the most talented reporter that had ever struck Enid. A big, loud fellow with a Bohemian air, he spoke patronizingly of our town, as became a city newspaperman bored with life in the sticks. From the off-hand mention of telegrams from other papers contending for his services, I took it that he'd not be with us long. The *Eagle* representative was a small, agreeable chap named Paul Hedrick, who, I was surprised to learn, had worked on the Kansas City *Journal* and the Dallas *Morning News.*

When our acquaintance progressed to a point where I could ask about reporting on the big papers, Hedrick would answer pleasantly and precisely, Humphrey banteringly and vaguely. His object seemed to be to expose my ignorance, Hedrick's to remove it. But I had to admit that Humphrey was the better writer. His copy had flair. He might misspell the names of well-known citizens. (Even I had to watch to see that Doctor Feild's name did not come out "Field" in copy.) And Humphrey would get facts twisted; but he could write. His contempt for personals also had my endorsement.

Against such formidable opposition I had to fall back on the fact that I was a hometown boy. Despite the influx of new people, old-timers held the public offices. Most of them I had known all my life. Laying aside the hail-fellow and slightly condescending approach which I imagined the best professional form, I addressed them as the small boy in the presence of his elders—pretty much as if I was still toting specials at the post office.

This method produced results—except where the sheriff's office was concerned. At that important fountain of news Humphrey had the edge. He'd scoop Hedrick and me regularly. In my case this may have been on account of the "Satire" in the *Events*. If so, you could hardly blame Sheriff Campbell. I had attempted to hold him up as a lover of cheap display. No description of Sam Campbell could have been less accurate. Long, lean, steely blue-eyed and with drooping sunburned mustaches, he looked the part of your typical southwestern sheriff of a day that was passing. More than that, he was such a sheriff.

What I lost in the sheriff's office I gained in the courts—County and District. I knew court procedure as well as my older rivals, and I knew the lawyers much better. Often an attorney would permit me to inspect, in advance of filing, a brief or answer or bill of complaint. If I could delay the filing until after Hedrick had made his round for the day I'd have a clear beat.

I am, however, getting ahead of my story as well as painting things in colors too favorable to myself. During my first week on the *Wave-Democrat*, with the courthouse beat anything but cinched, I learned one of the basic principles of newspaper reporting.

I was crossing the north yard of the courthouse when a desperate cry from above my head stopped me in my tracks. The cry came from a young lineman astride the cross-arm of an electric-light pole carrying wires into the courthouse. A little below him was a second lineman, with his safety belt on and his spikes dug into the pole. His back was toward me and he was leaning away from the pole clasping a wire. I saw this second lineman sort of straighten out. His legs straightened, his back straightened, his arms straightened: all without a sound from him. It was as if springs inside him were uncoiling. Then he collapsed. His spikes remained in the pole and the upper part of his body fell, face down, across the wires and stayed there. I recognized the man. His name was Jim Bloodsworth. This happened not too quickly, but in about the time it takes to tell.

The first lineman, the young fellow who had yelled and who kept on yelling, engaged his legs about the cross-arm, swung his body down and stretched his arms toward Jim Bloodsworth. He clutched Jim and then his cries ceased. He, too, performed the grotesque straightening motions and then he went limp. The two men clung together silently, swaying a little with the wires. It seemed a wonder they did not fall off.

Linemen on the ground were running toward the pole, their climbing irons clanking. One pulled on some rubber gloves and went up and cut a wire. By this time a crowd was gathering; people coming on the run. Jim Bloodsworth was lowered to the ground with ropes. Then the young lineman was lowered. Though this probably did not take more than a few minutes it seemed an unconscionably long time. Doctor Baker and Doctor Feild began working over the two men. They worked from before ten o'clock until after twelve and then said that the men had been dead from the first.

The north yard was filled with people. Everyone in town, it seemed to me, knew of the accident. Hedrick and Humphrey and I talked to the foreman of the linemen who gave his opinion of the cause of the fatal "short." The man who had lost his life trying to save that of his partner was June Weekly, twenty years old and the main support of his parents. Too shaken for professional stylistics, I went to the *Wave-Democrat* office and wrote four or five somber paragraphs on what I had seen and heard. The piece ran about half a column.

By the time the evening papers were out, the shock of my experience had begun to wear off. On picking up the *Eagle* I received a second shock, however. Hedrick had written rings around me, spreading himself to the extent of two columns. In next morning's *News* Humphrey did even better. He used vivid words I wished I'd thought of.

I walked into the *Wave* office with a humble apology, and also an excuse.

"Why, Mr. Harrison, everybody in town *knew* what had happened. That's why I didn't write more."

Mr. Harrison sucked his pipe and regarded me through his glasses.

"Son, just let me tell you something." I wished to heaven Mr. Harrison wouldn't call me "son." "The more people who know or see a thing, the more people, those same people, want to read about it. Who do you think are most eager to read an account of a ball game or a political rally or a shower for a prospective bride? Those who were there, of course."

This was instantaneously so obvious that my distress must have been plain to see.

"Don't worry about it too much," Mr. Harrison added. "You wrote a compact and clear story. But just try to remember what I've told you."

3

Still, I felt the only thing that saved me from a dressing down was the fact that Mr. Harrison was just a rube editor, lacking the cosmopolitan finish of a Hedrick or a Humphrey. I devoted myself to a study of newspaper style, Mr. Hearst's New York *American* and Mr. Pulitzer's St. Louis *Post-Dispatch* being the models most valued. I strove to illuminate my copy with marks of erudition and taste. A cow was a bovine quadruped. Ladies had finely chiseled chins and shell-like ears.

I labored to extract the gold of the unusual from the ore of the commonplace. On a dull day Hedrick and I listened to a prosy divorce suit in Judge Cullison's court. Going through my notes at the office my eyes hit upon these scrawled words: "He never did love me." Disregarding what had gone before or had followed in this complaining wife's drab tale, I slipped a sheet of paper in my typewriter and hammered out:

"A blush mounted her dimpled cheeks and her shy glance sought the floor as Bertha Hinkle confessed:

"'He never did love me. . . .'"

Next day Humphrey of the *News* approached me familiarly.

"You write that?" he asked, indicating the Hinkle item.

I said that I had.

"You're learning the ropes, my boy," was Humphrey's expansive observation. "That little piece took Campbell's fancy." Humphrey's tone became confidential. "James, how'd you like to work for a real newspaper?"

A story of mine had caught Campbell's fancy! How'd I like to work for the *News?* That was a lot to take at a gulp.

Campbell was the new publisher of the *Morning News,* replacing Mr. H. P. Crouse whose labors to re-educate Enid's preferences in journalism had been a financial disappointment. As I understood it, the Campbells of Ohio supplied the bulk of the money behind the *News.* To protect the investment they had sent down a member of the family to relieve Mr. Crouse. The Campbell who appeared among us had received the identifying touches of his craftsmanship not in Ohio but on the Colorado Springs *Evening Telegraph,* a journal embodying most special features. It was an imitation of Messrs. Bonfils's and Tammen's Denver *Post,* which, in turn, derived its inspiration from William Randolph Hearst.

Mr. Campbell had proceeded to liven up the *News* with larger headlines and boldface leads. All this I watched with an approving eye. Not for a moment did I credit the spiteful gossip I heard in the other offices: that Campbell had been sent down to sell the paper and if a sucker didn't come along pretty quick there'd be nothing to sell.

Humphrey launched into an exposition of the plans Campbell had for the *News.* Why did I think he, Humphrey, was sticking around in the face of that proposition from Gaylord on the *Oklahoman?* Would I be interested in a starting offer of twelve a week?

Twelve a week being double my current pay, I was interested. But by this time I had recovered a measure of composure. I said I'd think about what Humphrey had to say.

"We're going to get out a *news*paper," pursued the reporter. "Chance to land on the ground floor. Shall I tell Campbell you'll come over?"

"No. Just say I'll think about it. And thanks, Humphrey."

I walked into the *Wave-Democrat* office and hit the Old Man for a raise.

Doctor Kelso looked up from the editorial he was scratching out at the most disorderly desk I'd ever seen. Proofs and papers made a hodge-podge a foot high save for a cleared space just big enough to write on. The doctor seemed hurt at my request. He said he'd have to mull it over. "Awful lot of expense 'round here. Would you believe it, payroll last week climbed—*Ho-ly* smoke, and here it is Saturday—payday again!"

The doctor pawed the papers on his desk. "Markey, see the payroll anywhere?"

The Old Man darted into the business manager's office, demanding the payroll. The business manager, a sleek creature who had blown in with the boom, said he had delivered it to the doctor an hour ago.

"Seems mislaid," said the doctor. "Make out another and I'll write the checks."

When the doctor's back was turned the business manager rolled his eyes toward the ceiling and exhaled audibly.

Head down, the Old Man plunged back into his room.

"'Lo, Markey. What can I do for you? Quick, son; awful rushed today."

Hardening my heart I repeated the request for a raise, intimating that unless it was forthcoming I'd have to cast my line elsewhere.

"I'll think it over, Markey. Pretty short run for cash myself, just now."

Six months of journalism had brought M. A. Kelso neither the personal Elysium he had sought nor any discernible public benefits to Oklahoma. The man who had yearned for liberation from the treadmill of medicine demanded freedom as an editor. Contrary to the advice of an attorney, he refused to incorporate his newspaper, an act which would have limited his financial liability. In the manner of W. R. Nelson of the Kansas City *Star*, he carried in the masthead the legend:

M. A. KELSO
Editor and Owner

So far, the treadmill of journalism had proved as exasperating as that of medicine—not to mention expensive beyond all anticipation. Acting as his own architect, Doctor Kelso had built a brick building to house his plant. Had he consulted a printer on the back-room layout, the concrete foundation for the press would have been in the right place. And it would have been large enough for the press the doctor bought.

This piece of machinery was hardly needed. A serviceable press had been inherited from the *Wave*, but Doctor Kelso had run onto such a bargain that he could not resist. The new press was a bastard-size eight-column flat-bed Hoe—with alterations designed by its former owner, a Kansas editor and mechanical genius who had gone insane. A trial of the press suggested that this unfortunate event occurred before the innovator had perfected what he was trying to do.

One linotype of an old model had come with the *Wave*. The doctor bought another, second-hand, which proved to be obsolescent.

But for the temperament and capacity of the foreman, the mechanical end of the production of our paper would have been attended by more mishaps than we had. This foreman's name was Jack Morrow. A phlegmatic giant in his fifties who had spent a lifetime in poverty-ridden shops, Jack Morrow, like most printers of his generation, was a master of makeshift. No sooner would a linotype go out or the press break down than the Old Man, coatless and with his glasses dangling from a black cord, would streak from the front office as fast as his short legs could take him, asking questions in an unpunctuated stream. Tranquilly Jack Morrow would proceed with his repairs.

Though Mr. Harrison endorsed my request, no raise was forthcoming. Equally vexatious was Humphrey's behavior with reference to the *News* offer. One motive of my campaign for a raise on the *Wave-Democrat* was to put myself in a better position to talk salary to Campbell. But after his first sweeping approach Humphrey said nothing for several days. When he did bring up the matter it was to intimate that there had been some delay getting "fresh capital" for Campbell's program.

The librarian of the Methodist church was arrested for bootlegging. The county attorney confidentially informed me that more startling developments were in prospect. Enid's illicit liquor traffic had been gathered into the hands of the biggest politician in our parts—Josephine Barnabee's friend. The librarian was going to turn state's evidence and tell all about it. The prosecutor promised I'd have the scoop.

Burdened with this secret, that night I ran into a linotype operator named Clint. I kept him company on the back steps of the *News* where Clint was waiting for a printer friend to get through. The compositor had a half pint of corn. I wet my tongue a couple of times and Clint killed the bottle. Warmed by the corn, Clint fell to speaking of San Antonio, Texas. I asked him if he thought I could hold down a job in San Antonio.

My respect for a printer's opinion of a reporter's qualifications was not misplaced. Jack Morrow had been for a swim in University Lake when a young printer was drowned. I took my story to him to see if the facts were right. Jack spread the copy on an imposing stone, and, taking a stub pencil from the pocket of his apron, gave it the best piece of editing I had witnessed to that time. Little more than a word was changed here and there, but I could see the improvement every time. I had written "none were." Changing "were" to "was" he said quietly: "'None' is a contraction of 'no one.' It usually takes a singular verb." That lesson in grammar I was never to forget.

Clint said sure I could hold a job in San Antonio. I walked on home dreaming of pulling out for some place where my talents'd be appreciated.

4

McKinley Crouse quit the *Morning News* and went to Pawhuska where his father had re-established himself. Before he left Mike paved the way for me to call on Mr. Campbell. My interview with the man who was to make metropolitan journalism stick in Enid was brief. Mr. Campbell was a slight, narrow-faced man of twenty-eight or thirty with the pallid complexion of a night worker. His long, sensitive fingers were cigarette-stained. He wore a green eye-shade and looked past me while he spoke. Mr. Campbell offered ten dollars a week for "sports and a little local" and said to report to Mr. Wickersham.

Mr. Wickersham, a bald-headed old-timer lately arrived from Ohio, was the city editor. (In Enid city editors also handled the telegraph copy, read proof, made up, wrote a few editorials and when too many big stories broke at once they covered assignments.) I had been around long enough to recognize Mr. Wickersham as another bush-league editor, like Mr. Harrison of the *Wave.* I guessed that Mr. Campbell would have to depend mostly on Humphrey and me, and went over to Kress's and bought a green eye-shade.

Humphrey looked at things the same way. The keen edge of our zeal was blunted, however, by the way Wickersham devitalized our copy. Headlines shrank. Humphrey kicked to Campbell, but didn't get anywhere. It appeared that Wickersham had some sort of drag with Campbell's father back in Ohio. The last straw was when he started jumping Humphrey and me for more personals.

Yet work on the *Morning News* had its compensations. It was my first night job. I reported at two in the afternoon and was through at midnight. I covered the ball game and then a little local beat. After my trick on the *Wave-Democrat* this was a pipe. When the ball club was on the road I would voluntarily help

Humphrey at the courthouse because I enjoyed the courthouse crowd. Gradually I came to have a good deal to do with Mr. Wickersham. Seeing that any chance to make a real paper of the *News* had gone up the spout, I permitted myself to like him. Mr. Campbell did not know six people in Enid outside of the office and had no desire to enlarge his acquaintance. Wick had the hick idea that a local editor should know local people. I being the only bona fide Enid resident on the paper besides the society editor, he asked me to introduce him around. You couldn't help noticing the solid impression he made.

Often as I deplored the circumstance that I had spent my life in Enid, and greatly as I yearned to see the world so that I might speak of the places I'd been, as tramp reporters and tramp printers spoke, Mr. Wickersham's genuine impulse to know our town touched something genuine in me. Of the Square, shimmering in the glare of a southwestern sun which made even us natives squint, I was as proud as any Chamber of Commerce booster. So imperceptibly had this fair prospect emerged that one had to think twice to believe that the dust-blown, unpainted, pine-and-shingle rectangle of my childhood had existed in reality. In the center of the Square stood the hundred-thousand-dollar brick-and-limestone courthouse, never mentioned to a stranger without naming the cost. The maples and locusts on the grounds had come on so that their foliage shaded much of the five acres. Bermuda grass made a sun-defying carpet which the Garden Club had adorned with beds of brilliant geraniums.

With few exceptions the business buildings facing this park were brick, and two of them were five stories high. Wooden sidewalks had long since disappeared, wooden awnings over the sidewalks had lately gone and hitching posts were going. There had been some dissent to the removal of the awnings, but the boosters carried the day. Created a false impression of the climate for people to think you had to shade your walks. Nor did the Chamber of Commerce like the papers to print the temperature on a real warm day—say 108 in the shade. Given five or six days like that in a string and you could hear mutterings by the foes of progress: they shouldn't have been so hasty about the awnings. Such heresy ignored the plain fact that ours was a *dry* heat, which didn't hurt anybody.

All in all, as plains-country county seats went, it was a sightly town to which I introduced the interested immigrant from Ohio. More important than that esthetic consideration, it was a "live" town, pulsing with great expectations. The boosters had begun to talk of bringing a packing plant to Enid.

5

A satisfying feature of my new employment was the way morning-newspaper work disengaged a fellow's habits from those of the run of people. Ordinary folks' afternoon was a morning-newspaperman's morning, their sundown his noontime. At midnight he knocked off to take his recreation. In a community where two thirds of the people were in bed by ten and nearly all by eleven, this gave one a feeling of membership in an exclusive cult.

No matter how warm the day, night on the plains is almost invariably pleasant: so little moisture in the air to hold the heat. As soon as the sun dipped behind the roofs in the Weatherly Addition everyone who could got out of doors to cool off. Most of them sat on their porches, rocking and talking. Neighbors visited from porch to porch. By seven the after-supper crowd began to enliven the Square. Some took the air in their buggies and cars. Maybe the livery-stable tallyho would be out with a party.

The lights of the White Way went on. I think it was Humphrey who christened the Square the White Way in honor of the new street lights. They were mounted on fancy iron posts, nearly tall enough so the bugs wouldn't bother, three lights in white round globes to a post. The arrangement—one light above and two below—proved a little disturbing. Traveling salesmen observed the resemblance to pawnbrokers' signs and asked how much the town was in hock for.

Three picture shows and Delmar Garden, the roofless summer theater, soon filled up. The drugstores were open. Pool halls, lunch rooms, Parker's bookstore, and one or two cheap clothing and dry-goods stores which did not abide by the Merchants Association closing rules invited customers. Other stores showed lights only in their windows. Above the street level lights burned behind the windows of hotels and rooming houses, or here and there in an office where a lawyer pored over a brief or a real-estate man worked on a deal.

On Wednesday nights the churches were open for prayer meetings which ended before nine. The picture shows were dark before ten and Delmar a little after; lodge rooms, except the Elks, about the same time. Drugstores filled with the last contingent of soda-fountain patrons. The Peerless, current hangout of the high-school crowd, was a bedlam. By this time the night cop had completed his turn of the Square, extinguishing lights in the show windows. At eleven he unlocked and pulled a switch which put out the lower two White Way lights on each post, leaving only one burning. The drugstores and then the pool halls closed. At midnight the last street cars, the almost empty "owls," clattered on their runs. Hotel night clerks dozed at their desks; porters stacked chairs and mopped lobby floors. Block after block of houses in the residential streets was uninterruptedly dark. A light showing usually meant sickness. A lone drugstore, which bootlegged on the side, Cap Bond's restaurant, and the *News* office were the only ground-floor establishments open on the Square. The sleeping town belonged to the night people.

Aside from the residents of Two Street there were not many of us; and Two Street wasn't what it used to be. In a state of decline for years, the nocturnal life of Enid had practically been expunged by the advent of state prohibition. Time was when saloons and gambling houses never closed. The Midway Dance Hall closed only in the daytime. When we moved into the Cogdal-McKee building, the Red Front (two doors away) and Jim Utsler's were open until the small hours. Shortly thereafter the gambling departments of saloons were abolished by official edict. Next went the saloons themselves. By these means two important props were knocked from under Two Street. Jennie Hearn threw in her hand and departed for Fort Worth.

Thereby Enid lost a real pioneer, whose first business establishment in our midst was a tent. By 1909 those who could trace their Enid lineage to the tent era mentioned the circumstance with pride—sometimes on their letterheads. In appearance and demeanor rowdy, good-natured Jennie Hearn was the opposite of her chief professional rival, the fastidious Josephine Barnabee. Jennie had no political ties. She would fall for any hard-luck story. It used to be that when his own money ran out, my father would intimate worthy causes to Jennie. Papa was Jennie's attorney. Her contributions were donated in the name of "an anonymous friend." Some of the beneficiaries would have dropped dead had they known where the money came from. Jennie left town flat broke. A kitty was made up to see her to Texas.

Josephine Barnabee continued to reign in a down-at-the-heels realm. This rule had never been disputed, really. Not in her heyday had Jennie Hearn aspired to royal prerogatives. The story was that she and Jo got along none too well personally, because Jennie made fun of Jo's airs. Be that as it may, the sovereignty exercised by the queenly Josephine was an uneasy one these days. By the skin of his teeth her politician friend had escaped the exposure of his overlordship of the blind-tiger liquor traffic when the Methodist church librarian was arrested. His political power broken, the once-genial dictator had taken to the bottle.

For each admitted fancy house the reformers shut on Two Street, it seemed that a "rooming" house would open elsewhere. Two or three of them occupied second or third floors on the Square. You could see the lights in their windows wink on and off.

The paper to bed, the *News* bunch—printers, linotype operators, the stereotyper and the editorial people—would sift over to Cap Bond's to eat and chin. The night hack, with Jim Smart, its driver, half asleep on the box, would be standing in front. Inside you might find the cop, whose week it was to take the night watch, cooling his coffee in a saucer; Red Martin, the night operator at the Western Union; Kaintuck, the proprietor of a floating crap game; High Pockets, a pool shark and tin-horn gambler; a couple of chippies from a "rooming" house; Dirty Dozen guys from the Presserie; a table of players from Delmar keeping to themselves. Kaintuck also handled 'shine and he took offense at a remark of Red Martin's. Red said the stuff was all right to drink but he wouldn't want to spill it on his shoes.

Mizzou Edmundson might be there: an outmoded survival stranded by the tide of change—last of the old-time gamblers of the day when Enid was a wide-open town. I'm not sure what Mizzou did for a living any more—peddled a little rotgut, maybe, or played a little red dog or poker with the railroad boys on pay nights. He shunned such shallow characters as Kaintuck and High Pockets. Whatever its sources, Mizzou's income was not abundant. Gone were the heavy gold watch-chain and the rich attire which had been visible signs of a gambler's standing during Enid's gilded age.

I think Mizzou's residence was a second-floor room on Broadway, a piece east of the Square. Rarely did he appear before noon. Easing into his day gradually, Mizzou would lean against the Stephenson building, contemplating a world which had outrun him. He would shift his toothpick and spit. People used to joke about its taking a staunch building to bear the strain of Mr. Edmundson's afternoon constitutional. Mizzou was six feet two and, though diminished in flesh with the advance of years and the decline of his material fortunes, he must have tipped the beam to a good two-twenty.

Such were Cap Bond's after-midnight regulars. Casuals might be anybody: a bank teller who'd had trouble with his balance; lawyer; doctor; guffawing schoolboys back from a heavy date. A real-estate and insurance man doing a good business showed up for three nights running and brooded over black coffee. Then he went to his office and blew out his brains. No one ever learned why. My chief regret was that they found him in time for the evening papers.

A Negro called Happy Jack would shuffle up from Two Street with his guitar and depart a few coins richer. Our gang might chip in and acquire a pint of corn and cross South Grand to the courthouse yard to lounge under a tree and consume it. On such occasions I was grateful for the darkness which concealed the fact that I couldn't swallow that beverage.

Then, of course, I knew the ball players and loafed with them at the Salty Dog. As the Railroaders won the Western Association pennant that year our players were local heroes. Cincinnati bought Scissors Ashley. Earl Radcliffe of the *Eagle* scooped me on that.

6

However ardently reporters might oppose each other in the course of a day's work, there existed among us a bond entailing obligations honored at the occasional inconvenience of personal sacrifice. As the summer changed to autumn, it occurred to me that I might be able to finish my last year of high school without giving up my job on the *News*. Provided the authorities would waive a deficiency in Latin, I didn't need many credits for graduation. If I could get them in the forenoon I could keep on working. I had about decided to take what I could get in the morning, whether it meant graduating or not, when a reporter named Mellot blew in and was hired.

As we had no need for three reporters, it looked as if somebody was slated for the ax.

In a day or so Mellot took me aside.

"Did I hear you say you expect to work and attend school, too?"

I said yes, if the paper would have me.

"Campbell thinks you're quitting next week on account of school," said Mellot. "Better see him and straighten it out."

"What about you?"

"I hit this town without work and can hit another the same way."

Mr. Campbell said he'd keep me. Mellot caught a rattler for Oklahoma City. I never heard of him again.

CHAPTER FOURTEEN

The Packing-Plant Boom

MY LAST year in high school was one of perpetual variety. I lived two lives: that of an important high-school senior and of a newspaper reporter during the most stimulating episode in Enid's history since the North Town War. This was the packing-plant boom, the object of which was to make everybody rich without working. All you had to do was buy a lot, sell it for twice what you paid—and keep that up.

I have already mentioned that Enid was enjoying a boom. That was what we called it, for Westerners gloried in the word. In reality this earlier boom was a healthy growth, a flowering of Enid's valid resources, as far as they were known at the time. The Strip was a prospering agricultural and stock country. Wheat was king, corn a princeling. Fruit orchards were coming on. There was abundant feed for hogs, beef and dairy cattle, and poultry. Farm horses of good quality were bred for the market. What Garfield County raised it could send away. Railroads radiated from our town in ten directions. Two of these roads—the Arkansas Valley & Western and the Denver, Enid & Gulf—were monuments to local capital and enterprise.

Like land booms, the locally financed railroad was a recurrent phenomenon in the building of the West, and the product of established formulas. One way was for a promoter to turn up—an august and unctuous personage who might veritably wear a plug hat and spats, like a cartoonist's personification of the Trusts. He'd have Kansas City "connections," Chicago "connections"—"connections" to burn, this promoter. In confidence he'd mention to some of our influential men the great railroad which was to go—right—through—our—town. He had a map to prove it: a map in colors, showing a railroad that would make the Santa Fe look to its laurels. And, come to mention it ("if you gentlemen can keep a secret"), that's what was in the wind. The bunch of eastern capitalists who controlled the Santa Fe and another bunch of capitalists had had a falling out. The anti-Santa Fe crowd was backing the new road. Now it chanced that as a means of acquiring local goodwill ("and, between us, free right-of-way") the capitalists were willing to let a few local people in on the ground floor. If Enid people showed the proper response, there was a chance of making "Enid" a part of the name of the new trunk line. "Enid, San Diego & Pacific": how'd that be for advertising our town all the way to the Coast!

A variant of this was for the promoter to disclose that the big capitalists were just *thinking* about this new road. Here was a chance to get *ahead* of them and sell out at your own price. Or maybe, frankly, there weren't any big capitalists involved at all, except maybe one or two who were sitting on the fence. Here, then, was an opportunity for wide-awake *local* people to make a start on a railroad bound to attract scads of capital as soon as those eastern money men saw what a gold mine the Oklahoma Northern was bound to be.

Forehanded cartographers drew maps of the Cherokee Strip showing the Enid, San Diego & Pacific and the Oklahoma Northern as accomplished facts. Enid papers published the maps. We could almost hear the whistle of the locomotive.

It happened that the Enid, San Diego & Pacific and the Oklahoma Northern never got beyond the map stage. The Arkansas Valley & Western and the Denver, Enid & Gulf edged them out of the picture. And the promoter was no Wallingford from Chicago, but an Enid man we all knew, Mr. Edmund Frantz. Edmund Frantz was one of six brothers who came from Kansas and had much to do with making Enid the biggest town in the Strip. The Frantz clan opened a hardware store and a lumber yard. They started the brickyard on Jim Utsler's place and built the Frantz Hotel. Two Frantzes were the idols of all Enid boys: Frank who had been a captain in the Rough Riders and the last

Territorial governor of Oklahoma, and Walter who pitched for the Kansas City Blues.

When I say that the A. V. & W. and the D. E. & G. were built, I mean that a certain amount of track was laid. The Arkansas Valley & Western got as far west of Enid as Avard, sixty miles distant. The D. E. & G. got as far on its way to the Gulf as Guthrie and as far on its march to Colorado as Cherokee, in the next county. This took all the local money. The capital Mr. Frantz had hoped to attract from the outside was not forthcoming.

Such fragments of railroad could not live independently of the trunk lines. Nearly all their freight was consigned to points which could be reached only by transshipment at ruinous rates. When deep enough in the toils of amateur management and creditors little local roads would sell out, at bankruptcy prices, to big roads which could operate them as feeders. In this way the Arkansas Valley & Western became a part of the Frisco system and the D. E. & G. of the Santa Fe.

Sooner or later that was the history of all railroads financed by local boosters. It would come out in the wash that the promoter's select group had taken no gamble on the successful operation of the road, or at any rate had hedged plenty. They owned the construction company which had built the road and the supply company which had sold the construction company its stuff. These corporations conducted their affairs on a realistic plane. That was the almost universal technique. It was not, however, the technique employed by Edmund Frantz. His idea was to build the roads as economically as possible. His construction and supply companies had not made a cent. I heard a business associate of Mr. Frantz say in disgust that "Edmund couldn't make money if they gave him the mint."

Just the same he built the railroads, furnishing Enid with more outlets than any other town in Oklahoma. Among the tangible results were railroad shops; the Alton Mercantile Company and other wholesale establishments; grain elevators and flour mills; Oklahoma Christian University; the Stock Pavilion and the Garfield County Stock Show which was the biggest thing of its kind in northern Oklahoma. The town was spreading and real-estate prices climbing. The boosters overstimulated this climb somewhat. Healthy growth came to a halt, leaving property values in the air. This was what the banker we owed had in mind when he obliged Mama to sell the vacant lot and pay up before prices should begin to slide off.

2

The banker reckoned without the packing-plant boom.

Two or three of the Chicago meat packers had established branch plants in Oklahoma City and in Wichita. Our failure to get one of them was a sharp disappointment. The papers printed statistics on the carloads of livestock Enid shipped to Oklahoma City and Wichita. The Oklahoma Farmers Union cooked up a plan to build its own packing plant and keep at home the money that was lining the pockets of the Armours and the Swifts. Our papers began whooping it up for the Farmers' plant. Editors who had fallen over themselves to be cordial to the Chicago packers while trying to land a branch plant wrote indignant pieces about the Beef Trust.

The Farmers Union incorporated the Peoples Packing Company and awaited bids for a plant from the different towns scrambling for the plum. Enid bid two hundred thousand dollars and set forth the familiar story of our unexcelled transportation facilities. At this juncture an old-school railroad promoter appeared on the scene. He had a map of a railroad he called the Enid, Ochiltree & Western. This railroad would tap the Texas Panhandle and bring its cattle straight to Enid. Our town took the promoter to its bosom. A bumper wheat crop at high prices had everybody feeling good. In a whirlwind campaign Enid landed the Peoples plant and the boom was on.

Special trains brought hosts of people to the ground-breaking northeast of town. For a mile around farms had been staked off into lots which sold like hot cakes. Had money grown on trees it could not have been much more plentiful. Even the tottering *Wave-Democrat* took a brace on the strength of its share of the most bountiful advertising harvest our papers had ever known. One Sunday edition of the *Morning News* was twenty-eight pages, the largest regular issue of a newspaper that had ever been printed in Enid.

A strange assortment quartered themselves upon our town—fashionably dressed, glib-speaking gentry, who came to reap where they had not sown. The uppercrust lived out of trunks at the Loewen and the Billings (formerly the Frantz) hotels and opened real-estate offices on the Square. They introduced the practice of sending "readers" along with their display ad copy. A reader was a purported news story puffing up the firm and what it had to offer. At first Mr. Wickersham edited this phony news severely or tossed it to Humphrey or me to rewrite. The advertisers kicked. The editing became less meticulous.

Conspicuous among the Johnny-come-latelies was the firm I shall call the Eureka Realty Company, which maintained a floor of offices in town and an impressive establishment on the eighty it had bought in the Packing Plant Addition and cut up into lots. Automobiles carried prospective purchasers from the town to the Addition. Lunches were free. (Sometimes I went out just for the ride and the eats.) The advertising of the Eureka was spacious, which permitted it to submit lengthy readers. As a student of the written word I had to admire some of the Eureka's efforts, and wondered which of those well-dressed, hearty gentlemen could be the author of such sonorous prose. When I learned that it was cribbed, almost verbatim, from ads in the Los Angeles *Times*, a prejudice against the Eureka Realty Company was aroused in my mind.

Not that there was anything you could put your finger on. The Eureka people treated me fine. "Mr. James, this is a pleasure. I want you to meet our general manager, Mr. Blank. Joe, this young gentleman represents the press." Still, I had a funny feeling about the Eureka.

Then there was the boss man's wife. Hotels were a part of my beat and I used to see her sitting in the Loewen lobby, languidly turning the pages of a magazine. She was good looking. She was more than that: something I couldn't find a word for. One time she looked up and caught me glancing at her. She didn't even lower her eyes. Bending over the register to copy the arrivals, I pulled down the brim of my hat, afraid I might look her way again.

This lady had a dog, the like of which I had never seen before. It was a little snub-faced dog with long, fine, brown hair—about the color of the lady's hair. She would sit in the lobby of the Loewen with the dog on her lap. She would walk along the streets with the dog at the end of a lead, or she would carry the dog on her arm. When she did that you could hardly see that the dog was there for the lady wore a fur coat about the same brown color. Probably she was not the first woman to appear on Enid's streets in a fur coat, but she was the first I remember seeing. And she was the first lady I ever saw lug a dog around.

One Saturday Wick said Eureka was running a double-truck. This was so special I'd have to drop in to see Blank, the general manager, and interview him as if it was a legitimate news story. Mr. Blank received me cordially and started to spout away. I knew what he was going to say before he said it. He would explain the delay in building the plant. I could write that guff in my sleep. The weather was the cause of the delay.

A door opened behind me.

"Excuse me. Jack isn't in his office. Do you know where he is, Joe?"

It was the lady. Jack was her husband.

Joe said Jack was out at the property and, it being Saturday, he might stay late.

I had scrambled to my feet. Mr. Blank said:

"Mrs. Dash, do you know this gentleman? He represents the press. Mrs. Dash, Mr. James of the *Morning News*."

The lady advanced and held out her hand. "Mr. James and I scarcely meet as strangers. We have seen each other at the hotel, I think."

You could smell her perfume.

"Oh, sit down, you two," Mrs. Dash went on, "and finish your talk. If you don't mind I'll just wait here."

The lady took a chair where I could see her by turning my head ever so slightly. Then it was I noticed that she had green eyes. I restored my attention to the even flow of Mr. Blank's words. Mr. Blank was a large florid man. I was sure my face was as red as his. I made notes furiously.

When the interview was over the lady said: "Joe, I'll not wait any longer. See you and Jack at the hotel." In the hall she said to me: "Do you happen to be going my way, Mr. James?" Her voice was like velvet.

"Yes, ma'am," I said. "I'm going as far as the corner."

At the corner I was glad to escape. Trying to collect my thoughts I wondered what had got into me. Cripes!

Next day on my rounds I hesitated to enter the Loewen Hotel. But the lady wasn't in the lobby, after all. When I left I discovered that I felt deprived of something.

Then I saw her coming along North Grand, walking slowly, following the dog. She always walked slowly, as if to kill time.

"Why, how do you do, Mr. James," she said. I thought her step hesitated, as if fixing to stop.

Before I knew what had happened I'd tipped my hat and plunged past. Cripes! I guess I ought to have stopped. But I didn't know anything to say. Sure, I could've asked what kind of a dog that was she had. But that would've been a pretty dumb question. I could've told about the dogs I'd had. But she wouldn't've been interested in *them.* Just ordinary dogs.

After that I made up conversations to share with the lady. Sometimes, in rehearsal, they seemed quite satisfactory. This was mostly because the lady made interested responses. But whenever I saw her—in the Loewen lobby, on the street, and once in the Peerless having a coke—nothing I'd thought up seemed appropriate. I'd gulp "Good evening" and make off. What made matters worse, I sensed a diminution of warmth in the lady's greetings to me. She used to smile and show her pretty teeth; the petulant look of boredom would leave her face, and it would come alive. But not so much any more.

One day a chattering high-school girl and I passed the foot of the stairway leading to the offices of the Eureka Realty Company. The lady was standing there, her dog on her arm. I spoke and lifted my hat. The lady looked full at me—without a change of countenance, and without saying a word.

Thereafter I would cross a street to avoid passing the lady. Boy, had I been a sap! To think I might have shined up to her!

3

Shortly after the twenty-eight-page edition, chuck full of ads, the Enid *Morning News* was sold to Mr. Charles I. Stewart of Lexington, Kentucky, and Mr. Campbell left us. I could read Wick's disappointment. By and by, over an early-morning snack on a stool at Cap Bond's, he told me how it was. He had hoped to build the *News* into a property which the Campbells would not care to part with. At the same time Wick would be creating a nice berth for himself. Now Wick felt that the only result of his labors had been to get more money for the Campbells at the sale.

Mr. Wickersham said he was going to try to make himself indispensable to Mr. Stewart. "But I have a hunch he'll bring his own man from Kentucky."

Whenever a paper changed hands there was a to-do about the innovations the new owner would make. This was particularly true in the case of the *News* and Mr. Stewart, who went about his business with quiet assurance. He rented the second floor of the building we occupied and moved his office and the editorial room up there. Copy went down and proofs came up by way of a chute. The *News* was the only office in town where the editorial room was not a cramped, dingy, littered hole with desks so close together you could hardly get around. He bought a new rotary press and added pages to the paper in excess of those justified by advertising.

"Let's give them a *news*paper, Mr. Wickersham." His tone was not boastful. "Ads will catch up."

The additional space was filled with telegraph copy, including plenty of "grape," the N.E.A. picture service, and by padding our local stuff.

Mr. Stewart's model was the Lexington *Herald*.

"That's a good paper," Wickersham observed privately, "and the Old Man seems to know his business. But unless he has a barrel of money and this boom lasts he's going to end up Salt Creek without a paddle."

The second newcomer from Kentucky was Miss O'Brien who took over society. A little later she and Mr. Stewart were married.

Mrs. Stewart's brother Joe came from Lexington. He broke in on Humphrey's run and Humphrey was let go. The fourth Bluegrass invader was Barry Bullock. He broke in on my run. I thought that foreshadowed the end of me and told Mr. Bullock so. He said no, it was his impression that Mr. Stewart meant to keep me. After a while on my run Bullock switched over and Joe O'Brien began taking him around. By this time things were clearer. Barry had taken the two runs not only to learn the town but to learn the newspaper business. Barry Bullock had been principal of the high school in Lexington. His first day's work on a paper was the day he had started out with me.

Seeing he was the person ultimately threatened by the advent of this ex-schoolteacher, Mr. Wickersham began to work harder on his invention, which had to do with the engine of an automobile. In the bottom drawer of his desk he kept a number of steel parts made into interesting shapes. As fast as he could afford it he sent off and bought new ones, machined to his designs. In the small hours after the paper was put to bed he would get out the parts and study them. Night after night the last thing I saw in the silent city room was Wick's shirt-sleeved figure, in the cone of light from a shaded lamp, bending over his parts and his plans. With all my heart I hoped he would sell his invention to one of the big automobile companies and make a fortune.

Barry Bullock started breaking in on the desk: learning to evaluate the news, which looks a lot different trickling in in "takes" over a pony A.P. wire, or emerging page at a time from a reporter's typewriter, from what you see in the newspaper you unfold in your home; to "run the book" (of reporters' assignments); to edit copy; write heads; make up. About the same time Wick got bad tidings about his invention. Still, Mr. Stewart had been quite frank and quite considerate, Wick said. He hoped Mr. Wickersham would stay a month but not to do so if a good opening offered elsewhere.

The Sunday before Mr. Wickersham left for the *Kansan-Republican* in Newton we had quite a talk.

"The trouble with you, Markey," the old editor said, "is that the things that make you useful to this newspaper you don't give a damn about. You want to leave here. You want to make the rounds of the big city papers. I've had to wear out lead pencils on your copy because you try to ape the Sunday supplement of the St. Louis *Post-Dispatch*."

Wick tapped his pipe-stem against his teeth, and grinned. He said:

"Markey, what in hell do you want to be any kind of a newspaperman for?"

The question caught me unawares.

"Why, Mr. Wick, it's what I've *always* wanted. I mean to work on the *big* papers, too. And see the world. What—what would you do in my shoes?"

"Go to the A. & M. over in Stillwater for a couple of years, hire out on a farm, marry the farmer's daughter—and *raise Poland China hogs.*"

4

The Class of 1910 was the largest senior class in the annals of the Enid High School to that time: fourteen girls and nine boys, of whom all were graduated except the school's best athlete and one other boy. Scholastically I stood a little above the middle of the class, but had honors been awarded the senior enjoying the most privileges they would have gone to me. I was at school only long enough to attend three morning classes. At 1:30 P.M.

(two, before Mr. Stewart took charge) I reported at the *News* office and did my studying while covering my beat. Between midnight and one I got to bed. A time came when I had fallen so far behind with everything that I was staying up until two or three in the morning. This exhausted me so that I couldn't sleep well when I did turn in.

I arranged with Barry Bullock to take a week off and have Graham Young of the *Wave-Democrat* replace me—working for both papers. Doctor Kelso also consented to the unorthodox arrangement. Graham Young was an itinerant who had been in and out of Enid two or three times: a pinched, seedy little man twice my age. He tried to refuse pay for his week's work on the *News*.

We had a new principal—Mr. Bailey. My first meeting with Mr. Bailey had been as a reporter. I interviewed him about his plans for the academic year. "Got a good story," my diary discloses. "He is a fine young fellow." The fine-young-fellow attitude toward my principal I carried over as a student. It didn't make for the happiest of relationships between us. And there were other difficulties at school. To get by in his course I endeavored to presume on my friendship with the history teacher, Deming. He wouldn't stand for it. Because my notebook was incomplete he obliged me to take a midterm exam from which otherwise I should have been exempt on grades. I was furious. Unless I made 90 in the midyear I would be liable for the final. I cheated in the exam and was caught. My paper was marked zero and I was suspended from school. According to my diary I was the victim of an unfeeling conspiracy in which everyone but myself had acted from low motives. Still, I had to confess that Bailey took me back on decent terms.

The person who did most to awaken my mind that winter was Barry Bullock. It was not journalism that I imbibed from my city editor; it was general culture. A certain tenseness gave Barry Bullock the look of a restless scholar. He had a large forehead and thinning hair and he wore rimless nose glasses. He was of slight build, and I, six feet tall and thin as a bean pole, towered above him considerably. We got to taking long rambles in the dead of night, Barry holding forth on philosophy or ethics; a phase of history, with the emphasis on intellectual motivations; a writer or thinker; a book or sonnet. Like Karl Green, Barry Bullock could recite poetry by the hour. One night he asked about our "indigenous literature." I said we hadn't any; Oklahoma was too new.

Barry took to digging around. He came up with Alex Posey, the Indian poet and newspaper editor who had died a few years back. I felt a little disgraced that a Kentucky carpetbagger should acquaint me with a native poet. I went about acquainting others. This was not difficult, for I wager not ten persons in Enid had heard of Alex Posey before Barry Bullock sprang him on me.

I wrote a paper for English IV on the life and works of Alex Posey. It was a digest of one of Barry's midnight dissertations. A half-breed Creek, Posey had begun to use English when nearly grown. When he wrote he forgot his white-man learning, except the language. Some of that was a literal translation from the Creek, quaint and lovely. Posey's imagery was altogether Indian: every sound of nature was music to his ears. Barry Bullock's estimate stands up. No other Oklahoman has written anything so worthy of preservation.

One of the triumphs of my life was to discover Alex Posey to Karl Green, who had discovered so many of the glories of literature to me.

"If he had been born an eighteenth-century English country gentleman," Karl wrote, from Leland Stanford University, "and had gone to Oxford, he'd be in all the anthologies."

5

For a couple of weeks I filled in as society editor; and in that connection a remarkable thing happened. I was at a young people's party at Maurine Frantz's when I recalled that I'd clean forgot to telephone Mrs. Letson for the table decorations and list of guests at her dinner that evening. This was an affair of considerable social magnitude, Frank Letson being the banking partner of

O. J. Fleming, Enid's Morgan. As the Letsons lived only around the corner on West Pine, I excused myself to run over and get the story. Work on a morning newspaper was always overlapping my personal life. To arrive late, leave early, or disappear for a spell from a gathering of my contemporaries gave me a feeling of distinction.

This feeling dissolved when, standing in the wide doorway of the Letson drawing room, I had my first actual glimpse of one of those swell West Side adult affairs of which I could write so offhandedly. Probably never before had I seen a roomful of people —all the ladies, anyhow—in evening dress. White shirt fronts and rustling gowns endowed familiar figures with unfamiliar personalities. From the snatches of talk I judged that everything said was either witty or worldly.

And there I stood—in my good suit to be sure, but conscious that the sleeves and the pants legs needed letting out because I had grown so fast. What a relief when Mrs. Letson rustled up and crisply supplied the data required. I had turned to go when I heard:

"Why, this is Markey James, isn't it?"

The speaker was Mrs. O. J. Fleming. Funny how I always used to remember having seen her milking a Jersey cow—away back when we lived on the claim. Mrs. Fleming had a rather homely freckled face. It was a nice face, though.

I don't know what she said next, but it made me feel better. In a moment she said something about Ed, who was at Cornell. "One time Ed brought home from high school something you'd written. Some piece of foolishness. I laughed and laughed."

Ed Fleming had done that. Gee!

And what do you think happened next? Mrs. Harry Alton came up.

"Mama, I want to speak to Markey, too. I guess he doesn't know me any more."

Didn't know her!

Wouldn't you think that standing face to face with Blossom Fleming for the first time in my life would have made me tongue-tied? The funny part is that it didn't. I can't pretend to remember what she said, or what I said. But it all seemed friendly and natural.

Walking back to Maurine's, visions from the secret drama of my childhood infatuation swam before me. The impossible attachment was quite gone now. The memory of it that remained was agreeable. I wasn't ashamed of it, though not for the world, of course, would I have had anyone know.

My next meeting with Blossom Fleming was on the night of the Alumni banquet during Commencement Week. I talked to her longer than I talked to anyone else. To questions about my work I replied with no effort to show off. Not even when we spoke of reading did I feel a need to appear clever or profound, despite the fact that of late I'd been furrowing my brows over Hume and Kant and the Buddhist religion and trying to impress people all over the place.

CHAPTER FIFTEEN

The *Eagle*

JUST before I finished high school I switched over to the *Daily Eagle*, thereby swallowing an assertion that no self-respecting newspaperman would be found dead on that dull sheet. My reasons were practical: more pay and shorter hours. The glamour of night work had begun to pale. I could still see my friends at Cap Bond's one night a week if I cared to. The *Eagle* was an evening paper with a Sunday morning edition.

The *Eagle* covered the news of Enid more thoroughly than any other paper. Mr. Drummond would trim an A.P. report of

President Taft's cabinet troubles to make room for a four-line item about H. H. Champlin's hunting trip or Doctor Hellum's chicken farm. He made that policy pay, and I had reconciled myself to it.

What I could not reconcile myself to was the lack of sprightliness with which the *Eagle* presented this news. At the exchange table I had learned that while most prosperous small-town papers were as heavy-gaited as I thought the *Eagle* to be, exceptions did exist. The Atchison *Globe* had become a success before it had a telegraph service at all. Though I had never been in Atchison I loved to read the personals in the *Globe*. They dripped human nature. They acquainted you with characters whose counterparts could be found in any town.

At the end of a week Mr. Drummond complimented my work. I knew how to get the piddling little stuff he crammed his paper with. When I'd spread myself on a Police Court story or a fire, indulging in fine descriptive flourishes, he would cut my copy to the bone. That sort of reporting had helped to fill up the *News*. Incidentally, Mr. Stewart's inability to diminish the *Eagle's* lead in advertising was a factor I had weighed while turning over in my mind the question of changing papers.

The *Eagle* job was the first I'd taken without a specifically conceived mission to reform journalism in Enid. Giving up Enid as a hopeless case, I pointed my ambition elsewhere. I had taken up "outside" correspondence and was finding it a neglected garden. Already I had landed as the local correspondent for the Wichita *Eagle*, and for Oklahoma's leading newspaper, the *Oklahoman* of Oklahoma City, and its evening contemporary, the *Times*. I was angling for the Chicago *Record-Herald*, the St. Louis *Times*, the Kansas City *Post*, the Dallas *Morning News*, and the Omaha *Bee*. I sent them items by mail—"feature" rather than spot-news stories. Though none had been accepted I kept on trying. Especially was I desirous of impressing the Kansas City *Post*, a new venture of Bonfils and Tammen.

Mr. Drummond did not print feature stories unless verifiable, which meant that the dead spike was his idea of the place for a type of story I liked to see on page one. A farmer might come to town and tell about the cat which had fallen into the threshing machine and come out with only part of an ear snipped off, thus lending credence to the legendary indestructibility of cats. If the farmer bore a reputation for unimaginativeness Mr. Drummond would print a four-line item about it. In the hands of a good feature writer that incident could be elaborated a little. Give the cat a name, such as Carry Nation. Tell of some of its other experiences: as a kitten they'd tried to drown it but it clawed out of the sack; after which Carry had been struck by lightning, tossed on the horns of a bull, sucked up by a twister and deposited on a haystack in the next township, et cetera.

Mr. Drummond missed the whole point. A journalistic adaptation of the tall tale, this type of feature story wasn't supposed to be true—merely something to regale a Westerner's rangy sense of humor. Farmer Wilhite's cat was one with Paul Bunyan's blue ox, Babe.

2

When as a boy fresh from the claim I began to take notice of newspapers, little distinction existed among the business, editorial, and mechanical departments. Your old-time country proprietor did anything and everything. As our town and our papers grew, these functions tended to separate. The marked cleavage was in the front office, between the business and editorial sides. Editorial hands had more to do with the printers than with the people on the other side of the partition who rustled ads and circulation and kept the books.

The first business-office man I ever took more than passing notice of was one on the *Eagle* whom I addressed, with progressing familiarity, as "Mr. Taylor," "Mr. Will," and "Bill." Despite the fact that he hadn't been in Enid a year the whole town was beginning to know Bill Taylor. Mr. Taylor's title was business manager, and he had bought an interest in the paper. His principal job was to solicit advertising. But Taylor did something else, which I'd seen no business-office man do before. From his rounds of the Square he'd bring in a nice string of personals.

"John Dollar, the cobbler, says the more streets they pave in Enid the faster shoe soles wear out."

That was the kind of stuff you saw in the Atchison *Globe*.

In any event, Bill Taylor would have been hard to overlook. He was six feet tall, with broad and rather stooped shoulders, enormous ears, a big hooked nose, and a towhead. He had merry blue eyes, and a deep, infectious chuckle. Though he worked hard, returning to the office nearly every night after supper, Taylor spread an aura of fun about him. He liked to put up jokes on people in the office and when one was put up on him he'd enjoy it as much as anybody. When I joined the paper the particular target of his ribbing was Birdie McKenzie, the society editor.

I stood apart from this horseplay. Before coming to the *Eagle* I had known Birdie McKenzie only slightly, though all my life I'd known who she was: the old doctor's daughter and a younger sister of Miss Edna, my first schoolteacher. I meant to convey disapproval of Taylor's lack of chivalry; and I could have wished that Birdie had given me more support. The fact is she didn't seem to mind the teasing which kept all the office, except me, in a gay frame of mind.

So it was that my relations with Mr. Taylor started off on the cool side. One morning I wrote a little story about a scrap between an actor at the Loewen and a chorus girl, the particulars of which had been aired in Police Court. Here, again, my gallantry rose to the surface. The account gave the actor the worse of it.

In the afternoon when the last forms were being made up I was called to the telephone. The speaker introduced himself as the actor in question. He said he understood that I had written an article unfriendly to him. I replied that I had written what had been brought out in court. He said I'd better think twice before printing it. I said we were getting out a *news*paper and hung up.

A minute later Taylor strolled into the little editorial room. "By the way, Markey, what was that I heard you saying?"

I told him.

"Good for you," he said. "Got a proof of the story?"

Taylor glanced at the galley and whistled. "All I have to say is, boy, you got your nerve."

From the way he said it I began to feel that maybe I had too much nerve for the good of my health.

Pretty soon the phone rang again. It was the actor. His voice sounded ominous. He asked if I was still of a mind to print that piece. I said I was. "All right," he said. "I'll be at your office when the paper comes out and if that piece is in it, it'll be just too bad for you." This time the actor hung up.

He was a big fellow, the actor. I guessed maybe I'd get my hat and start home. Birdie McKenzie said brightly:

"Was that the actor again?"

Bill Taylor came in. "What's the matter, Markey? Anything wrong?"

"No, sir," I said.

"The actor called again," Birdie put in.

"What'd he want this time?" asked Taylor.

I said he wanted me to kill the story.

"And you told him you wouldn't do it?"

I said I had.

"That's the ticket," said Taylor. "Knew a case like that in New Mexico once. 'Bout a week later," he continued, with the detachment of reminiscence, "somebody took a pot shot at the reporter; only winged him, though."

Bill Nutt, the foreman, lounged in the doorway leading to the composing room. He had dark curly hair and a perpetual lump in one cheek from a quid of tobacco.

"OK to lock one?" he drawled, referring to the first-page form. Mr. Drummond having gone home, Taylor answered:

"It's up to Markey, here. Want to let that story ride or kill it?"

"Let me see the proof again," I said.

"No time for corrections," said Nutt, glancing at the clock on the wall. "The story goes as is, or not at all."

I hesitated.

"Which is it?" said Taylor briskly.

"Kill it," I said reluctantly.

"I guess, after all, that's the easiest way out," said Taylor. "Of course, some reporters I've known would have felt they had to stick to their guns——"

His voice trailed off.

I sort of wished I'd stuck to my guns.

When the papers came up front, my eyes skimmed page one and my heart went into my shoes. The story hadn't been killed. I became aware of a noise in Birdie's corner. Her shoulders were shaking with laughter.

An instant later Taylor's big form appeared in the doorway. A copy of the paper was in his hand and a look of concern on his face. But Birdie had given the game away and he commenced laughing, too. The threatening "actor" had been Bill Taylor—speaking over the business-office phone.

I took the joke pretty hard. Particularly was I resentful toward Birdie, whose champion I had been. Sometime afterward I stepped into Taylor's net again and once more the laugh of the office was on me. I took this hard indeed, not speaking to anyone in the shop for a day or so. One evening after press time I was viciously pounding away on outside correspondence when Taylor laid a hand on my shoulder.

"You know why we tease you, Markey? It's because we like you."

I felt like a fool. But I felt better.

3

I had been on the *Eagle* about long enough to get used to Taylor's ribbing when a great thing occurred. Milton H. Wright bought Drummond's remaining stock and assumed charge of the paper.

During his last year as principal of the high school Wright and I had developed a mutual attachment. This was strengthened in the year just closed when he was operating in real estate. We had long talks which usually began with those most absorbing of topics, my work and my plans. Mr. Wright expressed a deep interest in newspapers and their power in a community. Wright was an insurgent, or liberal, Republican. Together we had followed with enthusiasm the uprising in the House of Representatives which had shorn Speaker Cannon of much of his arbitrary power. In this fight Representatives George Norris of Nebraska (Mr. Wright's home state) and Victor Murdock of Kansas had taken the lead. Liberal newspapers had played inspiring parts: William Allen White's Emporia *Gazette*, Henry Allen's Wichita *Beacon*, Arthur Capper's Topeka *Capital*, and Congressman Murdock's Wichita *Eagle*. While not one of the insurgent pioneers, Mr. Drummond was backing Judge Garber for the Republican congressional nomination against the standpat incumbent, Bird McGuire. Mr. Wright and I were glad for the *Eagle's* stand, but thought that were we in Pete Drummond's shoes a lot more would be done for the cause of insurgency.

It was a time to captivate the fancy of a Republican insurgent with a yen to run a newspaper. Mr. Wright had made money in real estate. The packing-plant boom was on the wane. From a welter of conflicting reports it looked as if there was going to be no packing plant, after all. What better could Wright do than close out his real-estate business, put the money into a newspaper and join the exciting fight?

Though without newspaper experience, he had studied the Kansas City *Star* and such Kansas papers as the *Gazette*, the *Beacon*, the Atcheson *Globe*, the Hutchinson *News*. Better models did not exist. The Kansas City *Star*, the personal creation of William Rockhill Nelson, who had joined the Fourth Estate after his maturity, was one of the world's great newspapers. It was simply the best imaginable country newspaper expanded to Kansas City's size, and the antithesis of its evening rival, the Hearst-like *Post* (of which I was now the northern Oklahoma correspondent).

In a fortnight Mr. Wright made over the *Eagle* into the best newspaper published in Enid to that time. There was no attempt at copying metropolitan journalism, except of the Kansas City *Star* type. Enid was covered even more completely than under Mr. Drummond, and much more brightly. Earle Radcliffe, who had been working in Oklahoma City, became city editor. Humphrey and I were the reporters. Taylor continued his budget of personals and small sprightly items. Wright's editorials ranked with the best in our part of the country.

The *Eagle* imparted new zest to Judge Garber's campaign to unseat the reactionary Congressman McGuire. I felt myself a participant in a crusade that was convulsing the whole country and wrote a few editorial paragraphs which Mr. Wright printed without too much fixing. Unfortunately McGuire controlled the county machines. Nosing out Garber in a close contest, he won the nomination. All the same, the experience was a thrilling one to me.

Wright was learning the ropes as an editor. The *Eagle* got better and better. I continued to expand, and began to sell some of my tall tales.

Another achievement was the rescue of John Wilkes Booth from obscurity. I gave him his best season since 1864. This was simpler than you might think, for we had Booth right around the corner in the back room of W. B. Penniman's undertaking parlor on West Randolph. He had been there since 1902 when he took poison in the Grand Avenue Hotel and left a note saying who he was.

In a dozen other ways you could prove he was Booth, and that the fellow they shot in the Garrett barn in Virginia was somebody else. There was the testimony of Mrs. Harper, the Methodist minister's wife. In 1901, when the Reverend Mr. Harper was preaching in El Reno, they had boarded at a house where a gentleman named David E. George also boarded. This George was an educated man and he wore the air of a person with a past —not too rare a type in Oklahoma. The clergyman's wife liked him. One day George fell violently ill. In what Mrs. Harper thought a delirium he told her that he was the murderer of Abraham Lincoln. He related the details of his escape and subsequent wanderings. Then he recovered from his illness. Mrs. Harper mentioned the matter only to her husband. Thinking George a victim of hallucinations they said nothing about it.

Mrs. Harper identified the man who had killed himself in Enid as her El Reno acquaintance.

A lawyer named Finis L. Bates came from Memphis. He said that George was the same man he had met in 1878 in Texas under the name of St. Helen. When he thought himself dying, St. Helen had told Bates the same story George told Mrs. Harper in El Reno, except that in 1878 there hadn't been so much to tell.

Doctor Baker got measurements of Booth. Those of the corpse coincided and the small bone of the corpse's left leg had been broken where Booth's had been broken when he leaped from the President's box to the stage of Ford's Theater. As to facial resemblance, thirty-seven years will work changes in any countenance. Yet unmistakably there was a resemblance between the George of 1902 and the Booth of 1865. On top of that were the muddled and contradictory accounts of the capture and death of the man at Garrett's and of his secret burial. If they had got Booth in Virginia, why all the monkey business?

George left a will distributing substantial legacies. When it turned out that the property bequeathed had no existence, the embalming fee remained unpaid and Mr. Penniman kept the body. As a small boy I had become an authority on the evidence that George was Booth. I could deliver a lecture on the subject and take an auditor to Penniman's and show him the corpse, all for the consideration of ten cents.

The same material was warmed over as a Sunday story which I disposed of to several city newspapers. When Madame Inez, a clairvoyant, opened for a week's stand in Enid, I showed her clippings establishing me as Booth's press representative. I suggested that she clinch the fact that our Booth was the Ford's Theater Booth by communicating with his departed spirit. I said it would be worth five dollars for me to record this interview. She beat me down to three dollars and Taylor ran the interview at advertising rates.

Three months later we worked the same racket on a fortune

teller named Madame Belmont. At first I thought I was going to get nowhere with Madame Belmont. She had never heard of John Wilkes Booth or of Abraham Lincoln. So I gave the madame a lesson in American history documented with newspaper clippings. The clippings were the real convincers.

Though unaware of it at the time, I had caused Mesdames Inez and Belmont to give currency to a piece of historical fiction. The spook of our Booth had stuck to his story—the story he had told, when living, to Mrs. Harper and to Mr. Bates. However plausible, it was a fake. This I learned much later. They had got the right Booth at Garrett's. Identification was positive, of which proof exists in the files of the War Department. The cloudy work which obscured these facts at the time was deliberately done by Lafayette C. Baker, chief of the United States secret service, in an effort to euchre out of the reward the soldiers responsible for Booth's capture.

Though having the time of my life, there was a fly in the ointment. I could see that Taylor didn't like the way things were going on the paper. It wasn't the *Eagle's* militant political insurgency that he objected to. It was all the money Wright was spending. Journalistically, Taylor was neither an insurgent nor a reactionary; he was a money-maker: first of all a paper had to be solvent. Mr. Drummond began to reappear at the office. Disapproval of Wright and Wright's ways was all over the former proprietor's square, practical figure. The *Eagle* represented a cake which Pete Drummond was accustomed to eat and have, too. He made more money selling the paper than running it. Two or three times before he had sold out, only to buy the *Eagle* back when the purchaser got sufficiently into debt and discouragement.

If only the packing plant hadn't gone up the spout! The expiring agonies of the boom were long drawn out. To mention just one thing, a gigantic replica of a hammer, symbol of the knockers, was buried with ceremony in the Square. All the same, holders of Packing Plant Addition lots continued to get out from under. The Eureka Realty Company closed its doors and its crew departed, hastening the stampede of flush-times floaters toward greener pastures. On top of that a summer-long drought burned up the wheat and the corn.

4

From this dreary prospect it was a pleasure to turn to the delights of a reunion with a long-absent friend.

The tall, gangling, pimply-faced figure, resplendent in a flashy suit and yellow buttoned shoes, was lounging in the doorway of the smelly blind-tiger pool hall where High Pockets played for the house. Though he hadn't crossed my mind in years, recognition was almost instantaneous.

"Dewey Evans!" I cried.

A trifle startled by the warmth of my greeting, Dewey's splotched countenance went blank for a moment. Then the thick, loose lips parted in a grin which revealed a gold tooth.

"Markey—Markey James, ain't it?"

"Name I use in these parts," said I.

Dewey extended a limp, moist hand.

"Howyuh, boy?"

"Howyuh," I said. "Whereyuh been keepin' yourself?"

"Oh, evawheres," Dewey replied expansively. "Evawheres from hell t' breakfus'."

Over a couple of snorts of rotgut and a bottle of tin top (near-beer), which I drank, I drew from Dewey a summary of his odyssey. Dewey had achieved his goal in life. He was a short-order cook, a calling which lent itself to the broadening influences of travel. Oklahoma City, Fort Worth, Houston—names of towns dropped from his lips—Shreveport, Baton Rouge, Biloxi, Mobile; Montgomery, Atlanta, Waycross, Savannah.

"Been West any?" I asked tentatively. "Denver, Colorado Springs, Cheyenne?"

"No, but kinda headed thataway now. They say wages good out West."

"An' they're mighty right. Denver: there's a *town,* man. More going on than in Chi. Know what they got pasted up in the composing room of the *Rocky Mountain News?* Something clipped from a railroad ad and it says 'Tourist Stopover.' Hand-spiker can always grab a few days work on the *News.* 'Nough to carry him to Salt Lake."

Dewey took a fellow-traveler's interest in what I had to say.

"What say your lina work was?"

"Printer," I replied briefly. "Just now I'm in the front office, though. Reporter. On the *Eagle.*"

"Worked in a counter joint in Memphis where we fed a lotta printers."

Just now Dewey had the night shift at Cap Bond's. To see him in the discharge of his duties during the rush hour was to witness a transformation: loose-jointed, loose-minded two-bit sport into intent and purposeful expert.

With a deft rhythmic weaving Dewey Evans flipped a steak from the broiler to a plate, added a big spoonful of mashed potatoes and a dab of gravy and angled the whole through the slot in the partition between the kitchen and the dining room. He sang out: "Pick up small well!" and, in the same breath, acknowledged a fresh order from the other side: "Stacka w'eats; two in!"

"Chili!" came a voice from beyond the partition.

"Bowla hot!" called back Dewey.

"Milk toast!" came through, pronounced distinctly because the order was unusual.

"Graveyard stew!" acknowledged Dewey, starting to slip a couple of slices of bread into the oven before the words were out of his mouth. Dewey knew he'd made a contribution to the waiter's knowledge of the argot of his craft. "Graveyard stew's what they call it in Biloxi," he said to me. "*Some* town, man." The short-order cook's loose lips gave him a perpetual leer. His tone suggested nameless pleasures available in Biloxi, Mississippi.

With three or four orders on the fire and a couple of others in his head, Dewey'd shoot a glance in the direction of the slattern girl clattering crockery in a zinc-lined sink. "Side dishes up!" he'd bark, and throw in a lewd quip for good measure.

At this time I was the sergeant commanding K Company's machine-gun platoon, as we called the old battery. We drilled hard and I don't believe a platoon in the regiment knew its business better. As the time for camp approached I presented Dewey for enlistment. Captain Scott didn't want to take him unless he would sign as a cook. Dewey wouldn't do this. The captain yielded and Dewey went along with us to Fort Riley. The first two mornings he was late for reveille, giving the platoon a black mark. He dropped out on the first long hike. He won so consistently at craps that Mike Radford made a complaint of queer dice.

"Use your dice, then," I said, very much the sergeant.

One Saturday evening while slicking up to go to Junction City I found my clean socks—*the sergeant's socks*—on Private Evans's feet.

"Didn't think you'd mind none," said Dewey, hurt at the military crispness with which I ordered him to take them off.

Sergeant Jarboe missed a pocket knife and Harry Rector some change from his clothes at the bathhouse. Calling Dewey aside, I appealed to his better nature. As a little kid Dewey had been a competent fighter and I was afraid of him. Though a little uneasy now, I looked him in the eyes. The loose mouth twitched.

"Honest to God, Markey, I didn't taken 'em. I wouldn't taken nothin' offen a frienda yourn."

That made me feel better, even though I suspected he was lying by the clock.

Not long after our return I noticed a new night cook at Cap Bond's. To my inquiry concerning Dewey, Mr. Bond replied with incidental profanity:

"Flew the coop with three dollars belonging to the dishwasher."

Some months later, while looking over the exchanges, a familiar name caught my eye. In Missouri Dewey Evans had been sentenced to a term in the penitentiary for the theft of a stickpin belonging to the proprietor of a short-order house. Thus the first of my contemporaries to realize his ambition in life was also the first to go to the pen.

5

I used to think that this might not have happened except for the personal crisis which absorbed my attention on our return from Fort Riley, affording no time to look after Dewey. Bill Taylor had chosen the moment when the machine-gun platoon was making military history to install himself in the driver's seat at the *Eagle* and reorganize the paper, in the process of which I was separated from the payroll. An appeal to Wright brought only a vague promise of a future "opening." With something of a shock I realized that Wright himself felt none too secure. Drummond and Taylor had ganged him.

Turning to the *Morning News*, I got in a few days' work, after which Barry Bullock regretfully said that Mr. Stewart was too hard up to keep me. The *Wave-Democrat* was out of the question. Doctor Kelso's newspaper was *in extremis*, destined to survive only a few weeks. Accordingly, I matriculated at Oklahoma Christian University. The academic backbone of this raw little prairie school was a rigidly sectarian Bible College. The athletic department was conducted on more liberal lines. The coach enrolled football players who could write, but not very legibly. A member of the Enid Fire Department majored in penmanship. The result of this policy, plus some two-hundred-pound divinity students, was a team in which everybody took pride.

But I missed the newspaper office: the clatter of the typewriters, the clack of the linotypes, the roar of the presses; the local-room and the back-room banter. I even missed the jovialities of Taylor, the author of all my woes. Because I could not stay away, I hung around the *Eagle*, using the typewriters for outside correspondence and to contribute O.C.U. items free of charge. I submitted my first story to a magazine—McClure's. It was a sophisticated piece of fiction, beginning:

"'Cigarettes on the taboret,' said Arlington, gesturing carelessly."

I had read in *Smart Set* that a taboret was where the swells kept their smokes.

One night while I was using an *Eagle* typewriter Mr. Wright opened up and told how the land lay. The paper had been obliged to cut expenses five hundred dollars a month.

I tried to cultivate Mr. Taylor—to impress on him my value to the *Eagle*. The result was an offer of a job—soliciting subscriptions! Tactfully concealing the extent of his affront, I managed a civil if noncommittal answer. A few evenings later, chinning with Wright again, I happened to mention that the Board of Education must be having a hot time about now over the new-high-school-building question.

"Great Scott," said Wright, "is that up tonight?"

I said I thought everyone knew that it was.

Mr. Wright picked up the phone and called the Board rooms. The session had begun.

"Dig up there, Markey. I'll *make* Taylor give you a job."

It was a good story and Taylor agreed to take me back at six dollars a week—half my former pay. I shifted my O.C.U. schedule to make room for the *Eagle* work and was quite happy again.

Presently I landed the most spectacular scoop scored by an Enid newspaper in my time. Over a good part of the state it let loose a flood that extinguished an underhanded attempt to liberate John Cannon from the Oklahoma penitentiary where he was serving a sentence for shooting to death City Marshal Tom Radford. The exposé turned Enid upside down and for a few days made the *Eagle's* six-dollar-a-week reporter feel like the most important person in it.

I remembered well the shooting of Tom Radford, which had taken place the winter I was in the eighth grade at Central. The marshal was warming his hands at a radiator near the front door of the Tony Faust saloon. He had gloves on. His overcoat was buttoned over his gun. Cannon came in the side door of the saloon. Walking up to Radford, he said, "Bad day, ain't it?" Radford turned to face the speaker. Cannon pushed a .38 against the marshal's breast and fired. As the wounded man made a move to unbutton his coat Cannon fired again. Radford staggered through the front door. Cannon followed and fired again. Radford fell on the sidewalk. Cannon bent over him and seemed about to fire a fourth shot when a policeman rushed from Mills's barber shop, drew a revolver and backed the assailant off.

I saw none of this, but that night I mingled with the knots of armed men who gathered about the jail. After we boys had been chased off the streets I wrote in my diary: "I guess they will lynch John Cannon. I would like to see them hang him to a telephone pole." Next morning I was uptown early. The last of the armed men were reluctantly leaving the Square, their voices hoarse, their eyes underscored with blue and dull from dead excitement. By a fairly narrow margin they had failed of the gratification of their desires and mine. In his day Sheriff Campbell had faced down would-be lynchers. But this time he resorted to stratagem. Not until Cannon had been spirited out of town had the sheriff walked into the Square with an invitation to search the jail.

A confusing feature of the tragedy was the fact that John Cannon had been one of Enid's popular characters, and never in the slightest trouble until a few months before his crime. For years in the post of county jailer, his cracker-barrel jests had gained him a favorable reputation among the lawyers and local officialdom. On a wall of my father's office when he died was a group photograph comprising a veritable Who's Who in Enid. It had been taken in the jail yard and was labeled "Suckers' Convention, April 1, 1905." John Cannon had telephoned to lawyers that a prisoner wished the advice of counsel on a matter of great urgency; to doctors that a prisoner was sick; to undertakers that one was dead; and so on.

It being April Fool's Day, the prisoner represented as in need of these ministrations existed only in John Cannon's imagination.

Yet, at that moment, the jail did shelter a guest of the county who was well on the way to encompassing the downfall of the genial turnkey. Her name was Lillie Long. So interested did Mr. Cannon become in Lillie that, to safeguard the morals of the jail, Sheriff Campbell dismissed John from his employment. After Lillie's time was up Cannon married her. Lillie opened an establishment which became an object of police scrutiny when a man was killed there in an altercation involving rivalry for the friendly notice of one of Lillie's protégées known as Big Mae. During the official inquiry into this affair, words passed between Mr. Radford and Mr. Cannon. Lillie's husband threatened to kill the marshal, whereupon Mr. Radford observed that he didn't believe Cannon had the nerve to try it.

All this came out at the trial, in which Cannon was defended by Mr. Henry Sturgis. This disillusioned, hard-drinking man, whose shelves were filled with the classics of literature which he owned and with law books which he borrowed, had been my father's closest friend; and he was probably the most gifted of the legal luminaries of the early-day Strip.

Many stories have collected about the memory of Henry Sturgis as a courtroom performer. One deals with a time he was opposed by H. G. McKeever, a very good lawyer, always affable and rather glib in action. In his argument Mr. McKeever quoted a line from *Henry VIII.*

Henry Sturgis slouched before the jury.

"My learned friend McKeever has introduced a new party to this lawsuit, namely William Shakespeare. As submitted by my esteemed adversary, Mr. Shakespeare's testimony would appear to favor the pretensions of the plaintiff in this action. It wears that appearance because Mr. McKeever has quoted to you only a few words, only a scrap of what Shakespeare had to say on the point at issue. Gentlemen, permit me to refresh your recollections."

Mr. Sturgis quoted the scene entire, thereby establishing to the jury's satisfaction that William Shakespeare was on the side of the defendant.

Another courthouse yarn has Henry Sturgis opposed by Percy Simons, a large-domed, dead-earnest, capable little man who had been attorney general of the Territory.

"I will personally vouch," declared Mr. Simons with all the conviction he possessed, "I will personally vouch for the veracity of this witness!"

"You heard Percy Simons," drawled Henry Sturgis, "personally vouch for the veracity of the witness. Now, who'll vouch for Percy?"

An illiterate old codger named Jake Voorhees succeeded Judge Roach on the bench of the Police Court. Now and then Mr. Sturgis defended a client in the Police Court, sometimes to succor a friend and sometimes because he could use three dollars.

When D. W. Buckner was fresh out of law school a good deal of his practice was before Judge Voorhees. The young attorney was a silver-tongued Kentuckian with a bump of shrewdness. He learned the art of flattering the magistrate with high-sounding legal jagon. On the strength of this, Buckner got the job of substituting for the city attorney who was supposed to prosecute offenders the cops brought before Judge Voorhees.

The case in point involved a colored man. In his plea Mr. Buckner quoted Blackstone and Coke and cited opinions by Story and Marshall.

Henry Sturgis alluded to "the instructive citations offered by my eloquent and scholarly adversary." "But why—and I am confident this has occurred to your Honor—why did Mr. Buckner omit reference to Mr. Justice Marshall's opinion in the most celebrated case in the history of American jurisprudence bearing on the issue here involved, that is to say assault with an edged instrument, to wit, a razor? As your Honor has surmised, I refer to the case of Habeas *versus* Corpus."

6

The defense of John Cannon has been called one of Mr. Sturgis's masterpieces. Reading the record, it seems a miracle.

On a change of venue, the trial was held at Watonga. The prosecution was well conducted by County Attorney Dan Huett, who had an open-and-shut case of first degree murder. Mr. Huett showed that while under the spell of a harlot John Cannon had killed Tom Radford in cold blood. But this wasn't the Cannon Henry Sturgis defended. He kept before the jury a representation of the man Enid had long known: the decent guy, the hail-fellow everybody liked and wished well. A comparison of the accounts of witnesses who had seen John Cannon fire the shots into the body of the defenseless Radford presented the little discrepancies natural to honest testimony. Upon these trifles Henry Sturgis pounced with the ardor of a zealot. Of Lillie Long he made a Magdalen whose story would have moved a heart of stone.

The jury was sufficiently spellbound to bring in a verdict of first-degree manslaughter. Judge Garber, however, remained impervious to compassion and pronounced a sentence probably unprecedented for manslaughter in our part of the country—forty years.

Nearly four years had been served and the case was pretty well forgotten when Red Martin, the night operator, called me behind the counter at Western Union. Producing a sheaf of telegrams which had been filed at Enid and flimsies of the replies, he said:

"Read these and forget you ever saw them in this office, or it'll be worth my job. But this is so raw I got to do something."

Red Martin was the first sergeant of K Company of which two sons of the slain man were members. The telegrams told the story of negotiations for the pardon of John Cannon. At the Enid end were three well-known citizens; at the Oklahoma City end a politician close to Governor Haskell who had been said to grant pardons in exchange for political and other considerations. As Mr. Haskell had less than a month to serve, the Enid people were pushing matters—apparently with success.

Next day I broke the story—four columns with pictures. The effect was all a crusading reporter could have wished. Civic groups and labor unions filled the air with denunciatory resolutions. C. N. Haskell went out of office and John Cannon remained in the pen as long as I remained in Oklahoma.

When he did get out it was on account of Colonel McAlester's conviction that only horse thieves belonged in jail indefinitely. The colonel was lieutenant-governor under Mr. Haskell's successor. As a young man out of the Confederate Army, McAlester had gone to the Chickasaw Nation, married a Chickasaw girl, and become a Chickasaw citizen. Had he married a Choctaw girl and become a Choctaw citizen, a lot of inconvenience might have been avoided, for it happened that his trading post, later the town of McAlester, was a short piece over the Choctaw line. Arrested for a violation of the Choctaw laws having to do with trade, McAlester was sentenced to death. Ground was being cleared for the execution when the intervention of a white Choctaw citizen won a pardon from Principal Chief Coleman Cole. The incident disposed Colonel McAlester in favor of clemency as an item of executive policy.

Two weeks after my Cannon exploit I was back to earth. Taylor had tightened the screws again, giving Humphrey his walking papers. The next entry in my diary:

"December 31, 1910. I, too, got the official cleaver today. Wright explained matters in detail: The paper is hard up."

CHAPTER SIXTEEN

The Dull Day Items

NEW YEAR'S DAY, 1911, found your correspondent nursing a pair of sore feet and pondering the mutability of journalistic fame. The sore dogs came from tight shoes worn at the previous evening's function of the Congenial Dancing Club; the reflections from the fact that not only was I out at the *Eagle* but all 'round. While riding the crest of the Cannon affair I had quit the University: too small potatoes for a big newspaperman.

Before the day was over, though, a possibility of remedying this situation had begun to take form. Mr. Wright asked why didn't I hit Taylor for the circulation job? A week before, Wright had made the same suggestion and I had rejected it: a business-office job. This time the editor explained that there wasn't a Chinaman's chance of my getting back on the news side. "And, Markey, if I were you I wouldn't let any grass grow under my feet. You're not the only person out of work in Enid."

So I braced Mr. Taylor, putting all I had into a testimonial in favor of myself as a potential circulation builder. If the business manager was impressed he concealed it. He said he'd see. A few days later Mr. Taylor telephoned to inquire if I could keep a set of books.

"Yes, sir," I said, without asking what kind of books, for I wouldn't have known any more had he told me.

They turned out to be the advertising accounts, hitherto taken care of by Mr. Sexsmith, a business-office holdover from the Drummond regime. Taylor having cut the pay to six dollars a week, Sexsmith, who was an old printer, had gone to work in the composing room where he could draw the union scale. I took the job and engaged Mr. Sexsmith as my adviser. A part of the bargain with Taylor was that as soon as I got on to the run of things in the business office I could have a crack at circulation. This came sooner than expected. Hearing what was in the wind, the circulation manager quit and went over to the *Morning News*.

The way the *Eagle* handled its city circulation placed the circulation manager in business for himself. He bought papers for five-and-one-half cents per week and paid carriers three cents a week apiece to deliver them and collect ten cents from each subscriber on Saturday. The balance of one-and-one-half cents was the circulation manager's profit. He could increase this by getting new readers at ten cents a week, or by getting paid-up subscriptions on an annual basis. The price was four dollars in advance, of which the paper got half and the circulation manager half.

The Monday morning I took over, the *Eagle's* city list aggregated 1325 copies—368 paid-ups and comps (to heavy advertisers), and 957 currents. I began an energetic soliciting campaign and in the course of the week put on fifty or sixty subscribers. Yet when Saturday came my currents list was down to 918. "Stops" had exceeded "starts." This was in part due to the creeping paralysis of hard times. Railroad figures—which we did not print—showed fifteen families a week leaving Enid and taking their household goods. The other factor was the enterprise of my rival who had opened up with a burst of solicitation for the *News.*

The second week I made some headway and expanded the currents list to 972, thanks to the rudiments of a system I introduced into my canvassing. For a few evenings I'd send copies rubber-stamped "SAMPLE" to selected addresses. With each paper would go a printed "Personal Message" from "Marquis James, Circulation Manager," courteously inviting attention to the paper's specific and general excellence. Then I would call at those houses with my selling talk. It worked better than random door-thumping.

I learned to capitalize our news columns. In six weeks' time I'd adopted a business-office slant on news that should have shamed an ex-reporter. "Sensational divorce suit doing good things for circulation," reads my diary. "I put on about 15 today." Whenever we had a scoop or a particularly good paper I'd distribute sample copies and a "Personal Message" to a hand-picked list of non-readers. Birdie McKenzie's society column was exploited to a fare-thee-well. If a lady who did not subscribe gave a party or entertained the Madrigal Club, I saw that a copy of the *Eagle* with Birdie's write-up was on her porch that evening. Next morning I'd be there.

I wrote little items about non-subscribers. They didn't have to be spot news. Usually they were what Taylor called "dull day items." A sample of what he meant:

"Charlie Cansler is the best hand in town at judging the size of a crowd. He learned it taking tickets at the ball park."

My items didn't have to be about prominent citizens. A street-car motorman's ten cents was as good as a doctor's, and sometimes easier to get on Saturday. I'd keep plugging away until an object of my attentions subscribed or until I gave him up as a hopeless case. Once the latter decision was reached, the only way that individual could have got his name in the *Eagle,* with my connivance, would have been to land in the Public Square in one of the Wright brothers' flying machines.

Such measures proved effective enough to lift the currents list to 1055 in a month. In three months it was 1150 and the total list in the neighborhood of 1700.

This represented pretty hard work. Until mid-afternoon my day was devoted to soliciting, to individual subscriber and carrier problems, and to other activities of which I will speak presently. Then I would repair to the press room and "get out" the carriers as the papers came off the press. A route was never the same two days running. There would always be a certain number of starts and stops. On occasions a carrier would fail to appear. I would carry the route myself. (My predecessor had maintained, at his own expense, a substitute carrier.) One Sunday morning, in a howling blizzard, I carried two routes. I prided myself on a guarantee of delivery. Subscribers were asked to report non-deliveries by phone. An hour after the boys were out I'd stop by the business office, collect the skips and deliver them on a bike.

Saturday was a twenty-four-hour day. First off, I collected a route which had proved too tough for the boy who carried it. After that I took to my desk and settled for the week with each of the twelve carriers who had done his own collecting. Then I balanced my accounts and settled with the office, a detail involving considerable bookkeeping—fractional weeks to be considered, and so on. Owing to the fact that in my hands figures never behave normally, it was necessary to devise a system of my own for striking a balance and determining my indebtedness to the office.

Not once that I recall did my books come out exactly right. Either I had left in my hands a sum running from a few cents to a few dollars more than I knew by rights I was entitled to; or it would be the other way and the office would have too much. I knew better than to go back and try to find where the error lay. I'd just split the difference. If I felt that I had three dollars too much I'd give the office half of it. If I thought the figures showed the office share three dollars too high I'd pocket a dollar and a half. Sometimes I wondered what would happen should Taylor ask to see my books. Taylor could spot an arithmetical error on a page covered with figures by looking at it across a room. He never looked at my books, though, and seemed satisfied that with the bottom dropping out of everything else circulation revenue climbed.

Saturday afternoons and nights I worked as a reporter. From one until three Sunday morning, when the press began to roll, I might sleep on the exchange table, though usually the time was spent reading, chewing the rag at Cap Bond's or working up dull day items or outside correspondence. Papers counted and stacked according to routes, I'd await the coming of the carriers. Barring complications I'd be home by six-thirty or seven.

Having inherited a good bunch of carriers—mostly high-school or University students—I sought to improve their devotion to the paper by distributing comps to the shows and awarding prizes for getting new subs. No paper had successfully made carrier deliveries on the fringes of the town where houses were far apart. I built up a route there and got a boy with a pony to carry it. When one of the boys got in bad company and helped steal a valuable bicycle, I persuaded the county attorney to reduce the charge to petit larceny, to which the boy pleaded guilty and escaped with a fine. Otherwise he'd have gone to jail. The intercession made me ace high with the carrier corps.

All the while times were getting leaner and money scarcer. The exodus from town left rows of vacant houses and there were empty business buildings on the Square. A city circulation of 1700 represented the ultimate in human endeavor as far as my capabilities went. And I had to fight to hold it there. Consequently I turned my best efforts to getting annual paid-ups. My appeals were limited to people who had money. Such people are nearly always thrifty. I'd show them how they could save more than a dollar on a year's subscription. As my take was two dollars a subscription, some forenoons I'd make ten dollars. In all, I ran my circulation income to twenty-five or thirty dollars a week. That was more than the paper's owners were drawing down.

2

The first thing I knew a competition to see who could get the most dull day items had grown up between Taylor and me. Now that I was used to his ribbing, working with Taylor was fun. As the paper was down to one reporter, Earle Radcliffe, Taylor made a special effort to get news items and encouraged me to do so. On his rounds of the Square soliciting ads, Taylor would always come in with half a column. It was easier to get than ads. He would hunch his big shoulders over a typewriter and bat out as fast as his fingers could work the machine:

"Mayor Randolph tried for ten minutes to borrow a match this morning. . . . Harry B. Woolf wears copper wires around his wrists to prevent rheumatism. . . . J. A. Smith's family horse, when a colt eleven months old, fell to the bottom of a 50-foot well in Stevens county, Kansas."

At first items were made into individual paragraphs separated by three-em dashes, but as the drop in advertising frequently cut the paper to six pages Taylor took to "running in" the items to save space. He would pass a sheet of his items to me and say:

"Hey, Markey, quit loafing and match these."

I'd do my best:

"There are lots of people in Enid who think Jack McCutcheon can take apart or put together any machine which was ever made. . . . Col. Joshua Mathis is about as spry as any man his age in town. . . . H. G. McKeever is not superstitious but just feels a little better when he looks at the moon over his left shoulder. Mr. McKeever has not lost a case this term of court, which he attributes to the fact that he never uses the south stairs of the court house. . . . Happy Jack, an Enid negro, went away with the carnival. Happy got a job with one of the shows to do a little comedy singing and banjo playing. Happy has left before but he always comes back."

When Hap returned from that tour he told me that he had quit the carnival because he was tired of playing a banjo. On his own, Hap played a guitar. Notwithstanding the literature on the subject from Stephen Foster down, the result of my observation is that the banjo is not a favored instrument of the musical Negro. It is something put in his hands by showmen.

Mr. Taylor and I would save our items until we had about a column and then, two or three times a week, print them on the editorial page under the box head:

DULL DAY ITEMS

The column was signed "The Cub Reporters." Taylor believed the sum and substance of running a newspaper could be epitomized in an expression he'd heard from Ed Howe of the Atchison *Globe*: "A good reporter can get an item from everyone he meets." Starting out too poor to hire a reporter, Mr. Howe had gathered news as a by-product of his daily rounds shagging ads, subscriptions, and job printing. At first he set his items at the case, a form of training in expression which encouraged the conciseness of style most printer-editors had. In this way the Atchison *Globe* grew into one of the best small-town dailies in America. Taylor didn't think much of editors who had to brag about their telegraph service.

Ever since he had started to learn the printer's trade as a youth in Kansas, Taylor had seen newspapers curl up and die. He had seen Ed Howe, W. Y. Morgan of the Hutchinson *News*, Arthur Capper, Henry Allen, Victor Murdock, and William Allen White establish influential and paying properties. A primitive vigor emanated from those excellent newspapers, every one of them still in the hands of the man who had made it out of nothing but himself.

Though William Allen White was the only editor on the list who enjoyed a national reputation among the laity, Taylor always mentioned White's name last. "Take the editorials out of the *Gazette* and you don't have much of a newspaper." Taylor classed editorials below telegraph. Moreover, Mr. White was a literary figure, another species of little account about a newspaper office, in Bill Taylor's estimation.

Mr. Taylor's ideal was cynical old Ed Howe, who professed to believe "Booth Tarkington" too high-sounding to be a real name and who did believe one pack of politicians as bad as another. Though virtually unknown outside the newspaper fraternity, Howe had made his Atchison *Globe* one of the most widely quoted and imitated newspapers in the United States. All over the country ambitious columnists and paragraphers combed the *Globe*, reprinting, cribbing or rewriting with a local twist Howe's vinegary observations on human nature or finding local replicas of the Atchison characters who peopled his personals.

Joining the imitators, I had the advantage of working close to my models—close, I do believe, to the geographical center of the Golden Age of country journalism in America. A little of the precious dust blew across the Oklahoma line and stuck to my skin. Before long I could whip out copy of the Kansas school nearly as fast as Bill Taylor. The Dull Day Items grew into a daily feature of which I became the principal author. People read the column and talked about it. That made items easier to get. Folks would stop you on the street. One day Taylor went into the composing room and substituted my name for "The Cub Reporters." A greater thrill came a month later when Taylor, who watched expenditures like a hawk, let Wright squander a dollar for a half-column cut of me to adorn the Dull Day Items. It was sprung as a surprise one Sunday morning.

Although I was allowed to deduct from my weekly paper bill a dollar for my services as a reporter on Saturdays I wrote the Dull Day Items for nothing. So greatly did I love the column that I think I would have paid for the privilege of writing it. It is a pleasure to record this because I think it was one of the few business possibilities Taylor overlooked in those days.

When the column improved so that other papers began to quote from it I enjoyed another pleasant sensation. Surely it was something to see a batch of your stuff reprinted, with credit, in Kansas or Texas:

"Most men would rather catch fish than clean them but Red

Martin would rather catch them than eat them. . . . Bruce Sanders is getting his hands calloused from cranking his automobile. It used to be that when a man's hands were calloused he had been working. . . . Red Martin does not believe that he is the only person in town who can't tell how old a horse is by looking in its mouth. . . . Poor ventilation never kept Jim Smart away from church. . . . About the only thing Herschel Goltry hasn't claimed for his motorcycle is that it's a musical instrument. . . . When Jim Smart, the hack driver, works nights he learns things about people's private lives which he never tells because in Jim's circle they aren't any novelty."

Sayings and doings of Red Martin and of Jim Smart were reprinted so widely that once a stranger in town asked to have these homespun philosophers pointed out. Red Martin actually got off most of the quips attributed to him. Sometimes a rival paragrapher would pay the Items the sincerest of tributes—quotation without credit. To see an item I had borrowed from the *Globe* and lovingly restyled to fit the *Eagle* borrowed and rerestyled to fit the *Oklahoman* reduced my stock of faith in human nature. If plagiarism affected Ed Howe the same way, it is no wonder he had few illusions.

As time went on I didn't have to borrow so much as I did at first. And not all my items were short. Every now and then I'd write four or five hundred words of reminiscence I'd heard from some old-timer. When they tore down an old building, as they did the former Rex Hotel, I'd unwind about its history. Tramp printers' itineraries and experiences produced good copy. I made a practice of getting acquainted with the linotype operator who set the column and writing him up.

There was Harry Beckley who, when not carrying the banner, turned in as clean a proof as I have ever seen—and I mean to the date of this writing. "Carrying the banner" was an expression printers, and I suppose others, used for a hangover. The complete idiom was "carrying the banner for Colonel R E," meaning r-e-morse. Beck did more than any other operator I knew to perpetuate the folkways of the old-time tramp printer. Though a natty dresser who rode the cushions, Beck was always on the move.

His route was influenced by the bargains available in scalped railroad tickets. A scalped ticket was the return portion of a round-trip ticket which had been disposed of to a scalper by the original purchaser. Such tickets carried time limits—say sixty or ninety days. When these limits neared expiration a scalper would offer exceptional bargains. The only streak of thrift I ever discovered in Beck was his inability to resist such money-saving opportunities.

Beck's successor was Pittman Hinds, who looked part Indian. Anyhow, he had learned to set type in the old Choctaw Nation and had worked in the Choctaw and Cherokee languages. The Choctaws used the English characters but the Cherokees had an alphabet of their own, making theirs the only written Indian language. This was not pictography, by which all Indians could transmit simple ideas. It was writing by means of an alphabet of arbitrary characters, the inventions of an Indian named Sequoyah. Pittman Hinds told me about him. Though unable to speak any language except his own, Sequoyah had observed that the whites' ability to communicate by "paper talk" gave them an advantage over the red people. So Sequoyah sat down and after years of labor succeeded in classifying the Cherokee tongue into eighty-five sounds and giving each a symbol. It was one of the prodigious intellectual feats in the history of primitive peoples. Sequoyah lived to see a newspaper printed in the Cherokee language. It did not occur to him that he had done anything for which to be renowned. But nothing he or any other Indian could do stayed the greedy hand of the palefaces. A troubled old man, he wandered off to visit a band of Cherokees who had journeyed beyond the Rio Grande into Old Mexico to try to get away from the white people, printing and all. There Sequoyah died and no stone marks the unknown resting place of a genius of his race.

That was how I used to get long items out of the back room where the linotype was making its impress on the printing fellowship. The reign of the jaunty and unpredictable swift was over. Operators were kings of the composing room. All they did was sit and tickle a keyboard. That's what it looked like, though actually an operator was an exceedingly competent mechanic. Linotypes were more liable to stoppages than Colt machine guns. The men who kept them going comprised a different breed from the old hand-spikers. Better paid and steadier, they wore clean shirts and, the example of Harry Beckley notwithstanding, they stayed longer in one place. Young printers on the make wanted to become operators and settle down, not tramps and see the world.

So much for one legacy of the machine age. For my part you could have it. Though the tramp's sun was setting, it had lighted a spacious day.

3

The Dull Day Items had been running under my name for about a month when a letter came from Russel McKinley Crouse. Mike was on the big time—covering sports for the Cincinnati *Commercial-Tribune*. He wrote that the managing editor had sent for him. On the editor's desk was a copy of the *Eagle*. The editor asked Crouse how much I'd want to come to Cincinnati. Mike suggested I say twenty a week "and get out of the sticks."

I walked on air. Recognition at last! In imagination I was in Cincinnati already—a by-lined star on the *Commercial-Tribune*. Would they run my picture? I wondered.

Breaking the news to Mama brought me to earth with a jolt. Anxiety deepened the lines of her face, but all she said was, "Marquis, do study about it and decide what seems best for your future. Dear me, I don't know what to say—things happen so fast in this newspaper work."

I repaired to the low-ceilinged room to which I had carried so many problems. Flopping on the bed I cocked my feet in a loop of the fancy white ironwork and tried to think. Long ago the roof had leaked, spreading an irregular stain on the ceiling. When trying to concentrate, my attention had a habit of wandering to that stain. As in clouds, I could see so many patterns and enticing shapes that it required an effort to get my mind back to what it should be on.

Twenty bucks! There was the rub. Just a little more than half what I was hauling down in Enid, still it was above what a beginner could ordinarily hope for in the cities. Twenty dollars a week in Cincy would hardly more than keep me. What I made in Enid enabled me to live like a prince and salt away a hundred a month. The need for this saving—now that the debts Papa's death had left were paid? Well, going into that, there were two needs: first, Mama'd have to be taken care of whenever I *should* go off on my own, and, second, what about that year in college?

Provision for Mama was the without which nothing; college something I could do as I wished about, finances permitting. Trouble was, discovering what my wishes were. I faced one way and the other. Last fall, seeing so many of my high-school friends pull out for college had been a factor in my signing up at O.C.U. Then had come the Cannon scoop and my interest in college hit the vanishing point, to be rekindled during Christmas vacation by tales of life at Norman, K.U., Missouri, and Wisconsin. Again I felt that my life would be incomplete without a year of that. The heaviest weight in the scale was what Karl Green wrote from Leland Stanford. A few weeks before the arrival of Crouse's letter a letter from Green had decided me. I had applied for admission to Stanford and sent a deposit for a room. When receipt of the latter was acknowledged I regarded myself as a Stanford undergraduate.

Getting my mind off the stain on the ceiling long enough to survey the foreordained consequences of the Stanford move, it was clear that a year out there with Green would leave Mama so nearly broke that I'd have to scratch up another stake before I could launch myself on the city papers. And by *that* time I'd be practically *twenty-one years old!*

I almost wished Crouse hadn't written that letter and stirred all this up. Anyhow, I couldn't afford to take any measly little twenty-a-week job now. I'd just write old Mike so.

Guessed I'd better go tell Mama. She'd be on pins and needles.

Some pains were bestowed on the reply to McKinley Crouse. With satisfaction I noted the interest of his managing editor in the little column I managed to dash off each day amid other preoccupations. Without describing these preoccupations too minutely

I alluded to my responsibilities as northern Oklahoma correspondent for the Chicago *Record-Herald* and for the New York *World.* In view of my plans to return to college, money assumed a place in my calculations which would not permit of a fifty per cent reduction in income at this time. After some chit-chat about the old gang, I thanked Mike again for his act of friendship and his managing editor for the kindly interest shown and begged to remain. . . .

A month later I wrote Stanford not to expect me. I couldn't see deferring my career until old enough to vote.

What I told Mike Crouse about representing the New York *World* was no emanation of the mind. I also represented the New York *Morning Telegraph,* the theatrical and sporting paper, which enabled me to carry a card of identification good for admission to any place of entertainment. In all I suppose I had the most profitable string of city papers an Oklahoma newspaperman had built up outside the state capital, which was then Oklahoma City. To say that I was the northern Oklahoma correspondent for these journals does myself less than justice. Some of the things I did to geography to get news items within my jurisdiction would have puzzled the map makers. Most of my stuff I dug from obscure country papers and adorned the facts a bit, naturally. Much of it was stuff the Oklahoma City correspondents missed because no Bill Taylor had shown them how to find news when there didn't seem to be any.

4

For all my far-ranging ambitions and lifting of eyes to the hills, most of what I wrote was pure Oklahoma, grass-roots Cherokee Strip. It was the best and most genuine stuff I'd written yet; and it improved. The Dull Day Items were my trademark. They identified me—with Enid.

I was going with a girl who had been born in Enid. Her name was Dorothy Denton, and we used to laugh about the way her father, the late Scott Denton, and my father had failed to get along. Dorothy was as pretty as a picture. My attentions to her entailed a neglect of the social set I'd worked so hard to break into a few years back. Three years younger than I, Dorothy ran with a more juvenile crowd. As her friends were a bit immature for me, Dorothy and I got to going around by ourselves. My old set was breaking up anyhow—girls and fellows drifting away—getting married, even.

Dorothy and I didn't need anyone to help us have a good time. Sometimes she went with me on newspaper errands. I'd tell her about Mizzou Edmundson and Josephine Barnabee and the Dirty Dozen. She was the only nice girl I ever mentioned such people to. Dorothy said she was thrilled. Nearly everything thrilled Dorothy, who found little to criticize in life, or in me, and so made a beguiling companion.

Dorothy and another girl were the only persons young enough to have been born in the Strip and old enough to come within the scope of my serious notice. The other girl was Enid Purcell, Everett's youngest sister. She was born the day of the Run—in a tent on the Enid townsite during a blinding dust storm a few hours after Walter Cook had driven his stake. Every September 16 the papers would print something about her, just as on February 12 they would print something about shiftless old man Hanks, a second cousin of Abraham Lincoln. I'd known Enid Purcell by sight from the time she was getting her second teeth. But I *noticed* her just this summer, miraculously grown tall, with a lively, exciting face. Instead of being thrilled by the sparkle of my conversation she had a nifty comeback for every quip. I didn't feel so worldly in the company of Enid Purcell.

Around the time of her birthday there'd be a lot of speculation as to how Enid—the town, not the girl—got its name. The question has never been settled absolutely. Though disappointing to the romanticists, the most likely conjecture seems that an official of the Rock Island Railroad had been reading *Idylls of the King*. The Rock Island christened most of the Strip towns along its line before they were born. Pondcreek was the name of the stage stop on that site, where horses were changed before the days of the railroad. Some of the stage-station names were deemed a little rugged for the gentler culture of which the iron horse was to be the precursor. So Polecat became Renfrow and Skeleton, Enid.

Walter Cook was still with us and I liked the way Enid treated him—distinguishing between the man and the historical figure. It was the right way. To have mixed up the two would have done Walter no good and it might have marred the figure. By this time the historical character of Walter Cook was embedded in the locally accepted saga of the Run. An equestrian statue in front of the courthouse couldn't have made it any more so. No general account of the Run was complete without mention that the first man on the townsite was the kid cowpuncher from the Chickasaw Nation. On a range pony that looked like the kind any good trader could get for forty dollars, he had ridden into the ground fifteen thousand rivals and some of the fanciest horseflesh that could be imported from Kentucky. Pat Wilcox, also, was on hand —behind a desk in Art Stephenson's bank—to give you the stirring picture of little Walter on that little horse tearing down South Hill, across the Square, and to the claim that formed the Square's north boundary; swinging down as lightly as a cat, throwing off his saddle, looping his reins about the horn and then setting his stake a good two minutes ahead of Albert Hammer, the second comer.

That was your portrait of Walter Cook, the historical figure: undisputed winner of the Run, and by every rule of the game winner of the one hundred and sixty acres, worth, at the depression prices prevailing in 1911, more than a million dollars. Though the time had not come to put the story down in black and white, it was perfectly safe to *speak* of what had happened to dispossess Walter Cook of his claim: the swarming of the squatters: a clamorous spectacle of three hundred against one; and that one, a cocky little cowhand, unable to adjust his mental processes to the fact that overnight something had occurred to deprive cowhands of the influence they had been accustomed to exert in the Strip. Thus, as regards the contested hundred-and-sixty, matters had worked out according to the established precedents of Manifest Destiny.

So much for Walter Cook, the enshrined image, accorded honors usually reserved for a venerated personage long dead. There was no connection whatever between the image and the man, who might be seen walking the streets of the Square any day that he was free to walk them: a chunky, alert-eyed figure, moving at the stiff-legged gait which was a mark of the years he had been more at home in a saddle than on his own feet. Moreover he may have been troubled by corns, as were many cowpunchers, from an addiction to boots too small for them.

When Walter was not free to walk the streets you would have to climb the iron stairs to the top floor of the courthouse to see him. That was where we had our county jail. From the north windows you could get a better view of the claim Walter had won than you could from the streets below.

The years had worn Walter's cockiness down to a kind of brisk geniality. Without hard feelings he accepted the periodical sojourns in jail as an unavoidable hazard of his calling, which was selling liquor. There were no hard feelings on any side. The judge who usually sentenced Walter was one of his customers. As this jurist was a sly drinker, enjoying the support of the better element which kept the prohibition law on the books, he distrusted the integrity of the average bootlegger who might be inclined to talk too much with his mouth. So the payment of installments on Walter Cook's debt to society probably inconvenienced the judge as much as it did anybody.

You can see for yourself what would have happened had we not kept the figure and the mortal in separate compartments. Elementary journalistic rules of identification would have had me writing: "Walter Cook, who won the Run in '93, was sentenced to sixty days in jail on a bootlegging charge in County Court today. . . ." Or, getting up an anniversary feature: "Enid honors the name of her first pioneer, Walter Cook, who will be unable to be present in person because his current sentence won't expire in time."

Judge W. O. Cromwell—whose title, by some quirk of unofficial procedure, derived from his having been the last attorney general of the Territory—saw that Walter didn't go to jail *too* often. Judge Cromwell was Walter's lawyer. An uncommon bond united counsel and client, for Judge Cromwell had been Walter Cook's lawyer in the epic legal battles which had swirled about Cook's claim. The initial contest was no contest at all. Cook had got there first. That was the object of the Run. He was awarded the claim—hands down.

But there was too much at stake and too many after it for the case to end so simply. Albert Hammer, William Coyle, Ben Clampitt and three others—six in all—filed contests for the claim as a whole. The three hundred squatters who had split the claim into town lots and called their creation Jonesville jointly filed a contest. The Jonesville people reached an understanding with six of the seven individual claimants whereby, should the townsiters win, each individual contestant would get a good slice of lots. Walter Cook was the sole individual claimant to refuse to make such a deal. He gambled for all or nothing. He wound up with nothing. The highest authority in the Department of the Interior found that Walter Cook had "abandoned" his claim.

The facts seem to have been these. During the first round of the fight, which Cook won, Cook lived in a shack he had built on the land. It was one of three hundred shacks there. To fight his case he mortgaged the shack. Needing still more money he went to the Chickasaw Nation to raise it. Well within the permitted absence period of six months he returned and found his shack gone. Squatters had bought up the mortgage and at one minute after midnight on the due date they had torn down the shack. The reason Cook had not returned in time to care for the mortgage was that he was ill. Before he could put up another shack he got pneumonia. A settler living on a quarter north of the one in dispute took the young man in and nursed him through a desperate sickness. Before Cook was up and around the Jonesville clique made its master move. The clique included men prominent in town and county politics. They knew the ropes. They amended their petition to charge abandonment. At the end of a long and tortuous legal road they made the allegation stick.

By that time it was 1898 and Walter Cook joined Roosevelt's Rough Riders. Back from Cuba, he traveled with a Wild West show. Between seasons he married the widow of a policeman in

Kingfisher. She had two children. Settling down as a family man, Walter opened a little restaurant next to the Monarch saloon. It was famous for steaks. When state prohibition came in Walter took to purveying whiskey in his steak joint. The first thing Walter had to do when he finished a spell in jail was to broil his lawyer a steak. Judge Cromwell said no one else could turn out a T-bone that was half so good.

5

Anything I told Dorothy about the Dirty Dozen would have been carefully edited and a wholesome moral attached. Some of it would have been stretched—at any rate related from hearsay rather than experience. But to speak of the D.D. in anything like terms of familiarity was an earmark of a young man of the world.

The Dirty Dozen was a hardy institution. The name was of the members' own coining—a title they took pride in. The D.D. was one of the discoveries of the year of exploration when I was a resident of the Cogdal-McKee building. It was composed of boys of high-school age or older, but they did not go to school. They hung out at livery stables and pool halls. They made excursions to Two Street. Though few seemed to work regularly, they were the flashiest dressers in town. On occasions they could be seen riding or driving good horses. The father of one of their number owned a number of horses, including race horses. The father of another was a saloonkeeper. This boy had plenty of money and he was generous. During the roller-rink craze they produced some of the fanciest skaters we had. One summer they organized a baseball team, played a tough, tricky game, and went about the countryside cleaning up.

As years passed, membership in the D.D. changed. The usual proportion drifted away. One or two married, went to work and settled down. Another's wife went to work. Another started a small business and at the time of which I write he was on the way to becoming a well-to-do leader of the better element. Recruits took the places of those who dropped out.

What I liked about the Dirty Dozen was the way they stuck together. I don't think there was a closer bond among Masons. Let one of the gang run into hard luck and his pals would raise enough to send him to Hot Springs to be boiled out. The Dozen was always skirting the edge of trouble without falling in. I cannot recall a Dozener being so much as hailed into Police Court. I guess the D.D., like Arkansas, wasn't so bad as its reputation.

Still, I liked to think differently, and when it got so that I was tolerated around the Dozen's current headquarters I esteemed it a compliment. These headquarters were the Presserie, a cleaning and pressing establishment conducted by one of the older members in a basement near the Square. When I say I was tolerated I mean that when I dropped in, those who were hanging around would go on talking about their collective or individual concerns as if no outsider was present. In this way I learned some of their secrets, such as the practice of wearing customers' clothes. Neckties could be borrowed any time, but a suit was worn only after dark in company where the chance of meeting the owner was, by all sane calculation, remote.

The proprietor of the Presserie led the D.D. quartet and sang tenor. There had always been a D.D. quartet and the present one was real good. They sang the latest things out: "Oh You Beautiful Doll" and "Oceana Roll." But I still liked the old standbys: "Goodnight, Ladies," "Carry Me Back to Old Virginny," "Sam Bass," "Bury Me Not on the Lone Prairie," and "The Red River Valley."

It was getting so there were people in Enid who didn't know that the old cowboy songs were work songs, like sailors' chanteys. On the trail drives when an outfit stopped at night two punchers would ride slowly round and round the herd until daybreak, one going one way and one the other, singing. The songs soothed the cattle and made them less apt to stampede at a sudden noise in the dark.

In the Presserie basement I heard for the first time the classic "Frankie and Johnnie," "Christopher Colombo" ("He knew the world was round-o"), and others of that strain. Though titles elude me, snatches of words are remembered to this day. There was one that began:

> Rocks in the mountains,
> Fish in the sea,
> A red-headed gal
> Made a bum out of me.

At the Presserie I heard "Change the Name of Arkansas!" The performer of that gem of declamation was Pete Thomas, due to become one of the eminent medicine-showmen of the Southwest. Years afterward I used to get a pleasant glow from reading his name in the med-show column of *Billboard*.

The Presserie discussed the latest turn in the affairs of Josephine Barnabee, whom Dozeners called Jo. Jo had closed her house on Two Street and had bought a second-class hotel uptown. Though Two Street was nearing the end of its rope anyhow, Josephine was credited with an impulse to protect the man who had long protected her—her politician friend.

I looked upon this as another chapter in a story I had seen unfold from the time I carried specials. The chapter immediately preceding had been public and notorious: the politician's fight in the courts against a liquor-law charge. Old political loyalties had saved from prison the personage who was once a power in the Strip. He was given to understand, however, that the favor could not be repeated. The last vestige of his influence gone, the man went to pieces entirely.

A morbid desire for a closer view of the tragedy caused me to take to dropping in at Josephine's hotel to scalp the register for personals. One afternoon the proprietress walked from behind the desk and said:

"Sit down and visit a while, Markey—if you're not doing anything in particular."

"Thank you, Miss Josephine."

All at once I thought of her as Enid's *femme fatale*. Ever since running across them in Balzac I'd been looking for someone to fit those words.

Enid's *femme fatale* was of statuesque proportions. Beneath her glisteny black hair, dark eyes looked from a sultry pleasure-worn face. Of her origin I had heard conflicting accounts. One was that she was Louisiana creole, of good family, and had been educated in a convent. Too often had I seen Josephine's painfully scrawled signature to take any stock in the education part. The story that she was mixed-blood Osage seemed more probable. The French strain in the Osages could have given her features their Gallic cast.

We found so little to say to each other that I wondered the reason for Josephine's polite invitation. She mentioned my column but I could tell that she didn't read it. We talked about the hot spell and the dust storm last week. Mention of the dust storm provoked a line of reminiscence which didn't get very far off Oklahoma weather until Josephine alluded to the time I delivered specials.

"You know why I liked you when you were a boy?"

"I have no idea."

"Your manners. You had such nice manners."

The screen door of the little lobby slammed. It was the politician: face bloated, hat askew—tight as a tick. A glance of bemused entreaty rested on his mistress. Josephine answered with a look as hard as nails and he lurched toward the stairs.

So much for the great man whom once she had been required to court, had possessed utterly, and now sheltered—and despised.

In a moment he was gone and she turned to me with a warm smile.

6

So you see how wrong they were who said nothing ever happened in Enid.

A process of reorientation was at work inside of me. Heretofore I'd always thought of Enid as stuck away off on the rim of no where. Now there were times when it seemed to be the hub of everything.

Even the caprices of the weather could be regarded as investing the character of our country with distinction. Shortly before I discontinued my diary this entry appeared:

"When I came home was the most beautiful morning that could be imagined. Still and cool. The air moist and fresh with dew and a multicolored sunrise. I thought it gave promise of an exceptional Sunday. I awoke, however, at 11 a.m. and the wind was howling. I stayed up town all afternoon and a person could hardly see across the public square. It was a regular repetition of the famous old dust storms of pioneer days."

Ever since we'd left there I used to wander out to the claim. I liked to go alone. A shame Papa had to lose the claim. Gosh, what a pure inspiration Mama'd had: instead of the icehouse, a stock farm. It would have been a regular mint. Drought could take the wheat and the corn, but a good stock farm'd come through without turning a hair hardly: a little bigger feed bill, that's all.

Our claim was the county Poor Farm now. During the hard times right after Papa died, Mama and I had a grim jest about going back there. The management of the Farm seemed to be in the hands of those whose management of other things had made them public charges. Mama wouldn't so much as drive past the place and you couldn't blame her. Every time I went I saw a fresh despoliation: the rich bottom fields gone to weeds and brush; the orchard untended and most of the trees dead; the dam breached by a freshet and unrepaired, losing half the creek's water; the house a wreck; Mama's rambler roses gone first thing. The Bermuda-carpeted grove—"James's Grove"—the loveliest picnicking ground within miles of Enid was gone, the slim young trees cut for firewood. The inmates had begun to lay their axes to the stand of timber—cottonwood and elm of splendid growth and smaller hackberry, willow, and plum—that lined the creek. For the poor people themselves I felt no compassion. I hated them for the way they had debased the claim to the level of their own pointless lives.

Something within me cried to halt this vandalism, to recapture the prize my father had staked in the Run, restore it, take my mother there—behind a "fairly good horse"—and say it was hers. For years this had been just a boy's fantasy. Now—it came rather as a shock—I possessed the means for its realization. With a thousand dollars in the bank, I could have persuaded the commissioners to deed the place over right away. I knew Art Stephenson would take a mortgage for the balance.

I walked out toward the claim—walked rather than rode my bike. It may be that I didn't want to get there too quickly, for things were clashing around inside me. Ascending the gentle slope on the road that ran between the old Utsler place and Mr. Howell's, my glance rested on the horizon, awaiting the green silhouette of the top of the Big Tree. It would be stretching a point to imply that I awaited its appearance eagerly or expectantly, for it had always been there.

What? Oh, impossible! As soon the sun shouldn't rise in the east.

Not only was it possible; it was a fact. *The Big Tree was gone.*

Whether struck by lightning or chopped down I did not learn, for I approached no nearer than the top of the rise, a good quarter of a mile away. My eyes filled with angry tears. Ashamed, I blew my nose and stumped toward town. To hell with Oklahoma!

Which way to head?

There was that last tramp printer, a battered old hand-spiker who'd dropped half-starved off a freight. I'd kittied in a buck to help feed him up and see him to Oklahoma City, there being no work in Enid. The stories he told of New Orleans! And Jay Radcliffe: traveling with a circus, blowing a cornet in the band. The places *he'd* been! Horace Copple: a brand-new postmark every time he wrote. Fred Hall, the high-school debater whose platform manner had been an inspiration to me: punching cattle in Wyoming. Sam Godfrey: on tour with a stock company. Three or four ex-members of K Company in the Navy: picture postcards from Honolulu and Shanghai. Mike Crouse: in K.C. now: night police reporter for the *Star;* knew all the North End crooks.

And I? Sucking cider through a straw in Enid.

Guessed I'd write old Mike to expect me in K.C.

It wasn't so easy to write Mike, though, after the faintly cavalier way I'd treated the Cincinnati offer.

One evening Mr. Wright called me into his office and closed the door. Stewart, he said, was about at the end of his tether. I knew things were pretty bad on the *News*. Joe O'Brien had gone to Oklahoma City. Mr. and Mrs. Stewart and Barry Bullock got out the paper—all the editorial and business-office work. Yes, said Mr. Wright, Stewart was sunk and would have to listen to reason. The sensible thing would be for the *News* and the *Eagle* to cut overhead by getting out both papers from one shop. Wright and Taylor and Edmund Frantz had made an offer for the *News*. If Stewart had any gumption he'd call it a deal.

In that event Mr. Wright wanted to make me an offer: full charge of the editorial and circulation departments of the *News*, which would become the morning edition of the *Eagle*. Taylor would handle the advertising. Mr. Wright said a good deal more, calculated to fire my imagination—a thing he'd been first-rate at since my high-school days. The only promise he solicited was that I'd stay a year.

It was all I could do to adhere to a rule of prudence learned watching horse-traders: never snap up an offer, no matter how tempting.

Mama was spending the summer in Chicago. I posted a long letter, asking her advice, and at the same time making my own inclinations clear. Her reply was characteristic. Though it seemed a wonderful opportunity, she was not the person to judge. She could not pretend to know about "the newspaper business, as you call it." (Mama preferred "profession.") I had my own life to live and must make my own decisions. But should it fall out that I would stay in Enid I must know how happy it would make her to make a home for me until I should require one of my own.

My brother-in-law, Perry, a very busy corporation lawyer, wrote that the offer looked like a good one to accept.

I began to plan for the future as extravagantly as I had ever planned in my life. There was nothing I did not feel capable of doing with the *News*. It'd be insurgent in politics and, by Joe, we'd win the next city election.

We insurgents had just lost a city election by seventy votes. The first good rain in months had had to come on election day, giving the organization an edge and electing Peter Bowers mayor. I had really thrown myself into that campaign. A dramatist couldn't have asked for a finer figure of a reactionary, embodying the timidity that shrinks from change, than the retired frontier storekeeper grown prosperous and tamed by his possessions. Mr. Bowers had been one of the leading Jonesville townsiters. But as soon as Enid began to amount to something he'd sold out, planted the money in mortgages and sat down on his front porch to smoke his pipe and scheme to hold on to what he had. Every now and then he'd serve a term as mayor, and speak, in the tone of a philanthropist, of the fact that the office carried no salary. It was also Peter Bowers's boast that he'd not lost a cent in the packing-plant boom or in any of the railroads. That was only half of it: he'd not risked a cent. It was hard to believe that the same man could have had a finger shot off trying to close on Dick Yeager.

I thought him an old Scrooge. Didn't the very house he lived in stand on land pilfered from Walter Cook? I wasn't being very objective, but what crusader is? Perhaps the most maddening feature of the whole thing was Mr. Bowers's indifference to what I thought or what the *Eagle* said about him. He treated me as if I were still six years old and looking for a striped stick of candy.

Well, when I got to be editor of the *News* I'd show old Pete Bowers a thing or two. I'd go into politics myself, and I wouldn't stop with any piddling little municipal politics, either. I'd get myself elected to Congress, like Victor Murdock of the Wichita *Eagle*.

After such flights it was something of a chore to get down to the everyday details of planning the reorganization and conduct of the newspaper which any day now would be mine. There'd be practically no money to spend. Wright made that clear. No matter. I'd manage. I stayed up late nights figuring how; and for three days didn't see Dorothy.

After a couple of weeks Mr. Stewart was still "thinking over" the *Eagle* proposal. Cripes! What held him back?

7

J. L. Isenberg, one-time owner of the *Wave*, dropped in from California to look after his real estate. I printed a couple of items about him, but not the one I aimed to print eventually. I imagined the best way to settle the score I held against Isey, who had printed so much about my father that was uncomplimentary, would be to write up the Patterson-Williams killing. So I began to comb the back files and to interview old-timers.

One way to tell the story of the Patterson-Williams killing would be to ease into it by talking about Tammany Williams, the city marshal Enid hired to cope with the situation growing out of the North Town War in the early days.

Tammany wasn't his real name. It was a name Mr. Isenberg had given the marshal because he came from New York City. But Mr. Williams had been able to counteract the prevailing western opinion of New Yorkers. From what you heard, Enid had never seen a better snap shot. Ordinarily Mr. Williams fired from the hip and he fanned the hammer. To fan the hammer you used an old-style single-action gun with the "dog" filed so the hammer wouldn't stay cocked. You flipped it back with the first joint of the thumb and let it go—never touching the trigger. A stopwatch would have been required to register the time saved by shooting this way. It could happen that this was just the time a man needed.

Local tradition gave Tammany Williams two characters: one, of a law officer so peace loving and persuasive that he was able to talk enough people out of shooting at him to increase the life-expectancy within his official jurisdiction. But that wasn't the character Mr. Isenberg's *Wave* gave him.

A couple of cowboys rode into town and shot out the lamps in a saloon. Then they went to the Midway Dance Hall and escorted Ida Fisher and a young lady called Skeeter to Cap Bond's for a bite to eat.

"Boys," said Mr. Williams, "put up your hands."

The boys did not move.

"Boys," observed Mr. Williams, "this ain't no shooting matter. Put up your hands."

Miss Fisher suggested that the boys oblige the marshal, but one of them had to show off. He reached for his gun.

The marshal's hands dropped to his hips. The two reports sounded like one and the cowboys slid from their chairs. They were buried under the names of James Brown and Frank Smith.

That was the way Mr. William D. Fossett told the story to me.

Mr. Isenberg reported it differently, writing that Williams had been "possibly a little too quick" with his guns.

Judge Cromwell supported the editor's thesis. "Too much powder burned in those days." Cheyenne had taken a step in the right direction, with its ordinance making anyone who shot at another liable to a fine of ten dollars "whether he hit or missed." But Enid, under Williams, was unprogressive. The lawyer cited me an example of what he meant.

"There's going to be a killing this afternoon," he said the marshal had remarked by way of passing the time of day.

"Where?" Judge Cromwell asked.

Williams named a saloon.

"Who's going to do this killing?"

"Well, I'll be present," said the marshal.

Regardless of the disparity of opinion concerning the fine points of Mr. Williams's temperament, on the whole he was well liked. Another popular figure was Tammany Williams's friend, Colonel Robert W. Patterson, register of the land office and the ranking Government official in Enid. An urbane gentleman from Georgia, Colonel Patterson was noted for his attentions to the ladies. The *Wave* for June 26, 1895, contained an allusion to Colonel Patterson's gallant ways in which it was intimated that certain Enid husbands might do well to interest themselves in the premises.

Colonel Patterson read that evening's *Wave* while standing at the bar in the White Front. He finished his glass and announced his intention of interviewing the editor.

When Tammany Williams heard of this he started in search of Mr. Isenberg and the colonel. The quest proved fruitless until a little after eight oclock. Emerging from the Monarch saloon,

Williams saw both his men at the same instant. Patterson was walking north on South Grand and Isenberg was walking south. Before the marshal could attract the attention of either, Patterson fired and missed and Isenberg dived into Jenkins Brothers' notion store with the colonel a few jumps behind.

Williams drew a gun and took after Patterson. The marshal caught up with his friend in the store. Isenberg had fled through the back door. Williams called to Patterson to halt and, when the colonel kept on going, Williams clouted Patterson on the head with the butt of his pistol—probably the first time in his life Williams had used that end of a gun as a weapon. The marshal wished merely to distract the colonel.

Patterson wheeled and fired at Williams point-blank and resumed his pursuit of the editor. Williams groped his way to the back door of the store and leaned against the frame. Though June 26 is almost the longest day in the year, at eight o'clock it was nearly dark and the moon, four days old, gave no light. Mr. Isenberg was wholly invisible. Colonel Patterson was nearly fifty feet away and running. Steadying himself against the door frame, Mr. Williams, who was left-handed, lined the sights of one gun on the figure fleeing in the half light. No one had ever seen him take so long to get off a shot before. The ball struck Colonel Patterson behind the left ear. He was dead when they picked him up.

Mr. Williams stepped back into the store and would have fallen had not someone caught him. Blood was bubbling from his mouth. "I'm smothering," he said. Fifteen minutes later he died in a chair in Spencer Allen's drugstore.

Already the town was aboil. Friends of the dead men took up the quest for Mr. Isenberg. But the editor gave them the slip. Reaching North Town in a hack, he caught a train for Fort Worth where he stayed until the pursuit of Dick Yeager, which was just beginning to attract attention, gave Enid something else to think about.

That was the story I was fixing to write when one evening after supper I encountered Mr. Isenberg in front of the Frantz Hardware Company a few doors from the *Eagle* office. He peered at me through his thick glasses.

"Marquis James, aren't you?" he said. "Don't see so well any more."

It wasn't nearsightedness that bothered Mr. Isenberg so much as the fact that he was a little drunk.

I said who I was and Mr. Isenberg proposed a visit. We crossed Independence and sat on a bench under a tree in the Square.

Mr. Isenberg praised my column. Returning the compliment, I said I'd always liked the "Sons of Rest" items in the old *Wave*. "Sons of Rest" was a name Isey had given the courthouse loafers. Since his removal to Los Angeles Mr. Isenberg would sit in the parks and observe idlers and compose "Sons of Rest" items which General Harrison Gray Otis printed in the Los Angeles *Times*. I'd already told about this in my column.

"Didn't know you'd been much of a reader of the *Wave*," said Mr. Isenberg.

"Yes, sir; I read the *Wave*."

"Used to skin your ol' daddy, didn't I?"

"You were unjust to my father."

"O justice!" declaimed Mr. Isenberg. Then he laid a limp hand on my knee and his tone softened. "But I won't ridicule. I won't quarrel with you, boy. Let's admit that the judge wasn't exactly a beneficiary of my partisanship. But he had something else of mine, less prodigally bestowed. He had my respect."

"I'm glad to hear you say that, Mr. Isenberg."

Weaving slightly, the old man went on to speak of the old days and of the men who had made them what they were.

"And what are you going to do with *yourself*, Marquis?" he asked at length.

"Stay in the newspaper business," I replied.

"Here in Enid?"

"Sometimes I want to go away and see the rest of the country and sometimes I think I'll just stay right here."

"Marquis, the older I grow the less I'm inclined to offer advice —on the ground that a person bright enough to tell good advice from bad usually doesn't need any. I have no son. No chick nor child. But had I a son, I'd tell him what I tell you, and that is to move around a bit before you settle down. You know what ol'

Bacon said: 'Travel, in the younger sort, is a part of education; in the elder, a part of experience.' Of course, of course! You're going to tell me that Bacon also said, 'Reading maketh a full man, writing an exact man' and so forth. But before you get yourself too full and try to be too dam' exact give a thought to the difference between seein' a thing on the ground and just readin' about it. Are you a Latin scholar, Marquis?"

I confessed that I was not.

"Well, ol' Petronius really hit the nail on the head. 'Leave thy home, O youth, and seek out alien shores: a larger range of life is ordained to thee.' So I would say with the earnestness of one who wishes you well: 'Get out of this tank town and see the world; see it while you're young, while your sap's runnin'.'"

It was quite late, and Mr. Isenberg was soberer, when we walked away. At the door of the Billings Hotel the old editor held out his hand.

"Marquis, don't mislay my address. When you get to Los Angeles I'll take you around to General Otis."

8

Mr. Stewart rejected the terms for the *Morning News*. The visit with Mr. Isenberg cushioned the blow. I gave Mr. Wright my notice and wrote McKinley Crouse to expect me Monday morning, come two weeks.

Aunty, who did my wash and gave the house a going-over once a week, received in silence the enthusiastic announcement of my projected travels. Drawing thoughtfully on a pipe which had belonged to my father, at length she said:

"*Why* you gwine away, Ma'key? Don' you see you jus' brek yo' po' mammy's heart?"

"I know Mama's bound to take it hard for a while, and I hate to think about it. But she'll get over it. It's the way of the world, Aunty. You know that. Young'uns grow up and go off; always have and always will." This easy philosophy afforded some relief to me but made little headway with Aunty. I tried to stress another point. "Besides, Aunty, I just gotta go; gotta get out and see the world."

"Humph! Ah seed d' worl' in mah time. Been a sight better off t' stayed right home in Tennessee; an' so'd mah Daisy Lou."

Everything else that happened during the fortnight intervening before the day set for my departure seemed to confirm the wisdom of my decision. One morning I came to the office and Mr. Drummond was on the desk. When Mr. Wright was away Mr. Drummond often took the desk, gratis. I think he figured it wouldn't be long before he had the *Eagle* back again. This morning Mr. Drummond was telephoning his old city editor, Cod Harrison, secretary of the Oklahoma Bankers Association.

Blossom Fleming had died during the night, and Mr. Drummond fancied Mr. Harrison the only person in town qualified to do justice to an account of her life. From a professional point of view I resented this. But I was relieved. The last thing I really felt like doing was writing the obituary of Blossom Fleming.

In the welcome cool of Sunday's early dark, I rode to the Rock Island depot on Art Trexler's dray which also carried my trunk. While I was buying my ticket someone addressed me.

"Wintering in K.C., Markey?"

The speaker was Lon Crosslin, old Pap Crosslin's son and a dressy barber who traveled far and wide. Apparently a winter in Kansas City was no more to him than heretofore a week-end at Maybelle Stuart's farm had been to me. Suddenly I felt awfully flat, but, trying to be as nonchalant as Lon, I said I guessed I'd give K.C. a whirl this time.

Up to the moment of that accidental encounter I'd experienced two weeks of happiness such as seldom comes twice in this world. The troubled months of indecision over, the road lay before me, unobstructed and inviting. It stretched to the end of the earth. Concerning my imminent departure I'd done no bragging. Fact is, I'd mentioned it only to close friends. I suppose I wanted it the way it was with printers: here one day; next, long gone. But maybe I didn't want to run the risk of anybody else talking the way Aunty had.

The agent shoved the railroad ticket through the wicket. He was counting my change. . . . I couldn't back out now.

My weakness passed. A compensating surge of self-approbation, a threshold-of-great-things feeling, almost shook me physically. Pacing the station platform I wanted all Enid to know that here was a man bound for exciting destinations. What a sap I'd been! All that fake modesty! Should have built up my going into something half way commensurate with its importance (not to mention a sovereign deterrent of buck fever).

The coach was hot and half empty. I shucked my coat, turned a seat around, put my feet on it, and opened a book. It was a novel by Balzac. I'd been reading Balzac all summer and would have to mail this book back to Mrs. Vandever, the librarian. I hadn't told even her I was leaving.

The train slowed for Kremlin. Sa-ay! Maybelle Stuart might be down to the depot, seeing off week-end guests from Pondcreek or some place up the line. In their big, run-down farmhouse the Stuart family did a lot of entertaining, Virginia fashion. Maybelle'd be busting with questions. "Mark-James-I-do-declare-where-you-goin'-this-tima-night?" Chance to make up for neglected opportunities. When I'd tell her K.C., and from there on to the Coast, she'd spread the word far and wide. Maybelle could grasp an enterprise of bold portent—really make something of it.

The depot at Kremlin was on the west side of the track, the town's dozen houses on the east. The train came between them and I stepped off before it had stopped. An oil lamp shed a yellow light outside the station. But there was no Maybelle.

The conductor high-balled with his lantern. The train moved out; gathered speed. I let one car pass and expertly swung on a step of the next.

The brakeman came through, turning down the lamps with a long pole. Too dark to read. Suddenly I felt very sleepy. I folded my coat so its press would be fresh for Kansas City in the morning, stretched out on the two seats, and, for the last time in years to come, closed my eyes on a familiar world.